Kinderculture

THE EDGE: Critical Studies in Educational Theory

Series Editors   Joe L. Kincheloe, Peter McLaren, and
Shirley R. Steinberg

Kinderculture: The Corporate Construction of Childhood
edited by Shirley R. Steinberg and Joe L. Kincheloe

*Pedagogy and the Politics of Hope: Theory, Culture,
and Schooling (A Critical Reader)*
Henry A. Giroux

*Literacies of Power: What Americans Are Not
Allowed to Know*
Donaldo Macedo

FORTHCOMING

*Revolutionary Multiculturalism: Pedagogies of Dissent
for the New Millennium*
Peter McLaren

Education and the American Future
Stanley Aronowitz

*Teachers as Cultural Workers: Letters to Those
Who Dare Teach*
Paulo Freire

Kinderculture

The Corporate Construction of Childhood

edited by
Shirley R. Steinberg
and Joe L. Kincheloe

 WestviewPress

A Division of HarperCollins*Publishers*

The Edge: Critical Studies in Educational Theory

Copyright © 1997 by Westview Press, A Division of HarperCollins Publishers, Inc.

Published in 1997 in the United States of America by Westview Press, 5500 Central Avenue, Boulder, Colorado 80301-2877, and in the United Kingdom by Westview Press, 12 Hid's Copse Road, Cumnor Hill, Oxford OX2 9JJ

Library of Congress Cataloging-in-Publication Data
Kinderculture : the corporate construction of childhood / edited by
    Shirley R. Steinberg and Joe L. Kincheloe.
      p.   cm.—(The edge, critical studies in educational theory)
    Includes bibliographical references.
    ISBN 0-8133-2309-6.—ISBN 0-8133-2310-X (pbk.)
    1. Early childhood education—Social aspects—United States.
2. Popular culture—United States.   3. Critical pedagogy—United
States.   4. Curriculum planning—United States.   5. Child
development—United States.   6. Educational anthropology—United
States.   I. Steinberg, Shirley R., 1952–.   II. Kincheloe, Joe L.
III. Series.
LB1139.25.K55   1997
372.21—dc21   96-40376
                                                                                  CIP

The paper used in this publication meets the requirements of the American National Standard for Permanence of Paper for Printed Library Materials Z39.48-1984.

10   9   8   7   6   5   4   3   2   1

to john, paul, george, and ringo

Contents

Kinderculture

Introduction:
No More Secrets—Kinderculture, Information Saturation, and the Postmodern Childhood

Shirley R. Steinberg and Joe L. Kincheloe

THE THEME OF THIS BOOK IS VERY SIMPLE: New times have ushered in a new era of childhood. Evidence of this dramatic cultural change surrounds each of us, but many individuals have not yet noticed it. Unfortunately, many of the people who make their living studying or caring for children have not recognized this historical watershed. Furthermore, few observers have appreciated the fact that the information explosion so characteristic of our contemporary era has played a central role in undermining traditional notions of childhood. Those who have shaped, directed, and used the information technology of the late twentieth century have played an exaggerated role in the reformulation of childhood. Childhood is a social and historical artifact, not simply a biological entity. Many argue that childhood is a *natural* phase of growing up, of becoming an adult. The cardinal concept here involves the *format* of this human phase that has been produced by social, cultural, political, and economic forces operating upon it. Indeed, what is labeled as "a traditional Western childhood" in the last years of the twentieth century is only about 150 years old. In the Middle Ages, for example, children participated daily in the adult world gaining knowledge of vocational and life skills as a result. The concept of children as a particular classification of human beings demanding special treatment differing from adults had not yet developed in the Middle Ages.

1

Childhood as a Social Construction

Childhood, thus, is a creation of society that is subject to change whenever major social transformations take place. The zenith of the traditional childhood lasted from about 1850 to 1950. Protected from the dangers of the adult world, children during this period were removed from factories and placed into schools. As the prototype of the modern family developed in the late nineteenth century, proper parental behavior toward children coalesced around notions of tenderness and adult accountability for children's welfare. By 1900 many believed that childhood was a birthright—a perspective that eventuated in a biological, not a cultural definition of childhood. Emerging during this era of the protected child, modern child psychology was inadvertently constructed by the tacit assumptions of the period. The great child psychologists from Erik Erikson to Arnold Gesell to Jean Piaget viewed child development as shaped by biological forces.

Piaget's brilliance was constrained by his nonhistorical, socially decontextualized scientific approach. Whatever he observed as the genetic expression of child behavior in the early twentieth century he generalized to all cultures and historical eras—an error that holds serious consequences for those concerned with children. Considering biological stages of child development fixed and unchangeable, teachers, psychologists, parents, welfare workers, and the community at large view and judge children along a taxonomy of development that is fictional. Those children who don't "measure up" will be relegated to the land of low and self-fulfilling expectations. Those children who "make the grade" will find that their racial and economic privilege will be confused with ability (Polakow, 1992; Postman, 1994). *Kinderculture* joins the emerging body of literature that questions the biological assumptions of "classical" child psychology.

Living in an historical period of great change and social upheaval, critical observers are just beginning to notice changing social and cultural conditions in relation to this view of childhood. Categories of child development appropriated from modernist psychology may hold little relevance for raising and educating contemporary children. As childhood began to change in the 1950s, 80 percent of all children lived in homes in which the two biological parents were married to one another (Lipsky and Abrams, 1994). No one has to be told that families have changed during the last fifty years. Volumes could be written specifying the scope of the social transformation. Before the 1980s ended, children who lived with their two biological parents had fallen to merely 12 percent. Children of divorced parents—a group made up of more than half of the U.S. adult population—are almost three times as likely as children raised in two-heterosexual-parent homes to suffer emotional and be-havioral difficulties. Despite such understandings, social institutions have been slow to recognize different, nontraditional family configura-tions and the special needs they encounter. Without support, the "post-modern" family of the late 1990s, often with its plethora of working and single mothers, is beset by problems emanating from the feminization of poverty and the vulnerable position of women in both the public and private spaces (Polakow, 1992).

The Contemporary Crisis of Childhood

Changing economic realities coupled with children's access to informa-tion about the adult world have drastically changed childhood. The tra-ditional childhood genie is out of the bottle and is unable to return. Re-cent writing about childhood in both the popular and scholarly presses speaks of "childhood lost," "children growing up too fast," and "child ter-ror in the isolation of the fragmented home and community." Images of mothers drowning children, baby-sitters torturing infants, kids pushing kids out of fourteenth-floor windows, and trick-or-treat razor blades in apples saturate the contemporary conversation about children. Popular culture provides haunting images of this crisis of childhood that terrify us and engage our worst fears. The film *Halloween*, for example, at one level is a story of the postmodern childhood: fear in isolation. The isola-tion referenced here involves separation from both absent parents and a nonexistent community. No one is there to help; even on the once fes-tive Halloween night children are not present. Even in "safe" suburbia, the community has fragmented to the point that the safety of children trick-or-treating cannot be guaranteed (Ferguson, 1994; Paul, 1994). The crisis of contemporary childhood can be signified in many ways, all of which involve at some level the horror of danger faced in solitude.

New Sites of Learning:
Corporations as Educators

This crisis of childhood demands that we examine its causes. Although a range of factors have constructed the perilous situation that children must now face, this book analyzes one factor in particular: the corporate production of popular kinderculture and its impact on children. Such an effort falls under the umbrella term *cultural pedagogy*, which refers to the idea that education takes place in a variety of social sites including but not limited to schooling. Pedagogical sites are those places where power is organized and deployed, including libraries, TV, movies, newspapers, magazines, toys, advertisements, video games, books, sports, and so on. Our work as education scholars, we believe, demands that we examine both in-school and cultural pedagogy if we are to make sense of the educational process in the late twentieth century (Giroux, 1994). Operating on the assumption that profound learning changes one's identity, we see the pedagogical process as one that engages our desire (our yearning for something beyond ourselves shaped by the social context in which we operate, our affective investment in that which surrounds us), captures our imagination, and constructs our consciousness. The emergence of cultural studies (Grossberg, 1995) has facilitated our effort to examine the cultural practices through which individuals come to understand themselves and the world that surrounds them (McLaren, 1994). Supported by the insights of cultural studies, we are better equipped to examine the effects of cultural pedagogy with its identity formation and its production and legitimation of knowledge, that is, the cultural curriculum.

The organizations that create this cultural curriculum are not educational agencies but rather commercial concerns that operate not for the social good but for individual gain. Cultural pedagogy is structured by commercial dynamics, forces that impose themselves into all aspects of our own and our children's private lives (Giroux, 1994). Patterns of consumption shaped by corporate advertising empower commercial institutions as the teachers of the new millennium. Corporate cultural pedagogy has "done its homework"—it has produced educational forms that are wildly successful when judged on the basis of their capitalist intent. Replacing traditional classroom lectures and seatwork with dolls with a history, magic kingdoms, animated fantasies, interactive videos, virtual realities, kick-boxing TV heroes, spine-tingling horror books, and an entire array of entertainment forms produced ostensibly for adults but eagerly consumed by children, corporate America has revolutionized childhood. Such a revolution has not taken place in some crass manner with Leninesque corporate wizards checking off a list of institutions they have captured. Instead, the revolution (contrary to the 1960s idiom) *has been televised*, brought to you and your children in vivid Technicolor. Using fantasy and desire, corporate functionaries have created a perspective on late-twentieth-century culture that melds with business ideologies and free-market values. The worldviews produced by corporate advertisers to some degree always let children know that the most exciting things life can provide are produced by your friends in corporate America. The economics lesson is powerful when it is repeated hundreds of thousands of times.

The broad argument here is that it is our parental, civic, and professional responsibility to study the corporate curriculum and its social and political effects. Indeed, we maintain that as parents, citizens, and teachers we must hold corporations accountable for the pedagogical features of their activities, for the kinderculture they produce. As Jeanne Brady argues in Chapter 12, we must intervene in this cozy relationship between popular culture and pedagogy that shapes our identities. In the interest not only of our children but of the larger society we must exercise our personal and collective power to transform the variety of ways corporate power—gained via access to media—oppresses and dominates us. We must cultivate an awareness of the ways cultural pedagogy operates so that we can scold when appropriate and rewrite popular texts when the opportunity presents itself. Kinderculture is primarily a pedagogy of pleasure and, as such, cannot be countered merely by ostracizing ourselves and our children from it. Strategies of resistance must be formulated that understand the relationship between pedagogy, knowledge production, identity formation, and desire. This book attempts to open a public conversation about such issues.

Situating Kinderculture in Cultural Studies

Questions concerning kinderculture and its relationship to cultural pedagogy can be clarified and discussed within the academic field of cultural studies. This book resides at the intersection of educational/childhood studies and cultural studies. Attempts to define cultural studies are delicate operations in that the field has consciously operated in a manner that avoids traditional academic disciplinary definitions. Nevertheless, cultural studies has something to do with the effort to produce an interdisciplinary (or counterdisciplinary) way of studying, interpreting, and often evaluating cultural practices in historical, social, and theoretical contexts. Refusing to equate "culture" with high culture, cultural studies attempts to examine the diversity of a society's artistic, institutional, and communicative expressions and practices. Because it examines cultural expressions often ignored by the traditional social sciences, cultural studies is often equated with the study of popular culture. Such an equation is misleading; although popular culture is addressed by cultural studies, it is not its exclusive concern. Indeed, the interests of cultural studies are much broader and include in particular the "rules" of academic study itself; that is, the discursive practices (tacit regulations that define what can and cannot be said, who speaks and who must listen, and whose constructions of reality are valid and whose are unlearned and unimportant) that guide scholarly endeavor.

Thus, cultural studies holds exciting possibilities for new ways of studying childhood education specifically, with its attention to the discursive dynamics of the field. How do children embody kinderculture? How do the power dynamics embedded in kinderculture produce pleasure and pain in the daily lives of children? How do critically grounded parents, teachers, child psychologists, and childhood professionals in general gain a view of children that accounts for the effect of popular culture in their self-images and worldviews? Such questions open new domains of analysis in childhood studies, as they seek out previously marginalized voices and the vantage points they bring to both the scholarly and practitioner-based conversation (Grossberg, 1995; Nelson, Treichler, and Grossberg, 1992). We are enthused by the benefits of cultural studies of childhood yet critical of expressions of elitism within the discourse of cultural studies itself—a recognition made more disturbing by the field's claim to the moral high ground of a politics of inclusivity. Unfortunately, the study of children has traditionally been regarded as a low-status exercise in the culture of academia. So far, at least, the field of cultural studies has reproduced this power/status dynamic in its neglect of childhood study. Indeed, few students of cultural studies have targeted children as the subjects of their scholarship. Kinderculture attempts to address this absence and promote new literature in the area.

Value of Studying Popular Culture

The study of traditional forms of kinderculture—fairy tales, for example—has granted scholars insights into hard-to-reach domains of child consciousness. Moreover, the more disturbing and violent the fairy tale, some would argue, the more insight into the "primitive" feelings that arise and shape us in early childhood and, in turn, in adulthood. The connection between kinderculture and childhood desire/feeling blows the rational cultural fuse, thus connecting adults to the *Lebenswelt* (life world) of children and granting them better access to childhood perceptions (Paul, 1994). Not only does the study of children's popular culture grant insights into childhood consciousness, it also provides new pictures of culture in general. Kinderculture, in this context, inadvertently reveals at a very basic level what is disturbing us in our everyday lives, what irritants reside at the level of our individual and collective subconsciousness. The objective of this book is to promote understandings of kinderculture that lead to democratic pedagogies for childhood at the cultural, familial, and school levels. Cultural studies connected to a democratic pedagogy for children involves investigations of how children's consciousnesses are produced around issues of social justice and egalitarian power relations. Thus, our analyses focus on exposing the footprints of power left by the corporate producers of kinderculture and their effects on the psyches of our children. Appreciating the ambiguity and complexity of power, our democratic pedagogy for children is committed to challenging manipulative and racist, sexist, and class-biased entertainment for children. It is equally opposed to other manifestations of kinderculture that promote violence and social and psychological pathologies. Children's entertainment, like other social spheres, is a contested public space where different social, economic, and political interests compete for control. Unfortunately, Americans are uncomfortable with overt discussions of power. Such unease allows power wielders to hide in the recesses of the cultural and political landscape—all the while shaping cultural expression and public policy in their own interests, which may conflict with those of less powerful social groups such as children.

Americans have not been good students of power. All too often references to power are vague to the point of meaninglessness in the worst literature produced by critical scholars. For the purpose of clarification, when we refer to "power wielders" in America we are not merely referencing a social class or a category of human beings. Picking up on John Fiske's (1993) use of the term *power bloc*, we are referring to particular social formations designated by race, class, gender, and ethnicity that hold special access to various resources (e.g., money, information, cultural capital, media, and so on) that can be used for economic or political gain. Power, as we use the term, involves a panoply of operations that work to maintain the status quo and keep it running with as little friction (social conflict) as possible. Therefore, it is beneficial to those individuals and groups who profit most from existing power relations to protect them from pests like us. When studying this power bloc, we employ Fiske's notion that it can be better understood by "what it *does* than what it *is*" (11). Importantly, our use of the concept of the power bloc in the production of kinderculture is not meant to imply some conspiracy of diabolical corporate and political kingpins churning out material to harm our children. Rather, our notion of the power bloc revolves around alliances of interests that may never involve individual relationships between representatives of the interests/organizations in question. Power-bloc alliances, we believe, are often temporary, coming together around particular issues but falling apart when the issue is no longer pertinent.

If one perceives power to be a complex issue, she will encounter little disagreement from us. Power and power-bloc alliances are nothing if not complex and ambiguous. But because of the power bloc's contradictions and ephemerality, it is never able to dominate in some incontestable manner. Along the lines of its contradictions may exist points of contestation that open possibilities of democratic change. Larry Grossberg (1995) contends that since power never gets all it wants, there are always opportunities for challenging its authority. In this context we begin our study of the corporate production of kinderculture, analyzing the ways power not only represses the production of democratic artifacts but also *produces* pleasure for children. If power was always expressed by "just saying no" to children's desires, it would gain little authority in their eyes. The power of Disney, Mattel, Hasbro, Warner Brothers, and McDonald's is never greater than when it *produces* pleasure among consumers. Recent cultural studies of consumption link it to the identity formation of the consumer (Warde, 1994), meaning that to some degree we are what we consume. Status in one's subculture, individual creations of style, knowledge of cultural texts, role in the community of consumers, emulation of fictional characters, internalization of values promoted by popular cultural expressions—all contribute to our personal identities. Popular culture provides children with intense emotional experiences often unmatched in any other phase of their lives. It is not surprising that such energy and intensity exert powerful influences on self-definition, on the ways children choose to organize their lives.

Obviously, power mixed with desire produces an explosive cocktail; the colonization of desire, however, is not the end of the story. Power enfolds into consciousness and the unconsciousness in a way that evokes, no doubt, desire but also guilt and anxiety. The intensity of the guilt and anxiety a child may experience as a result of her brush with power is inseparable from the cultural context in which she lives. Desire in many cases may take a back seat to the *repression* of desire in the construction of child consciousness/unconsciousness and the production of identity (Donald, 1993). The cocktail's effects may be longer lasting than first assumed, as expression of the repression may reveal itself in bizarre and unpredictable ways. To make this observation about the relationship among power, desire, and repression of desire and the way it expresses itself at the psychological level is not a denial of human agency (self-direction). Although the power bloc has successfully commodified kinderculture, both adults and children can successfully deflect its repressive elements. The role of the critical childhood professional involves helping children develop what John Fiske (1993) calls the affective moments of power evasion. Using their abilities to "reread" Disney films along fault lines of gender or to reencode Barbie and Ken in a satirical mode, children take their first steps toward self-assertion and power resistance. Such affective moments of power evasion certainly do not constitute the ultimate expression of resistance, but they do provide a space around which more significant forms of critical consciousness and civic action can be developed.

Media/Popular Cultural Literacy
Needed in Hyperreality

The information explosion, the media saturation of the late twentieth century with its access to private realms of human consciousness, has created a social vertigo. This social condition, often labeled hyperreality, exaggerates the importance of power wielders in all phases of human experience. Hyperreality's flood of signifiers in everything from megabytes to TV advertising diminishes our ability to either find meaning or engender passion for commitment. With so much power-generated information bombarding the senses, adults and children lose the faith that they can make sense of anything (see Kincheloe, 1995, for an expansion of these themes). Thus, the existence of hyperreality forces us to rethink our conversation about literacy. Children, Henry Giroux argues in Chapter 2, who have been educated by popular culture approach literacy from a very different angle. Media literacy becomes not some rarefied add-on to a traditional curriculum but a basic skill necessary to negotiating one's identity, values, and well-being in power-soaked hyperreality. In many schools such ideas have never been considered, not to mention seriously discussed. Media literacy, like power, is not viewed in mainstream circles as a topic for children (or even adults). As Peter McLaren and Janet Morris argue in Chapter 6, the same educators who reject the study of media literacy or kinderculture are the ones who have to cope with its effects.

Jan Jipson and Ursi Reynolds in Chapter 13 refer to their classroom efforts to cultivate a critical media literacy among educators. As their course progressed, they watched students shift their analysis of the effects of media-based kinderculture from vague women and children in "TV Land" to themselves—and through themselves to their own children and students. As a result of the course, the students were motivated to teach their own students ways of analyzing media and the effects of its cultural pedagogy. In particular, early-education teachers in the class came to define one aspect of their educational task as encouraging media literacy among the parents of their students. The point made in this context is extremely important: as Peter McLaren et al. (1995) argue in *Rethinking Media Literacy: A Critical Pedagogy of Representation*, a critical understanding of media culture requires students not simply to develop the ability to interpret media meanings but to understand the ways they themselves consume and affectively invest in media. Such an attempt encourages both critical thinking and self-analysis, as students begin to realize that everyday decisions are not necessarily made freely and rationally. Rather, they are encoded and inscribed by emotional and bodily commitments relating to the production of desire and mood, all of which leads, in Noam Chomsky's famous phrase, to the "manufacture of consent."

Devil or Angel? The Commercial and Democratic Impulses of TV

Commercial TV in America has always been structured by conflicting demands of commerce and democracy. Any study of kinderculture will find these competing dynamics at work at various levels in the texts examined. When analysts and consumers begin to understand the cultural authority mustered by children's TV and other entertainment forms, the bifurcated imperatives for the medium begin to take on unprecedented significance. The democratic moments of TV are profound but far too rare. The exposure of the insanity of Joseph McCarthy, the evils of racial segregation, the perils of pollution, the most obvious abuses of patriarchy, the inhumane excesses of Vietnam, and the criminality of Watergate undoubtedly represented the zenith of TV's democratic impulse. The unfortunate consequence of such successes has been corporate constraint and governmental regulation of attempts to replicate such achievements (note the Bush administration's successful efforts to curtail the press coverage of the Gulf War so as to prevent another "Vietnam"). When such media management is combined with TV's tendency to fragment and decontextualize the issues it does choose to cover, events are often stripped of their meaning. Children who depend heavily on TV for their entertainment and thus their worldview are cognitively impaired by this dynamic (Kellner, 1990). Make no mistake: TV's curriculum for children in the last gasps of the twentieth century is not crafted by media moguls' fidelity to the principles of democracy. Commercial concerns dictate media kinderculture; profit margins are too important to bother with concerns for the well-being of kids.

Society's most important teachers don't ply their trade in schools, just as the nation's "official" children's policy is not constructed by elected officials in Washington, D.C. America's corporate producers of kinderculture are the most influential pedagogues and policymakers. In Chapter 2 Henry Giroux writes of the blurring boundaries between entertainment, education, and commerce, as Disney Imagineers inject their teachings into the dreamworld of children. There is nothing transparent about children's TV or movies, but messages are being delivered to our children with the intent of eliciting particular beliefs and actions that are in the best interests of those who produce them. Bifurcated as TV's imperatives may be, democracy takes a backseat to the logic of capital. In comparison to the promotion of the multiple "products" of kinderculture, child advocates have limited access to the airways. Those corporations who advertise children's consumer paraphernalia promote a "consumption theology" that in effect promises redemption and happiness via the consumptive act (ritual). Such advertising and pleasure-production grant a direct line to the imaginative landscape of our children—a mindscape that children use to define their view of America.

Thus, child professionals and parents must understand that humans are the historical product of the mechanisms of power—an appreciation often missed in the everyday world. This paradox of human consciousness confounds observers with its Zen master double-talk—folks make culture, yet culture makes folks. Meaning emerges from this maze at the level of the social, and individual consciousness is shaped by this interaction and the ways of seeing (ideologies) it produces. As a social and ideological phenomenon, consciousness is constructed not simply by its contact with culture but by an interaction with a view of culture—a view "edited" by ideological refraction. Refraction involves the manner in which the direction of light is changed when it passes through one medium to another—for example, from a crystal to a wall. The refracted light we see on the wall is different from the light that originally encountered the crystal; one aspect of the light's "reality" has been displaced. Ideology is like the crystal in that it refracts perceptions of the lived world. This is not to say that the light (world perceptions) prior to its encounter with the crystal (ideology) is some Godlike, pristine light (reality). Our view of ideology understands that no transcendental, totalizing view of the light (reality) exists; we always perceive it from some position in the web of reality. Leaving our metaphor behind, the salient point here is that kinderculture serves as a mechanism of ideological refraction—a social force that produces particular meanings that induce children (and adults) to interpret events within a specific range of possibilities (Thiele, 1986; Donald, 1993; Mumby, 1989).

Kinderculture, like all social texts, speaks with an authorial voice that is neither up-front nor covert about its ideological inscription (Lincoln, 1995). Not surprisingly, corporate-produced kinderculture chooses Monty Hall's covert ideological curtain number three. In this way kinderculture colonizes American consciousness in a manner that represses conflict and differences. Thus, the critical childhood professional understands ideology, its refraction, its effect on consciousness construction as the conceptual basis for his or her effort to expose kinderculture as a politically pristine, uncontested sphere of social activity. Just as classroom teaching and the school curriculum are never simply neutral, disinterested messengers/transmitters of data, corporate kinderculture harbors an agenda. Our recognition of, say, the Mc-

Donald's ad campaigns promoting family values during the early Reagan years, and the company's financial ties to the right wing of the Republican Party, is important to our understanding of the way politics works and the context within which kinderculture is conceived and displayed. Such a recognition does not necessarily mean that we deprive our five-year-olds of their Happy Meals or their fascination with the Hamburglar. Our understanding of the patriarchal depiction of Kevin's (Macauley Culkin) mother as failed caretaker of children in the two *Home Alone* movies while excusing his equally culpable father of blame for his part in the abandonment grants insight into the way misogyny is transmitted across generations. It doesn't mean that we have to, as gender police, bar our eight-year-olds from renting the movie. Maybe an explanation of what is happening along gender lines and a mutual celebration of Kevin's self-sufficiency may turn *Home Alone* into a positive experience of (as our daughter puts it) "family bondation."

Childhood professionals have not traditionally been students of power, but given the power of kinderculture they now have to be. As students of the power dynamics of children's popular culture, parents and professionals begin to understand the actions of children from a new perspective. Given their power to sink their tentacles deep into the private lives of children, the corporate producers of kinderculture constantly destabilize the identity of children. At the same time, however, new products—toys, movies, TV, video games, fashion, texts—attempt to restabilize new identities through the consumptive act. The study of power vis-à-vis children and contemporary kinderculture provides a conceptual tool for criticizing social, economic, and political practices and explaining the ways young people's life choices are restricted. Artifacts of culture, whether toys or automobiles, have always worked to help us create ourselves and our social affiliations. Our task as kinderculturalists is to expose these invisible yet influential forces, the micro-practices that shape our children's lives. Our task is complicated by the fact that those practices that are the most visible and unquestionable in commonsense observations of children at play are those most fully saturated by the humidity of power. The ability to appreciate these realities provides us the wisdom to distinguish between just and unjust kindertexts, manipulative and liberatory corporate activities. Thus empowered, we can begin to piece together the complex and often ambiguous ways that corporate actions modify children's behavior, the ways advertising and its promotion of childhood hedonism produce an ethic of pleasure and a redefinition of authority. Such issues reside at the core of who we are as a people and who we want to become (Kellner, 1992; Wartenberg, 1992; Seiter, 1993; Ball, 1992; Grossberg, 1995; Abercrombie, 1994).

Corporate Power and Kinderculture

The study of power and kinderculture reveals insights into American politics that may at first glance seem only incidental to parents and child professionals. When one begins to explore child-activist avenues, he or she is immediately confronted with the concentration of power into fewer and increasingly corporate hands. Such a reality cannot be ignored by child advocates and concerned parents, since the corporate-dominated power bloc is unafraid to retaliate against those who would question the impact of its products. In light of the failure of oppositional institutions to challenge corporate hegemony, corporations to a large extent have free reign to produce almost any kinderculture that is profitable. Of the 7,000 interest organizations that are active in Washington, D.C., most are business- or corporate-sponsored. Public-interest organizations are typically outnumbered ten to one in formal congressional proceedings on regulatory issues. The antidemocratic implications of the system with its corporate curriculum designed to adjust public opinion to support business agendas are chilling (Greider, 1992).

This expansion of corporate power has occurred over the last couple of decades. When pollsters in the 1970s uncovered a decline in public confidence in businesses and corporations, corporate leaders jumped into action. To counter public perceptions of themselves as greedy and uninterested in the public good, corporations dropped extra hundreds of millions of dollars into public relations advertising designed to promote corporate images and ideological dispositions. Designed to engineer consent, these legitimation ads focused on treasured common experiences in our lives, family, childhood, and parental events in particular. Among many others, the Ethan Allen furniture company latched on to the family, childhood, and parental triad, attaching its corporate identity to a right-wing notion of traditional family values. The Ethan Allen legitimation ads talked about the rise of juvenile delinquency and its threat to those of "us" who care about "our" children. Our treasured ways of raising our children, the ads asserted, are under threat by an unidentified group who just don't care about traditional family values and the sanctity of old-fashioned ideals.

Chapter 14, in which Joe Kincheloe analyzes the McDonald's family values–oriented legitimation ads, documents one of the highest expressions of the corporate colonization of family values and parental and child consciousness. In one particular McDonald's ad a young boy and a younger girl stroll along a tree-lined trail in a park. The camera watches them walk away from the TV viewer. The small girl runs to catch up with her big brother. Both are wearing oversized baseball uniforms with Tigers spelled across their backs. With baseball caps worn backwards, they are obviously "adorable" *American* children. The little sister loves her older brother, who waits for her when she gets too far behind and allows her to grab his baseball shirttail for her support on the way home. The musicover sings "You, you're the one. You're moms and dads and brothers, sisters, and sons. We're stronger for each other." The attempt here, of course, is for McDonald's to connect its image with the best interests of children and to legitimate itself as a company with a heart, an organization that would never do anything not in the best interests of the family. Viewers don't have to remember the specifics of the ad for it to work as McDonald's intended—the emotional valence it imprints, the positive connection between treasured childhood memories and the golden arches is all that matters in the legitimation strategy.

Corporations and the free enterprise system that protects their right to operate in the best way they see fit make possible these warm, familial moments of our lives. Maybe "we" should protect them from those meddlers who want to regulate them and interfere with all the good that they do. Of course, the truth is obviously irrelevant in these legitimation ads. Indeed, General Motors was audacious enough in the early 1980s to run a multimillion-dollar ad campaign demonstrating the extraordinary amount of input line workers had in the automobile production decisionmaking process. As far as McDonald's veracity, Kincheloe reveals in Chapter 14 founder Ray Kroc's demands that McDonald's employees keep concern for their families far down the list of their priorities if they hoped to climb Kroc's corporate ladder. McDonald's corporate culture is by no means unique in the pantheon of American corporations. Indeed, the decline of traditional family life and the safe climate for children is a casualty of corporate development (Goldman, 1992). After the end of World War II corporate America pursued a variety of policies jeopardizing traditional family arrangements, including everything from its expectations of employees, the promotion of hedonistic and individualized life courses, and opposition to government aid to families fragmented by economic need to the promotion of childhood consumption designed to pit children versus parents and parents versus children in a battle for consumer satisfaction. Despite all of this, the legitimation ads have worked well enough to protect companies from calls for some authentic form of social responsibility.

The Power to Represent:
Corporate Historical Revisionism

As parents and child advocates become more attentive to the pedagogical locales where child consciousness is shaped, out of necessity they begin to attend to the influence of giant corporate organizations such as Time-Warner, Disney-ABC, Rupert Murdoch's News Corporation, and other conglomerates that control information and entertainment. So powerful are these and hundreds of smaller corporations that they can rewrite American history to suit their particular ideological needs. Being that all political positions embraced in the present are reflections of particular ways of viewing the past, the power to rewrite history is not trivial. Children who study the Disney Frontierland curriculum, for example, with its uncomplicated portrayal of brave and pure Europeans fighting the savage Indians in the quest to fulfill God's plan of Manifest Destiny are more likely to be insensitive to questions of justice because of their acceptance of the divinely sanctioned European conquest of "Frontierland." Boys and girls who drink at the Disney Foundation of Eurocentric Knowledge have taken part in a political curriculum with serious implications for the formation of their ideological consciousness. Jeanne Brady's analysis (see Chapter 12, "Multiculturalism and the American Dream") of the corporate historical revisionism of the American Girl Dolls curriculum makes clear that its removal of conflict and repression contributes to the production of unquestioning citizens unaware of even the mere existence of struggle and imperialism. Even when, Brady writes, the Pleasant Company included an African American doll, Addy, a former slave living during the Civil War, managers removed illustrations of Addy that were deemed "too graphic and depressing" for children. Brady tells us that the company concluded that slaves should have smiling faces.

Such curricular sanitization is evidence of America's end-of-millennium crisis of democracy. The threat is fueled by a pervading unwillingness on the part of political leaders and corporate producers of the civic curriculum to address growing divisions between classes, racial polarization, accelerating poverty, an expanding underclass of hopeless individuals living in urban ghettos, and an increasing percentage of children who are poor. Weaned on the corporate curriculum, Americans' civic awareness of these and other issues of democracy continues to fade. When the corporate takeover of TV in the 1980s is examined in this context, the power of cultural pedagogy is further clarified. During the Reagan-Bush era, corporate America recognized a golden opportunity to capture the major TV networks and to use them to advance their own political and economic interests. Stories that would grant children and their parents insight into the self-interestedness of the corporate world were not broadcast. The TV airwaves are in effect a "public utility" required by law to serve the public interest; TV is an institution designed to be separate from and critical of the agendas of state and corporate interests. With corporations securely in control of TV and other forms of information and entertainment production, these institutions have gained unprecedented power to represent the world to both children and adults. Whereas great military powers once had the capacity to militarily and economically occupy geographical territories for exploitation and gain, national and international corporations now occupy mindscapes, the realm of consciousness (Kellner, 1990; Fiske, 1993). As the colonizers of the new millennium, such organizations derive great benefit from the occupation of the human psyche—advantages that mirror those of their military forebears.

Changing Childhood Via Kinderculture/Popular Culture

There is no doubt that childhood has changed, often as a result of its contact with kinderculture and other, more adult manifestations of media culture. Although all audiences of popular culture play an important role in making their own meanings of its texts, kinderculture and adult popular culture exert specific affective influences, mattering maps that emerge in the social contexts in which children encounter it. Since parents are no longer in control of the cultural experiences of their children, they have lost the role that parents once played in shaping their children's values and worldviews. In the 1920s, for example, with the protected childhood firmly established, children had few experiences that fell outside of either parental supervision or child-produced activities shared with other children. Since the 1950s more and more of our children's experiences are produced by corporations—not as much by parents or even children themselves. TV shows, movies (now on pay/cable TV), video games, and music (with earphones that allow seclusion from adults) are now the private domain of children. The key theme of this book rests here: Traditional notions of childhood as a time of innocence and adult-dependency have been undermined by children's access to popular culture during the late twentieth century.

The Dilemma of the Postmodern Childhood

Such a new reality presents adults (parents and teachers in particular) with a complex problem that might be called "The Dilemma of the Postmodern Childhood." Contemporary children's access to commercial kinderculture and popular culture not only motivates them to become hedonistic consumers but also undermines the innocence, the protected status from the tribulations of adult existence children have experienced since the advent of the era of protected childhood in the 1850s. Advocates of traditional family values and severe discipline for children understand that something has changed, that for some reason authority has broken down. Such advocates often attribute the breakdown of authority to feminism and its encouragement of mothers to pursue careers outside of the home and to permissive liberals who oppose corporal punishment and other harsh forms of child control. Unfortunately, for the welfare of children, they are wrong. Adult authority over children, no doubt, has broken down, but not because of feminist mothers or wimpy liberals. Children's access to the adult world via the electronic media of hyperreality has subverted contemporary children's consciousness of themselves as incompetent and dependent entities. Such a self-perception does not mix well with institutions such as the traditional family or the authoritarian school, institutions both grounded on a view of children as incapable of making decisions for themselves.

Why are children so defiant, so hard to control in the last decades of the twentieth century? The answer involves the fact that they don't see themselves in the same way as adults in these institutions view them. Postmodern children are not accustomed to thinking and operating as little tikes that need adult permission to operate. We understand that not all children react to kinderculture and their access to popular culture in this way, for diverse groups of children will respond differently. The reality remains, however, that adults have lost the authority they once held because they knew things that purportedly sheltered kids in fact did not. Adult information is uncontainable; children now see the world as it is (or at least how it is depicted by corporate information producers). Daily examples of the effects of children's information access and the new view of themselves it produces are ubiquitous. In the *Home Alone* movies Macauley Culkin's Kevin character is constantly embarrassed and bothered by adult assumptions that a ten-year-old is a child. In the *Problem Child* movies, the problem child performs knowing looks for the camera (and his fellow kids-with-adult-knowledge), indicating his adult take on an unfolding situation. Movie depictions of this real-life dynamic dominate movies about children from the early 1970s to the present.

This change in children's access to adult knowledge about the world and the changes in the nature of childhood that it produces have undermined the conceptual/curricular/managerial bases on which schooling has been organized. We do not believe it hyperbolic to argue that in light of these cultural changes schools must be reconceived from the bottom up. Currently the school curriculum is organized as a continuum of experience developmentally sequenced as if children learned about the world in school in progressive increments. Right-wing efforts to protect outmoded school organizations and the traditional notions of child-

hood that come with them are in some ways understandable but ultimately doomed to failure. We cannot protect our children from the
knowledge of the world that hyperreality has made available to them.
Such a task would demand a form of sequestration tantamount to incarceration. The task that faces us is intimidating but essential. We must
develop education, parenting skills, and social institutions that will address this cultural revolution in a way that teaches our children to make
sense of the chaos of information in hyperreality. In this context school
becomes not as much an institution of information delivery as a
hermeneutical site, that is, a place where *meaning* is made, where understanding and interpretation are engendered. The task is difficult, but
road maps to negotiate it are already being produced (see Kincheloe,
1995, for a detailed picture of what this *meaning making* education
might look like).

The Backlash: Hating the Worldly Child

The postmodern child is worldly, often presented in popular culture as a
"smart-ass." As know-it-all wise guys, such children are often easy to
hate—a theme Joe Kincheloe traces in movies about children over the
past several decades. Children with power are especially threatening to
adults—a fear that manifests itself particularly in horror films since the
early 1970s. *The Exorcist*, which presented the evil child Regan as a monster in need of punishment, encouraged an entire school of evil-children
movies, including *The Omen, It's Alive, It Lives Again, Firestarter, Children of the Corn, Halloween, The Brood*, and others. The precocious
child is a threat to what Valerie Polakow (1992) calls the order paradigm,
a way of seeing that demands pedagogical adherence to the established
developmental sequence and reward for the docile and obedient student. Indeed, there is something frightening to the established order
about the child-savant who learns about life "out of sequence" from TV
and other electronic media. Independent and self-sufficient youths with
an "inappropriate" insight into the adult world constitute the monsters
in the evil-children movies.

Rhoda, the precocious child-murderer in *The Bad Seed*, is simply "too
adult" in her frequent manifestations of self-control and self-discipline.
A conversation between Rhoda's mother and Miss Fern, the head-
mistress of Rhoda's private school, is revealing:

MOTHER: I don't know how to say it, but there's a mature quality
about her [Rhoda] that's disturbing in a child, and my husband and
I thought that a school like yours where you believe in discipline

and the old-fashioned virtues might, well, perhaps teach her to be more of a child.

MISS FERN: Yes, yes, I know what you mean.

Interesting here is that Miss Fern, a stickler for strong discipline, is agreeing with the mother that Rhoda needs to be *less* mature. Concurring with the mother without equivocation, Miss Fern tacitly shares the mother's recognition that Rhoda's evil revolves around her maturity, her precociousness. The mother and Miss Fern see their roles as reestablishing control of Rhoda in an adult-child power hierarchy. The recent film history of demonization of such children is impressive: in *Halloween* we have the six-year-old murderer; in *Firestarter* the power of the young female protagonist, Charley, is best used in the destruction of those around her; in *The Other* the evil child kills his father and carries around his severed finger; and in *The Exorcist* the rebellious students are portrayed as objects of revulsion who must be controlled at any cost (Paul, 1994).

The list could continue. Obviously, something involving fear of knowledgeable children is being expressed in these films, these cultural artifacts. An important theme in the recent history of childhood thus emerges: parents becoming fearful of the latent monster in all children, a parental fear of what their children may become. The middle-class concern with order and equilibrium is reasserted in light of these repressed parental fears. The precocious child must be rendered obedient; the body must be regulated in the it's-for-your-own-good discourse of justification. Parental fears find legal expression in new laws defining new classes of juvenile crime, making juvenile records public, establishing boot camps for young criminals, outlawing the sale of spray paint to curb graffiti, and eliminating age guidelines in treatment of youth offenders (Vogel, 1994). Recently published children's books attempt to frighten precocious children who become "too big for their britches" into not only obedience but a new form of dependency. Written to counteract too much child identification with Macauley Culkin's precocious, independent, and successful Kevin character in *Home Alone*, Francine Pascal's *Ellen Is Home Alone* (1993) paints a gruesome picture for children who want to stay home alone. Her message is simple and straightforward: Staying home alone is scary; as a child you are incompetent; if you try to act like an adult you will be severely punished; if you resist parental control you may *die*. Pascal's infantiphobia and the "hellfire pedagogy" she uses to enforce discipline is not unlike Jonathan Edwards's imagery of children in the hands of an angry God, or the conclusion of *The Bad Seed*, where the precocious Rhoda is killed by a lightning bolt.

Family Values: Code Words for Child Neglect

The double-speak of the right-wing call for family values is in actuality a misleading code for an antifamily and antichildren agenda. The antifamily reality of "family" values establishes discouraging obstacles for working-class families—working single mothers in particular—and great suffering in the everyday lives of their children. During the Reagan-Bush administrations of the 1980s, as well as during the Gingrich-Dole "revolution" of the 1990s, family values were a cover for greed and excess, in the case of the former, and mean-spirited punishment of the poor in the latter. As a cover for more malevolent goals, family values has served the right-wing agenda gloriously. Erecting a facade of concern, conservatives are able to convince millions of Americans that new moneys for education, antipoverty programs, and child care are pointless when the real problem is the absence of family values. A central but often unasked question involves how many families struggling in poverty would be saved if they embraced traditional family values. The answer: very few. To understand the economic problems that plague an alarming proportion of America's children one must explore a panoply of structural changes in the global economy in the 1970s, 1980s, and 1990s. Traditional family values and structures characterized by working fathers and homemaking, child-caring mothers are inconsistent with new economic realities.

The family, Norman Denzin (1987) reminds us, has been a locale of political and ideological struggle since the late eighteenth century. Such struggles have worked in the second half of the twentieth century to the realization that the all-American nuclear family is no longer the social norm. Such a structure is not now and may *never* have been the familial model experienced by most Americans. In the present era the nuclear family is a site of submerged hostilities as precocious children wrestle with their parents for adult privileges and material goods. The *Home Alone* movies, for example, work diligently to cover up the familial fault lines introduced by the plot. As a result, screenplay writers and directors must walk a political tightrope over a canyon of family- and children-related issues. The seismic waves emanating from these family battles—from the fear of precocious children—are clearly reflected by the right-wing family-values rhetoric. Precocious behavioral problems, the conservative argument goes, are the direct product of a liberal age of permissiveness. Such problems of undisciplined youth, the right maintains, are especially true among the poor and the nonwhite, and the only way to deal with these "sociopaths" is to get tough (Griffin, 1993). With the help of feminists in particular, the story continues, family values and traditional family structures continue to erode to the point that jailing youth is our only alternative to utter chaos. In this context the rhetoric of family values does not connote a loving, supportive approach to child advocacy.

The political climate for children is indeed hostile in the late 1990s, what with Gingrich's Boys Towns and Republican social services cuts in the name of "tough love." Incarceration for criminal children is virtually antithetical to crime prevention, rehabilitation, or the reduction of repeat offenses. Juveniles in adult institutions are five times more likely to be sexually assaulted, twice as likely to be battered by institutional staff, and 50 percent more likely to be beaten with a weapon than young people in juvenile facilities. Repeat offenses by juveniles placed in adult institutions are significantly higher (Vogel, 1994). Equally depressing is the discourse of many liberal child-advocacy groups premised on an instrumental view of children that demands public investments in children must eventuate in quantitative cost-benefit outcomes. In this context childhood intervention programs are invaded by unending tests for academic progress, social appropriateness, crime reduction, and decreased welfare dependency. Such a mind-set is often indifferent to the need for a quality child care system in a nation where over half of children under six years old have working mothers. Funds for such a service are withheld on the family-values belief that mothers, not child care workers (or husbands) should care for their children at home. Thus, right-wing pro-family policies continue to throw up obstacles for working families—single mothers in particular—that cause children to suffer unnecessarily (Polakow, 1992).

The Cold Reality of Violence in Families and Among Children

As much as we may highlight problems within the discourses of family values and child advocacy and deplore the fear/hatred of children we find in the crevices of the public unconsciousness, in no way do we mean to discount the difficulties of child rearing and the frustrations of parents and teachers at the end of the millennium. Child and juvenile crime is a fact of life that continues to escalate in American society in urban, rural, and suburban settings. In this context every other home in America is a scene of family violence—not typically perpetrated by children—at least once per year. How surprising can child violence figures be when we learn that kids in 60 percent of American homes confront child abuse yearly, including sexual abuse, hitting, and battering—not to mention emotional violence (Denzin, 1987)? Whatever the context, the reality is unavoidable: Children in the late 1990s are increasingly involved in acts of violence. It is our argument here that kinderculture and popular culture in general constitute a social dynamic that contributes to violence by young people.

It is not possible to establish statistically valid causal connections between media violence and violent behaviors in children—variously worded research questions will produce divergent results. From a more qualitative perspective, however, violent kinderculture privileges violence as the most effective method of problem solving in the daily lives of children. Sponsors of children's TV and producers of cinematic kinderculture are pushed by competitive pressures to manufacture more violent products that turn higher profits. Doug Kellner argues in Chapter 4 that such pressures will accelerate as the number of TV channels grows and competition intensifies. Also, Aaron Gresson (1997) maintains in Chapter 9, on wrestling, that the "sport" is tailor-made for postmodern audiences searching for the spectacle of brutality and violence. Like other forms of media violence, wrestling glorifies barbarity—indeed, it lays the foundation for a larger aestheticization of violence with blood and guts flying through the air to the strains of a romantic melody. Watching our children glued to the TV, as gunshots explode torsos and spew brains, is a sobering but all-too-common parental experience in hyperreality.

As the video-game industry establishes the rules for the development of interactive TV, new forms of aesthetic violence couched in racist and sexist contexts will reinforce already established manifestations. In Chapter 5 and in his previous research in *Video Kids: Making Sense of Nintendo*, Eugene Provenzo traces the escalating violence of early video games (*Pac-Man* and *Space Invaders*) to those of the mid-1990s (*Double Dragon II* and *Streets of Rage*). To win such games one must immerse oneself in the battle-for-survival virtual cosmos and learn to maim and kill all rivals. A mind-set of aggressiveness is established, as violence becomes a "natural" amphetamine, a sanctioned entitlement to "get high on death" and *kill* the boredom of the postmodern childhood. Virtual violence is an abstracted violence that removes brutality from its IRL (in real life) consequences. Some children imitate the actions of interactive characters, even though they well understand the fantasy of the games and videos—there is nothing simplistic, linear, or cause-effect in the ways children reproduce media violence in their lives. Pathologies hidden in a particular child's subconscious may be triggered and brought to the surface by violent imprints of video games, wrestling, movies, or TV; other children, at the same time and with the same kindercultural experiences, may be relatively unaffected.

Kinderculture and Questions of Justice

Any analysis of childhood in the late 1990s must attend to questions of race-, class-, and gender-related injustices that plague segments of kinderculture's child audiences and shape the format of the media, print, and interactive dimensions of kinderculture. From the perspective of many poor and minority children, the world they have been encouraged to trust no longer works. Poor American children have seen their dreams stolen from them, replaced by a hopelessness that narrows their choices and undermines their sense that their actions can make a difference. Youth suicide was not even a category before 1960; by the 1980s it was second to "accidents" as the leading cause of death among young people (Ferguson, 1994). By the 1990s suicide among kids was described as an epidemic. What kind of hopelessness must a child feel to take his or her own life? By the time many children enter middle school, they are world-weary, drained of a sense of possibility. Many have heard it all, the charlatans with their manipulative pseudohope grounded on everything from televangelism to drugs to schooling (Ferguson, 1994). Kinderculture must often provide a welcome escape from such harsh realities—no wonder TV viewing time is so high among poor and dispossessed children.

These sobering descriptions of marginalized children's experiences in America are not to be found in corporate-produced kinderculture. In Chapter 6, on the Mighty Morphin Power Rangers, Peter McLaren and Janet Morris instruct us that children's media culture rarely takes into account the perspectives of the poor and racially or ethnically marginalized. Too often, kinderculture refuses to challenge patriarchal power structures or provide alternative vantage points on the world. The "good *guys*" of kinderculture are too often white males who fight the good fight for neoimperialist causes. The advertising of children's consumer products that supports TV programming for kids is uncritical of the gross economic inequalities that characterize it (Seiter, 1993). In the name of a *common culture* kinderculture ignores experiences of economic inequality and lived understandings of oppression endured by too many American children. In this context questions of children's differences in opportunity and privilege are erased. An important distinction here involves the fact that cultural racial differences may be represented by TV, movie, or print producers, but they are dehistoricized and stripped of any depiction of the power differences that cause suffering among marginalized children and their parents.

TV heroes typically are inscribed with dominant and mainstream cultural values. As white, male, classless (read: middle-class) protagonists, they carry WASP values to violent villains who remarkably often are non-white or non-American. White heroes frequently are provided with a nonwhite or female sidekick to overtly signify the value of diversity—a strategy that covertly registers the need for white male control of a diverse society (Fiske, 1993). Thus, the presence of difference can be noted in kinderculture; indeed, advertisers and marketers have enthusiastically embraced difference—from Jamaican Barbies to ethnic snack foods. Mattel's multicultural Barbies or American Girl Dolls' Addy constitute a corporate "containment policy," not (this time) of communism but of creeping multiculturalism. A post-Fordist niche marketing strategy is at work here that uses diversity as a method of reaching beyond standardized mass production's economies of scale. It is, however, a safe, common-culture type of diversity that sanitizes and depoliticizes any challenge to the harmony of the status quo.

Racialized Kinderculture

Analysis of commercials on cable TV for children and Saturday morning network programs reveals advertising set in a WASP-oriented, middle-class reality. The homes that serve as backdrops for toys are spacious, with kid-dominated play areas—suburban utopias. Casts for the ads are reported by talent agents to be chosen around the "all-American" standard of appearance (read: white). When nonwhites are cast they frequently are placed in the periphery (the left one-third of the TV screen) of the action, leaving leading and instigating roles to white boys. Black characters in children's commercials often dance and play basketball and often display vivacious and loose characteristics—they are not the scholars, the kids with a secure vocational future. McDonald's, more than most children's corporations, employs African American children in its ads—but rarely in lead roles. Often, nonwhite children in McDonald's commercials are shown on the edges of the TV picture, slightly out of focus. Outside the conscious realization of their viewers, children's commercials that use nonwhite actors reproduce racial hierarchies that privilege whites. In one McDonald's ad connecting the corporation to traditional family values, the lyrics "families like . . ." in the songover are visually accompanied by a picture of an early-century immigrant family arriving in America. By the time the song's lyrics get to ". . . yours" the visual scene has shifted to a WASPish, upper-middle-class family. While referencing the great American melting pot the commercial covertly labels "your" family, the normalized all-American family, as white and upper middle class (Seiter, 1993; Goldman, 1992).

Gendered Kinderculture

It is amazing, given all the gender analysis and reconceptualization that has taken place over the past few decades, kinderculture can remain as gender-differentiated as it has. Yet whereas the gender analysis of popular culture advances and grants important insights into media constructions of gender, kinderculture continues to promote delineated gender roles. Advertising for girls' toys has changed little since the 1950s—missing are the allusions to how well the toy stoves provide training for home economics and the demands of motherhood. Similarly, toy ads for boys have witnessed only minor alterations during the last forty years. The adult-male voiceover is gone, but close-ups of the toys, and boys' voices making engine and weapon sound effects, continue uninterrupted. Boys still become one with their toys, whereas girls take care of theirs—ever the adoring spectators of their dolls in girl commercials. In Disney animated films, as Henry Giroux points out in Chapter 2, girls and women are depicted within constrictive gender roles. In *The Little Mermaid* and *The Lion King* women characters are subordinate to men: Mermaid Ariel appears to be on a liberatory journey against parental domination, but in the end she gives up her voice in a deal to trade her fin for legs so she can pursue her fair prince; in *The Lion King* all leaders are male, recipients of patriarchal entitlement. After King Mufasa dies, the duplicitous Scar becomes the new monarch. The lionesses are powerless, granting Scar the same deference as they had Mufasa. The female lions have no agency, no moral sense—they are merely backdrops to the action that the males initiate and in which they take part. Similar gender dynamics are present in *Aladdin* and *Beauty and the Beast*.

At work in these films and other manifestations of kinderculture is what Linda Christian-Smith and Jean Erdman refer to as "hegemonic masculinity" (see Chapter 7). Such a patriarchal form obviously holds serious implications for women, but it distorts male development as well. Boys are encouraged by various forms of the kinderculture curriculum to assume patriarchal roles that allegedly entitle them by birthright to define reality and enjoy the rewards of privilege through their domination of subordinates. Such an identity, unfortunately, is often formed through the young boy's denial of his connections with other people. Late-twentieth-century American patriarchal culture defines manhood in terms of separation and self-sufficiency—Clint Eastwood's no-name character comes to mind, as in *High Plains Drifter*. Here was a man who was such a loner he had no use for a name. Setting the standard for male disconnection, Eastwood's characters in this genre repressed their hurt feelings and learned to hide and disguise them from the world. Indeed, in hegemonic masculinity the only approved techniques for dealing with one's emotions involve evasiveness, bravado, boasting, bluster, lying, and various forms of aggression. In their attempt to master such techniques, young boys in our culture begin to cultivate a "cool and detached male pose" around the time they enter the fifth or sixth grade. In its fullest manifestations such a pose negates public emotional display—obviously crying is forbidden and even smiling and displays of enthusiasm are restricted (Nightingale, 1993).

The emotional repression and lack of interpersonal connection that this hegemonic masculinity breeds among boys creates severe social dysfunctionality. Boys who are unable to deal with emotional conflict and the interpersonal dynamics of family and peer relationships grow up to be men who have difficulty loving. They often become the types of men who leave and/or abuse their wives and families—an ever-growing trend in the last third of the twentieth century (Nightingale, 1993). Such sociopsychological issues push the kinderculture gender curriculum to the front burner. Such dynamics should induce teachers, parents, and other citizens to take seriously McLaren and Morris's disturbing picture of the gender issues at work in the *Mighty Morphin Power Rangers* with its patriarchal construction of the macho-military warrior prototype for boys. Some observers of the Power Rangers may take solace in the fact that there are both male and female characters; unfortunately, female Rangers are weak characters who constantly rely upon males for support. Girl Rangers relinquish feminine ethics of connectedness for patriarchal principles of macho, "kick-butt" competitiveness. In this ethical universe they are relegated to low status positions in the warrior hierarchy and are guilty of "traditional female tendencies" such as boyfriend identification and jealous competition with other girls over love interests. A home or school curriculum that takes kinderculture seriously involves children in the recognition and analysis of such gender issues and their effects on the pedagogical formation of their own self-concepts.

What Do We Do? Learning to Understand Kinderculture

What often inhibits understanding of the pedagogical power of popular culture in general and kinderculture in particular involves this society's failure to recognize that power plays an exaggerated role in the shaping of personal experiences. This relationship is so apparent that it is often lost in its obviousness (Grossberg, 1995). Power produces images of the world and the people who inhabit it that make meaning for those who receive the images. The films, books, video games, and TV shows of kinderculture shape the way white children, for example, understand the poor and racially marginalized—and in turn how they as white people come to recognize their own privilege. Language patterns connect with this production of images to reinforce power's influence, its ability to provide the context in which children encounter the world. The advent of electronic hyperreality has revolutionized the ways knowledge is produced in this culture and the ways children come to learn about the world. Parents and educators need to appreciate the nature of this revolution and its role in identity formation. Simple condemnation of kinderculture à la Bob Dole accompanied by calls for censorship is insufficient; equally ineffective is a policy of benign neglect. Concerned individuals should begin with an attempt to understand these dynamics in all their complexity and ambiguity, followed by an effort to involve themselves in the public conversation about them. In this context adults may come to appreciate the fact that postmodern children's confusion and identity disorientation may be a reasonable reaction to the incongruity between kinderculture's and schooling's positioning of children.

What Do We Do?
Rethinking Childhood Education

As we begin to understand these issues, the need for a reconceptualization of childhood education presents itself. At the foundation of this rethinking is the rejection of a child psychology predicated on the adjustment of children to the existing social order. Valerie Polakow (1992) argues that this adjustment in psychology demands an "order ideology of schooling" that is structured around the removal of the child from any experience of conflict. Inherent in this psychological model is an infantilization impulse that denies children the autonomy to make decisions about issues that affect their lives and to negotiate their relationships with conflicting imperatives. Rejection of the order ideology does not mean that we embrace anarchy but instead understand and learn even to appreciate the desire, the libidinal impulse that begins to bubble in childhood and reaches full expression in adolescence. Kinderculture in this context does not incite rebellion or violence; it pokes and irritates the beast of desire—an affective force that is present in romantic love, the bond between parent and child, and our spiritual proclivities (Ventura, 1994). A critical pedagogy of childhood is aware and unafraid of childhood desire, often connecting it to children's efforts to understand the world and themselves. As Paulo Freire maintained years ago, a critical childhood education is interested in the knowledge and intuitions children bring to school. In hyperreality such a pedagogical principle means that educators are obligated to study kinderculture, its effect on its consumers, and its relationship to desire. If we are interested in knowing our children, such a pedagogy provides us a direct line into their consciousness as well as their perceptions of themselves and the world. What happens when children nurtured by kinderculture encounter the certified knowledge of the school? The answer to such a question leads us to new forms of learning, new insights into the construction of contemporary childhood around which we can restructure schools and rethink the role of parenting in hyperreality.

References

Abercrombie, N. 1994. "Authority and consumer society." In R. Keat, N. Whiteley, and N. Abercrombie, *The authority of the consumer.* New York: Routledge.

Ball, T. 1992. "New faces of power." In T. Wartenberg, ed., *Rethinking power.* Albany, New York: SUNY.

Brady, J. 1997. "Multiculturalism and the American Dream." In S. Steinberg and J. Kincheloe, eds., *Kinderculture: The corporate construction of childhood.* Boulder: Westview.

Christian-Smith, L., and J. Erdman, 1997. "'Mom, it's not real!' Children constructing childhood through reading horror fiction." In S. Steinberg and J. Kincheloe, eds., *Kinderculture: The corporate construction of childhood.* Boulder: Westview Press.

Denzin, N. 1987. "Postmodern children." *Caring for Children/Society* (March/April): 32–25.

Donald, J. 1993. "The natural man and the virtuous woman: Reproducing citizens." In C. Jenks, ed., *Cultural reproduction.* New York: Routledge.

Dorfman, A. 1971. *How to read Donald Duck: Imperialist ideology in the Disney comic.* Trans. International General: Paris, 1975, 1992.

Ferguson, S. 1994. "The comfort of being sad." *Utne Reader* 64 (July/August): 60–61.

Fiske, J. 1993. *Power plays, power works.* New York: Verso.

Giroux, H. 1994. *Disturbing pleasures: Learning popular culture.* New York: Routledge.

_____. 1997."Are Disney movies good for your kids?" In S. Steinberg and J. Kincheloe, eds., *Kinderculture: The corporate construction of childhood.* Boulder: Westview Press.

Goldman, R. 1992. *Reading ads socially.* New York: Routledge.

Greider, W. 1992. *Who will tell the people? The betrayal of American Democracy.* New York: Touchstone.

Gresson, A. 1997. "Professional wrestling and youth culture: Teasing, taunting, and the containment of civility." In S. Steinberg and J. Kincheloe, eds., *Kinderculture: The corporate construction of childhood.* Boulder: Westview Press.

Griffin, C. 1993. *Representations of youth: The study of youth and adolescence in Britain and America.* Cambridge, Massachusetts: Polity Press.

Grossberg, L. 1995. "What's in a name (one more time)." *Taboo: The Journal of Culture and Education* 1 (Fall): 11–37.

Jipson, J., and U. Reynolds. 1997. "Anything you want: Women and children in popular culture." In S. Steinberg and J. Kincheloe, eds., *Kinderculture: The corporate construction of childhood.* Boulder: Westview Press.

Kellner, D. 1990. *Television and the crisis of democracy.* Boulder: Westview Press.

_____. 1992. "Popular culture and the construction of postmodern identities." In S. Lash and J. Friedman, eds., *Modernity and identity.* Cambridge, Massachusetts: Blackwell.

_____. 1997. *"Beavis and Butt-Head:* No future for postmodern youth." In S. Steinberg and J. Kincheloe, eds., *Kinderculture: The corporate construction of childhood.* Boulder: Westview Press.

Kincheloe, J. 1993. *Toward a critical politics of teacher thinking: Mapping the postmodern.* New Hampshire: Bergin and Garvey.

_____. 1995. *"Home Alone* and 'Bad to the Bone.'" Paper presented at the *Journal of Curriculum Theory* and Classroom Practice Conference, Chattanooga, Tennessee, September 29.

_____. 1997. "McDonald's, power, and children: Ronald McDonald (aka Ray Kroc) does it all for you." In S. Steinberg and J. Kincheloe, eds., *Kinderculture: The corporate construction of childhood.* Boulder: Westview Press.

Kunzle, D. 1992. "Dispossession by ducks: The imperialist treasure hunt in the Barks-Disney comics." Unpublished paper.

Lincoln, Y. 1995. "If I am not just one person, but many, why should I write just one text?" Paper presented at the American Educational Research Association, San Francisco, April 13.

Lipsky, D., and A. Abrams. 1994. *Late bloomers.* New York: Times Books.

McLaren, P. 1994. *Critical pedagogy and predatory culture.* New York: Routledge.

McLaren, P., R. Hammer, D. Sholle, and S. Reilly. 1995. *Rethinking media literacy: A critical pedagogy of representation.* New York: Peter Lang.

McLaren, P., and J. Morris. 1997. *"Mighty Morphin Power Rangers:* The aesthetics of phallo-militaristic justice." In S. Steinberg and J. Kincheloe, eds., *Kinderculture: The corporate construction of childhood.* Boulder: Westview Press.

Mumby, D. 1989. "Ideology and the social construction of meaning: A communication perspective." *Communication Quarterly* 37(4): 291–304.

Nelson, C., P. Treichler, and L. Grossberg. 1992. "Cultural studies: An introduction." In C. Nelson, P. Treichler, and L. Grossberg, eds., *Cultural studies.* New York: Routledge.

Nightingale, C. 1993. *On the edge: A history of poor black children and their American dreams.* New York: Basic Books.

Paul, W. 1994. *Laughing and screaming: Modern Hollywood horror and comedy.* New York: Columbia University Press.

Polakow, V. 1992. *The erosion of childhood.* Chicago: University of Chicago Press.

Postman, N. 1994. *The disappearance of childhood.* New York: Vintage Books.

Provenzo, E. 1991. *Video kids: Making sense of Nintendo.* Cambridge: Harvard University Press.

_____. 1997. "Video games and the emergence of interactive media for children." In S. Steinberg and J. Kincheloe, eds., *Kinderculture: The corporate construction of childhood.* Boulder: Westview Press.

Seiter, E. 1993. *Sold separately: Parents and children in consumer culture.* New Brunswick, New Jersey: Rutgers University Press.

Steinberg, S. 1997. "The bitch who has everything." In S. Steinberg and J. Kincheloe, eds., *Kinderculture: The corporate construction of childhood.* Boulder: Westview Press.

Stewart, M. 1993. *Ellen is home alone.* New York: Bantam Books.

Thiele, L. 1986. "Foucault's triple murder and the development of power." *Canadian Journal of Political Science* 19 (June): 243–260.

Ventura, M. 1994. "The age of endarkenment." *Utne Reader* 64 (July/August): 63–66.

Vogel, J. 1994. "Throw away the key." *Utne Reader* 64 (July/August): 56–60.

Warde, A. 1994. "Consumers, identity, and belonging: Reflections on some theses of Zygmunt Bauman." In R. Keat, N. Whiteley, and N. Abercrombie, *The authority of the consumer.* New York: Routledge.

Wartenberg, T. 1992. "Situated social power." In T. Wartenberg, ed., *Rethinking power.* Albany, New York: SUNY Press.

1 Home Alone *and "Bad to the Bone": The Advent of a Postmodern Childhood*

Joe L. Kincheloe

Home Alone (1990) and *Home Alone 2: Lost in New York* (1992) revolve around Kevin McAlister's (Macauley Culkin) attempts to find his family after: (1) being left behind on a family Christmas trip to Paris; and (2) being separated from his family on a Christmas trip to Miami. Wildly successful, the two movies portray the trials and tribulations of Kevin's attempts to take care of himself while his parents try to rejoin him. In the process of using these plots to set up a variety of comedic stunts and sight gags, the movies inadvertently allude to a sea of troubles relating to children and family life in the late twentieth century. As we watch the films, an entire set of conflicts and contradictions revolving around the lives of contemporary children begins to emerge. In this way both movies take on a social importance unimagined by producers, directors, and screenplay writers. In this essay I will use the family dynamics of the *Home Alone* movies as a means of exposing the social forces that have altered Western childhood over the past couple decades. In both films a central but unspoken theme involves the hurt and pain that accompany children and their families in postmodern America.

A Generation of Kids Left Home Alone

Child rearing is a victim of the late twentieth century. Given the prevalence of divorce and households with two working parents, fathers and mothers are around children for less of the day. As parents are still at work in the afternoon when children get home from school, children are

31

given latchkeys and expected to take care of themselves. Thus, we have seen generations of "home-aloners"—kids that in large part have had to raise themselves. The past thirty years have witnessed a change in family structure that must be taken seriously by parents, educators, and cultural workers of all stripes. Since the early 1960s the divorce rate as well as the percentage of children living with one parent has tripled. Only one-half of today's children have parents who are married to each other. By the twenty-first century only one-third of U.S. children will have such parents. Among children under six years old, one in four lives in poverty. The stress that comes from the economic changes of the last twenty years has undermined the stability of the family. Family incomes have stagnated, as costs of middle-class existence (home ownership, health care, and higher education) have skyrocketed. Since the late 1960s the amount of time parents spend with their children has dropped from an average of thirty hours per week to seventeen (Lipsky and Abrams, 1994; Galston, December 2, 1991). Increasingly left to fend for themselves, contemporary children have turned to TV and video games to help pass their time alone.

Any study of contemporary children must analyze the social conditions that shape family life. Rarely do mainstream social commentators make reference to the fact that Americans' standard of living peaked in 1973, creating a subsequent declining economic climate that demanded mothers work. Although the effects of international competition, declining productivity, and the corporate reluctance to reinvent the workplace all contributed to a depressed economy, not all recent family problems can be ascribed to the declining post-Fordist economy. The decline of the public space and the growth of cynicism have undermined the nation's ability to formulate creative solutions to family dysfunction. The 1970s and 1980s, for example, although witnessing the birth and growth of a family-values movement, represented an era that consistently privileged individual gratification over the needs of the community (Paul, 1994; Coontz, 1992). Such an impulse justified the privatistic retreat from public social involvement that has been institutionalized in the 1990s as part of a larger right-wing celebration of self-reliance and efficient government. Unfortunately, it is often our children who must foot the cost of this perverse abrogation of democratic citizenship.

One scene in *Home Alone* highlights the decline of the public space in postmodern America. While Kevin's parents attempt to arrange a flight from Paris to their home in Chicago, the rest of the family watches *It's a Wonderful Life* dubbed in French on TV. This positioning of movie within movie confronts viewers with the distance between the Americas of Jimmy Stewart's George Bailey and Macauley Culkin's Kevin McAlister. Kevin has no community, no neighbors to call for help—he is on his own in his "private space." George Bailey had a score of neighbors to help bail him out of his financial plight and to help him fight the capitalists' efforts to destroy the community. Kevin is not just home alone—he is socially alone as well. But such realizations are not present in the conscious mind of the moviemakers. On the surface the McAlisters live in a desirable community and are a perfect family. Like millions of other late-twentieth-century families, they are physically together but culturally and emotionally fragmented. Plugged into their various "market segments" of entertainment media, they retreat into their "virtual isolation booths."

Like millions of other kids, Kevin feels isolated in such an existence—isolation leads to powerlessness, hopelessness, and boredom. How could kids with everything handed to them, adults ask, become so alienated from their parents, schools, and communities? The answer to this question involves on some level the pervasive violation of childhood innocence. Popular culture via TV promised our children a Brady Bunch family circus, but they had to settle for alienated and isolated homes. The continuing popularity of *The Brady Bunch* is testimony to the mindset of American children—the Brady Bunch with its family values and two engaged parents seemed to provide what our children found lacking in their own homes. This melancholic nostalgia for suburban family bliss indicates a yearning for a lost childhood. All those hours home alone have taken their toll (James, December 23, 1990; Rapping, 1994; Ferguson, 1994).

The Unwanted

Although the *Home Alone* movies work hard to deny it, they are about a child unwanted by his family—as with other films of the 1980s and early 1990s. The comedic forms of the movies supposedly render the unwanted theme harmless, in the process revealing contemporary views of parenting and the abandonment of children. In one particular scene in *Home Alone*, Kevin's mother (Catherine O'Hara) pays her penance for abandoning her son by riding home to Chicago through midwestern snowstorms in a truck carrying a polka band and its leader (John Candy). In one dialogue mother and bandleader engage in a confessional on bad parenting and child abandonment:

MOTHER: I'm a bad parent.

BAND LEADER: No, you're not. You're beating yourself up. . . . You want to see bad parents. We're [i.e., the band] on the road forty-eight to forty-nine weeks out of the year. We hardly see our families. Joe over there, gosh, he forgets his kids' names half the time. Ziggy over there hasn't even met his kid. Eddie, let's just hope none of them [his children] write a book about him.

MOTHER: Have you ever gone on vacation and left your child home?

BAND LEADER: No, but I did leave one at a funeral parlor once. Yeah, it was terrible. I was all distraught and everything. The wife and I, we left the little tike there in the funeral parlor all day, all day! We went back at night when we came to our senses and there he was. Apparently, he was there alone all day with the corpse. He was okay. You know, after six or seven weeks he came around and started talking again. But he's okay. They get over it. Kids are resilient like that.

MOTHER: Maybe we shouldn't talk about it.

BAND LEADER: You brought it up.

So comfortable are marketers with the theme of abandonment that promos on the home video of *Home Alone 2: Lost in New York* present a *Home Alone Christmas Album*. Commodifying child abandonment, promoters urge viewers to "begin a tradition in your house." Something is happening in these movies and the promotions that surround them that is not generally understood by the larger society. By the early 1990s social neglect of children had become so commonplace that it could be presented as a comedic motif without raising too many eyebrows. There was a time when childhood was accorded protected status—but that time is growing obsolete, as safety nets disintegrate and child-supports crumble. Now, as children are left to fend for themselves, few public institutions exist to address their needs.

In the *Home Alone* movies not only is Kevin left to take care of himself, but when his parents and family are on-screen they treat him with disdain and cruelty. In one scene Kevin's uncle unjustifiably calls him a "little jerk." After understandably asking why he always gets "treated like scum," Kevin is banished to the attic, at which time he proclaims for his generation: "Families suck." These early experiences set up the comedic bread-and-butter of *Home Alone*: Kevin's transference of his anger toward his family to burglars Marv (Daniel Stern) and Harry (Joe Pesci) and his subsequent torture of them. Both *Home Alone* movies are not the only movies of the era that address child abandonment and child revenge. In horror-thrillers *Halloween* and *Friday the 13th* the only individuals spared from violence are those who give time to and care for children. Those who neglect children must ultimately pay with their lives. As neglected social rejects, children are relegated to the margins of society. It is not surprising, therefore, that in *Home Alone 2* Kevin forges an alliance with a homeless pigeon-lady who lives in Central Park—after all they are both social castoffs. Together they learn to deal with their cultural status.

The American Ambivalence Toward Children

After World War II Americans began to realize that childhood was becoming a phase of life distinctly separate from adulthood. This distinction was most evident in the youth culture that began to take shape in the 1950s; it was this youth culture that convinced parents that they were losing the ability to shape the culture in which their children lived. As a result, they were losing control of their sons and daughters. This fear has informed the academic study of youth in the second half of the twentieth century, often focusing attention on children as "the problem." Too often refusing to question the dominant culture and values of the adult world and the tacit assumptions of the field of childhood studies itself, mainstream scholars have often viewed conflict between children and parents as dysfunctional. Childhood "experts" and the mainstream education establishment have often insisted in this academic context that children need to be instructed to follow directions. This functionalist orientation assumes that the order and stability of environments must be maintained (Paul, 1994; Lewis, 1992; Griffin, 1993; Polakow, 1992). This, of course, ensures that institutions such as schools become unable to accommodate change, as they regress into a state of "equilibrium," that is, rigidity.

The virtual ubiquity of parent-child alienation and conflict is rarely perceived at the individual level of human interaction as a social phenomenon. When such conflicting dynamics occur in almost all parent-child relations, it is not likely that fault rests solely with individual parents and individual children. As we said before, something larger is happening here. It seems as if individual children cannot help but judge parents for their inconsistencies and shortcomings. Yet parents cannot help but resent their judgment and strike back with equal venom (Ventura, 1994). Adults must understand the social nature of this familial phenomenon and, based on this recognition, attempt to transcend the demand for order inscribed into their consciousness by the larger culture. Indeed, Americans don't understand their children or the dynamics of children's culture. Kids understand that adults just don't get it, as they listen and watch adults express and act on their misunderstandings of the differences between generational experiences and mind-sets.

Schools are perceived by children as virtually hopeless—indeed, they are institutionally grounded on a dismissal of these differences. Little has changed since the 1960s when Kenneth Keniston wrote that adult misunderstanding of youth contributed to the conclusion reached by many children: American mainstream culture offers us little to live for (Lewis, 1992).

Understanding this adult-child alienation, children slowly begin to withdraw into their own culture. Culkin's Kevin has absolutely no need for adults, as he shops (with newspaper coupons even), takes care of the house, and defends himself against robbers all by himself. This is quite typical for the films of John Hughes, whose children and teenagers rule in a world where youth culture is the only one that matters. Parents in these films are notoriously absent—they are either at work or on vacation; their advice is antiquated, consisting generally of pompous pronouncements about subjects they obviously know nothing about. Typical of the genre is *The Breakfast Club*, which revolves around the stupidity of parents and adult authority. Although it is a flagrant attempt by Hughes to commodify and exploit youth culture, the film does point out the width and depth of the chasm that separates kids and adults (Rapping, 1994). Children's culture, of course, takes shape in shadows far away from the adult gaze—as well it should. The point here is that it behooves parents, teachers, social workers, and other cultural workers who are interested in the welfare of children to understand the social dynamics that shape children and their culture in the final years of the twentieth century. When parents intensify their anxiety about the threat of postmodern kinderculture and strike out against it, they simply widen the chasm between themselves and their children. In this situation, the assertion of parental control becomes simply an end in itself, having little to do with the needs of children.

As adults in the 1950s and early 1960s began to understand the power of children's culture and the separations between childhood and adulthood it represented, parent and educator anxiety levels reached new highs. Adult fears that the kids were out of control expressed themselves in a variety of ways, none more interesting than in two British films of the early 1960s, *Village of the Damned* and its sequel, *Children of the Damned*. *Village of the Damned* is based on an invasion by an intergalactic sperm that impregnates earth women to produce a new race of mutant children who mature quickly and are capable of reading adult minds. Reflecting adult anxieties of the era concerning the growing partition between childhood and adulthood, the movie offers a "solution" to the youth problem. Although they embrace it with great difficulty, adults in *Children of the Damned* ultimately decide that they must kill their children. Understanding that child murder by necessity is suicidal in that it involves killing a part of oneself, parents sacrifice themselves in order to eradicate the iniquity their children embody. The youth rebellions of the mid- and late 1960s that followed *Children of the Damned* would serve to raise the emotional ante expressed in the movie's fantasized infanticide.

The adult hostility toward children is omnipresent in the *Home Alone* movies, but such issues are consistently hidden from overt recognition. Previous films—*The Other, The Exorcist, The Bad Seed, Firestarter, It's Alive*—recognized adult hostility but projected it onto evil children as a means of concealing it. The abundance of these evil-children films points to a social tendency of parents to view their children as alien intruders. This child-based xenophobia positions children as foreigners whose presence marks the end of the family's configuration as a couple (Paul, 1994). Old routines are undermined and new demands must be met, as the child's power as manipulator is experienced by harried adults. Such familial dynamics set the scene for the postmodern child-custody case where lawyers, judges, and parents decide who *has* to take the kids.

Commercial children's culture understands what parents and educators don't—children and adolescents are wracked by desire that demands stimulation and often gets out of hand. We see its manifestation in children and children's culture with the constant struggle to escape boredom. Of course, most adults view this childhood desire as a monstrous quality to be squashed by any means necessary even if it requires the stupidification of young people in the process. In the *Home Alone* movies Kevin constantly feels as if he has done something terribly wrong, as if he were a bad kid. In *Home Alone 2* Kevin prays to the Rockefeller Square Christmas tree: "I need to see my mother, I need to tell her I'm sorry." Exactly for what he should be sorry, no one is quite sure. One can only conclude that he is sorry for being a child, for intruding on the smooth operation of the family, of being goaded by his monstrous desire.

If we equate children with that which is monstrous, it is not a long jump to the position that the manipulative aliens are evil. In *The Bad Seed*, a successful novel, play, and movie of the mid-1950s, Rhoda is an eight-year-old murderess endowed with a greed for material things—childhood desire run amuck. As the first work that explored this homicidal dimension of childhood, *The Bad Seed* equates youth with absolute malignancy—concealed at first in an innocent package. As Rhoda's landlady says of her: "She never gets anything dirty. She is a good child, a perfect child. She saves her money and keeps her room clean." The appearance of evil so close to goodness and innocence made the child monster that much more horrible. Children who are so evil (or at least so capable of it) in a perverted sense justify child abuse. By 1990 this image of the bad child would be used for comic effect in *Problem Child* and *Problem Child 2* a year later. The way adults in *Problem Child* reacted to the problem child is revealing:

> SCHOOL PRINCIPAL: Being a principal's great 'cause I hate kids. I have to deal with the weenies.

> SCHOOL TEACHER to principal after he brings problem child to her class as a new student: O God, another one. How many kids are they going to make me teach?

> LAWANDA, the owner of the bank: What's this thing [referring to problem child]? This kid's a nightmare. . . . Kids are like bum legs. You don't shoot the patient, you cut off the leg.

> PROBLEM CHILD'S GRANDFATHER to father: You little psycho— you're an evil boy. You got to learn to respect your elders.

> LAWANDA: Listen you little monster. I'm going to marry your father and send you to boarding school in Baghdad.

> SCHOOL PRINCIPAL: You rotten kids should be locked in cages.

> LAWANDA: I hate children. They ruin everything. If I had enough power I'd wipe them off the face of the earth.

Child-murderer Sharon Smith never stated it this clearly and unambiguously.

Whenever the problem child seeks to subvert the order of the status quo, viewers are alerted to what is coming by George Thorogood's blues guitar riff from "Bad to the Bone." Such innate "badness" cannot be indulged. As with the neo–folk wisdom in 1990s America that criminals cannot be rehabilitated, there is no hope for the growth and development of the problem child. *Home Alone*'s Kevin, who is certainly capable of "badness" and sadistic torture, is still struggling with parental forgiveness; the problem child is beyond all that. Parental and educational authority is concerned simply with control; the issue is naked power— there is no need for ameliorative window dressing in this realpolitik for children. In this context kindness becomes the cause of juvenile delinquency, child advocacy the response of dupes and bleeding-heart fools. Movie audiences want to see the problem child punished, if not physically attacked. Not too far from such sentiments looms child abuse.

In John Carpenter's *Halloween* the camera shows the audience an unidentified murderer's point of view of a middle-America suburban house occupied by two teenagers making love in an upstairs bedroom. As we watch from the murderer's eyes, he picks up a carving knife in the kitchen, observes the teenage boy leave the house, and walks back up the stairs to the bedroom where the teenage girl is now in bed alone. Looking directly into the gaze of the camera the girl expresses her annoyance with an obviously familiar character wielding the knife. At this point the hand carrying the knife stabs the girl to death, principally focusing the attack on her bare breasts. It is only after the murder that we are granted a reverse-angle shot of the killer, who is a six-year-old boy. In 1978, when *Halloween* was made, reviewers made little note of the age of the murderer (Paul, 1994). So accustomed was the American audience to the "innate" evil potential of children that moviemakers perceived no need to explain the etymology of the child's violent behavior. By the end of the 1970s headlines such as "Killer Kids" and newspaper copy such as "Who are our children? One day they are innocent. The next, they may try to blow your head off" (Vogel, 1994, 57) had made an impact. No more assumptions of innocence, no surprises. A new era had emerged.

The Blame Game

Clusters of issues come together as we consider the role of mothers and fathers in the family wars of the late twentieth century. The battle to ascribe blame for family dysfunction in general, and childhood pathology in particular, plays out on a variety of landscapes: politics, religion, and popular culture. On the political terrain in the 1990s, we have witnessed the Dan Quayle–Murphy Brown showdown over single mothers as parents; on the religious battleground right-wing Christian fundamentalists have fingered feminism as the catalyst for mothers' neglect of their children. The analysis of this blame game as expressed in popular culture offers some unique insights.

In the *Home Alone* movies Kevin's mother has internalized the right-wing blame of women for the neglect (abandonment) of Kevin in particular and family pathology in general. Though they are uncomfortable with a negative maternal figure, the screenplay writers leave no doubt as to who's to blame. Banished to the attic because he has been *perceived* as a nuisance, Kevin is (justifiably) hurt and angry.

KEVIN: Everyone in this family hates me.

MOTHER: Then maybe you should ask Santa for a new family.

KEVIN: I don't want a new family. I don't want any family. Families suck.

MOTHER: Just stay up there. I don't want to see you again for the rest of the night.

KEVIN: I don't want to see you again for the rest of my whole life. And I don't want to see anyone else, either.

MOTHER: I hope you don't mean that. You'd be pretty sad if you woke up tomorrow morning and you didn't have a family.

KEVIN: No, I wouldn't.

MOTHER: Then say it again. Maybe it'll happen.

KEVIN: I hope I never see any of you again.

The mother here is the provocateur, the one who plants the ideas that emerge as Kevin's wishes. Insensitive to his emotional hurt, she induces him to request a new family, she is the first to speak of not wanting to see him, she is the one who dares Kevin to tempt fate by wishing away his family (Paul, 1994). There is little doubt left by the *Home Alone* movies that child care is the mother's responsibility. John Heard's father-character is virtually a nonentity. He is disinterested in Kevin, condescending and hostile. He knows (along with the audience) that he is not responsible for Kevin's abandonment even though he was present during the entire episode. He has no reason to gnash his teeth or rent his garment in displays of penitence—this is the domain of the mother. And pay she does with her polka-band trip in *Home Alone* and in her frenzied running through the nighttime streets of New York calling for her son in *Home Alone 2*. In an era when child abuse and child murder by mothers occupy national headlines, Kevin's mother's quest for forgiveness may signify a much larger guilt. The right-wing male's blame of women for the ills of the family, however, is grotesquely perverse, implying as it does that battalions of strong but tender men are struggling with their wives to let them take charge of child rearing—not hardly (Rapping, 1994).

Feminist research and analysis of child abuse and domestic violence have subverted the happy depiction of family life as a safe haven far removed from pathologies emanating from internal power inequities. As such scholarship documented the ways that family life has oppressed women and children, profamily conservative groups responded by calling for a reassertion of patriarchal control in the home. Women, they argued, should return to child rearing. Some conservatives have even maintained that women who don't adequately perform these "maternal" chores should have their children taken away and placed in orphanages. The most optimistic estimates place the number of children who would be institutionalized under this plan at over 1 million—the costs of such care would run over $36 billion (Griffin, 1993; Morganthau et al., December 12, 1994). The male backlash to the assertive feminist critique has only begun with its depiction of women's political organizations as the rise of a dangerous special-interest group. Protectors of male power are waging an effective public relations battle: Any campaign that is able to deflect blame for family failure from absent and often abusive fathers to mothers possesses a superior penchant for persuasion and little concern for truth (Griffin, 1993).

Home Alone displays these gender dynamics in its complete refusal to implicate the father in the abandonment. Upon learning that Kevin is not in Paris with the family, his mother exclaims "What kind of mother am I?" The lack of effect on the part of the adult males of the family, Kevin's father and his uncle, is perplexing. The careful viewer can only conclude that they neither like nor care about the eight-year-old. An explanation of the father's dismissiveness is never provided. All the viewer can discern is that the father and uncle seem to be fighting for their manhood, expressing it perhaps in their resistance to the "breadwinner-loser" male character who forfeits his "male energy" in his domestication and subsequent acceptance of fidelity in marriage, dedication to job, and devotion to children (Lewis, 1992). Such a male figure was ridiculed by beatniks as square, by *Playboy* devotees as sexually timid, and by hippies as tediously straight. The search for a hip male identity along with a healthy dose of irresponsibility has undermined the family as a stable and loving environment. Indeed, to "do the right thing" in regard to one's family as a man is to lose status among one's fellow men.

An examination of adult-male behavior in families indicates that many men are desperately concerned with peer-group status. For example, recent media reports indicate that men on average pay pitifully inadequate child support to their former spouses (if they pay it at all). Only half of women awarded child support ever receive what they are owed; another quarter receive partial payments, and the remaining quarter get nothing at all (Galston, December 2, 1991). This ambiguous role of the father in the family highlighted by the indifferent father of *Home Alone* is addressed in a more overtly oedipal manner in other movies of the past couple of decades (Paul, 1994). *The Shining*, for example, retrieves that which has always been repressed in Western culture—a father's hostility toward his own son—and builds an entire plot around it. Danny, the child protagonist in *The Shining*, develops the psychic power to see beyond the limits of time and space after his father (Jack Nicholson) in an alcoholic stupor broke Danny's arm. Danny's power, his shining, is expressed through his imaginary friend, Tony, who lives in Danny's mouth. Tony exists to help Danny cope with his violent and abusive father. Danny's presence and growth remind his father of his emasculation, his stultification by the family. The father's solution to his problem—the attempted ax-murder of his wife and child—allows for none of the *Home Alone* ambiguity; the movie jumps into the maelstrom of the conflict between virile masculinity and the demands of domesticity.

As the screen image of the crazed, ax-wielding Jack Nicholson fades into our blurred image of *Jurassic Park* (1993), the continuity of the child-hating adult male remains intact. Even in this "child-friendly," Spielberg-produced dinodrama, the paleontologist (Sam Neill) holds such an extreme hatred of children that he won't ride in the same car with them. At one point in the film, in response to a prepubescent boy's sarcastic question about the power of dinosaurs, Neill evokes the image of the violent Nicholson, circling and threatening the child with the ominous claw of a velociraptor. The difference between *Jurassic Park* and *The Shining*, however, involves Neill's moment of epiphany; when the children are endangered by the dinosaurs, Neill sheds his hatred and, like a good father, risks mutilation and death to save their lives. As in the *Home Alone* movies, the issue of the father's hatred is buried in a happy ending: the safe children celebrating with the "reformed" Neill and the happy McAlister family celebrating Christmas in a frenetic present-opening ritual. The demand for family values in the 1980s and 1990s had changed the cultural landscape: family values must triumph; adult men must be depicted as ultimately devoted to their children; the feminists' portrayal of the "bad father" must not be reinforced.

And as if the Ambiguity Wasn't Bad Enough, Some Kids Matter More Than Others

It doesn't take long to discern that with the class dynamics of the 1990s poor children in America don't matter as much as upper-middle-class children, that is, privileged children like the ones portrayed in the *Home Alone* movies. The frequent assertion that America is not a class society, uttered so confidently by mainstream politicians and educators, holds profound psychological and political consequences. This class silence undermines the well-to-do's understanding that they were granted a head start while paralyzing the less successful with a feeling of personal inferiority. At the political level, as the belief sustains the fiction it reifies the status quo: When the poor are convinced that their plight is self-produced, the larger society is released from any responsibility (Rubin, 1994).

An overt class silence pervades the *Home Alone* movies. Even newspaper reviewers referred to the upper-middle-class, white, and Protestant "bleached and sanitized" microcosm of the two movies (Koch, December 27, 1990). The McAlisters are very wealthy, living in their enormous brick colonial in a generic Chicago suburb filled with extravagant furnishings and conveniences. Indeed, they are an obnoxious and loathsome crew, but being so privileged they believe they can act any way they want. The filmmakers go out of their way to make sure viewers know that the family deserves its money—as father McAlister drinks from crystal in the plane's first-class cabin on the way to Paris he alludes to his hard work and humble origins. The message is clear—the American dream is attainable for those willing to put in the effort. The McAlisters deserve their good fortune.

It is a restricted world of affluent WASPs. Harry and Marv (two small-time robbers with an attitude) make their appearance as the only poor people and the only non-WASPs in the two movies. Harry (Pesci) and Marv (Stern) are quickly positioned as "the other" in both screenplays: They speak in specific lower-socioeconomic-class accents; obviously ethnic, Pesci exaggerates his working-class Italian accent; and just so we are not confused Stern signifies his Jewishness with a curiously gratuitous "Happy Hanukkah" reference as he steals money from a toy store. They are ignorant and uneducated—Pesci makes specific reference to the fact he never completed the sixth grade; they also hold an irrational hatred of the affluent—their modus operandi is to flood the affluent homes they rob (thus they are known as the "wet bandits"). These class- and ethnic-specific traits set Marv and Harry apart to such a degree that the audience can unambiguously enjoy their torture at the hands of Kevin.

The *Home Alone* movies pull their weight in the larger social effort to erase class as a dynamic in late-twentieth-century American life. Under interrogation the movies confess their class complicity, as evidenced through the "otherization" of Marv and Harry. Compare Marv and Harry with Mr. Duncan, the toy-store owner who appears in *Home Alone 2*. Imbued with the sweetness and generosity of Clarence, the guardian angel in *It's a Wonderful Life*, Duncan is the most charming character in the *Home Alone* movies. After the McAlister family's reunification in *Home Alone 2*, he showers them with scores of presents. His only motivation for being in business is that he loves children and wants to see their happy faces when they open presents from his store. His loving smiles prove that capitalism cares and the status quo is just. He deserves every penny of his profits just as much as Marv and Harry deserve their torment. Such characterization gently dovetails with the dominant political impulses of the moment, marked by a callous acceptance of poverty, child poverty in particular, in the midst of plenty.

More than 12.6 million children live below the poverty line, making one out of every five American children poor (Polakow, 1992). Too often unaware of even the existence of such class realities, Americans and their institutions are far removed from the insidious effects of such poverty. Poor children too infrequently escape the effects of living with parents scarred by their sense of shortcoming, of having to negotiate movie and TV images of the poor and working class as dangerous and oafish caricatures (as in *Home Alone*), and of confronting teachers and social workers who hold lower expectations for them than their middle- and upper-middle-class peers. A key feature of the class dynamic in the *Home Alone* movies involves the public reaction to the McAlisters' child abandonment episodes as "good fun," as opposed to the real-life home-alone cases that keep surfacing in the 1990s. When Kevin's parents report his having been left alone in New York to the police after they reach their vacation destination in Miami, it's no big deal. Even when they admit that abandoning the child has become "a family tradition," no one is excited—after all, the McAlisters are upper class, well-to-do people. Almost daily, parents (especially single mothers) who leave their young children home alone for sometimes just a few hours are arrested and forced to relinquish their offspring to foster care. With child care often costing $200–400 per month, poor mothers are placed into virtually impossible circumstances (Seligman, August 1, 1993). The society's refusal to address poor and single mothers' need for child care has contributed to the feminization of poverty (Polakow, 1992). The *Home Alone* movies indicate the double standard that dominates the American view of the rich and the poor and the mean-spirited class bias of some expressions of popular culture in this conservative age.

The Postmodern Childhood

Within the bizarre *Home Alone* mix of child abandonment, child-parent alienation, children caught in the crossfire of gender wars, crass class bias, and comedy resides something profound about the role of children in contemporary American culture. The movies could have been made only in a culture that had experienced a profound shift in the social role of children. To all individuals who have a stake in understanding childhood—parents, teachers, social workers, family counselors, and so on—knowledge of these changing conditions becomes a necessity. A no-growth economy has mandated that all adults in the family must work outside the home; because of such needs, children find themselves saddled with daily duties ranging from housecleaning, baby-sitting, and grocery shopping to cooking, laundering, and organizing car pools. With the "family values" agenda of right-wing movements of the 1990s threatening to eviscerate government's economic support of poor and middle-class families, the poverty problem of children looks to get worse before it gets better.

The new era of childhood—the postmodern childhood—cannot escape the influence of the postmodern condition with its electronic media saturation. Such a media omnipresence produces a hyperreality that repositions the real as something no longer simply given but artificially reproduced as real. Thus, media-produced models replace the real—simulated TV kids on sitcoms replace real-life children as models of childhood. In this same, media-driven, postmodern condition a cultural implosion takes place, ripping apart boundaries between information and entertainment as well as images and politics. As media push the infinite proliferation of meaning, boundaries between childhood and adulthood fade as children and adults negotiate the same mediascape and struggle with the same impediments to meaning-making. Children become "adultified" and adults become "childified" (Aronowitz and Giroux, 1991; Best and Kellner, 1991). Boundaries between adulthood and childhood blur to the point that a clearly defined, "traditional," innocent childhood becomes an object of nostalgia—a sure sign that it no longer exists in any unproblematic form (Lipsky and Abrams, 1994; Postman, 1994).

There is nothing childlike about a daily routine of child care, cooking, and shopping. In the *Home Alone* movies Kevin is almost completely adultlike in meeting the demands of survival on his own. He checks into hotels, uses credit cards, orders pizzas, and shops for groceries (even with coupons)—all as a part of a day's work. He needs no adult figure; he can take complete care of himself. In the postmodern childhood being home alone is an everyday reality. Children now know what only adults used to know: postmodern children are sexually knowledgeable and often sexually experienced; they understand and many have experimented with drugs and alcohol; and new studies show they often experience the same pressures as single working mothers, as they strive to manage the stresses of school, work at home, and interpersonal family dynamics. When the cultural dynamics of hyperreality collide with post–baby boom demographics and the economic decline of the early 1970s, 1980s, and 1990s, the world changes (Lipsky and Abrams, 1994). The daily life of media-produced family models such as the Cleavers from *Leave It to Beaver* is convulsed. June must get a job and Wally and Beaver must take care of the house. No longer can Beaver and his friends Larry and Whitey leisurely play on the streets of Mayfield after school. Anyway, it's dangerous—Mayfield is not as safe as it used to be.

In the mid-1990s children under twelve belong to a generation only half the size of the baby boomers. As a result, children as a group garner less attention in 1996 than they did in 1966 and exert a correspondingly diminished voice in the society's social and political conversation. In such a context, youth issues are not as important as they once were. Add to this a declining economy complicated by rising expectations. As

American manufacturing jobs have disappeared and dead-end service jobs have expanded, advertising continues to promote higher and higher consumer desire. Frustration levels among children and teenagers rise as a direct result of this socioeconomic contradiction. Given the centrality of TV in the lives of this postmodern home-alone generation, the awareness of the desirability of children's consumer goods becomes a central aspect of their lived reality. Consumer desire, however, is only one aspect of the effect TV and other electronic media have upon American children. TV is where children find out about American culture. Indeed, one doesn't have to be a movie critic to know how often Hollywood has drawn on the TV-taught-me-all-I-know theme. In *The Man Who Fell to Earth*, David Bowie as an alien learns all about earth culture from TV; in *Being There* Peter Sellers as idiot-savant Chauncey Gardner knows nothing about the world but what he has learned on TV. The movie ends with Chauncey on his way to a possible presidential candidacy—life imitates art? The robot in *Short Circuit*, the mermaid in *Splash*, the aliens in *Explorers*, and the Neanderthal in *Encino Man* all are completely socialized by TV (Lipsky and Abrams, 1994).

What does the repeated invocation of this theme say to observers of childhood? With the evolution of TV as a medium that attempts to more or less represent reality, children have gained an adultlike (not necessarily an informed) view of the world in only a few years of watching TV. Traditional notions of childhood as a time of sequential learning about the world don't work in a hyperreality saturated with sophisticated but power-driven views of reality. When a hotel porter asks Kevin McAlister in *Home Alone 2* if he knows how the TV in his hotel room works, Kevin replies, "I'm ten years old; TV's my life." The point is well taken, and as a consciousness-dominating, full-disclosure medium TV provides everyone—sixty-year-old adults to eight-year-old children—with the same data. As postmodern children gain unrestricted knowledge about things once kept secret from nonadults, the mystique of adults as revered keepers of secrets about the world begins to disintegrate. No longer do the elders know more than children about the experience of youth; given social/technological changes (video games, computers, TV programs, etc.) they often know less. Thus, the authority of adulthood is undermined, as kids' generational experience takes on a character of its own.

The social impact of such a phenomenon is profound on many levels. As discussed in more detail in Chapter 14 on McDonald's, a subversive kinderculture is created where kids, through their attention to child-targeted programming and commercials, know something that mom and dad don't. This corporate-directed kinderculture provides kids with a body of knowledge adults don't possess even while their access to adult themes on TV at least makes them conversant with marital, sexual, business-related, criminal, violent, and other traditionally restricted issues. When combined with observations of families collapsing, the dynamics of the struggle of a single mother to support her family, parents involved in the "singles" scene, and postdivorce imposition of adultlike chores, children's TV experience provides a full-scale immersion into grown-up culture.

In the context of childhood education the postmodern experience of being a kid represents a cultural earthquake. The curriculum of the third grade is determined not only by what vocabulary and concepts are "developmentally appropriate" but by what content is judged to be commensurate with third-grade experience in the lived world (Lipsky and Abrams, 1994; Postman, 1994). Hyperreality explodes traditional notions of curriculum development—third-graders can discuss the relationship between women's self-image and the nature of their sexual behavior. And while parental groups debate the value of sex education in the public schools, their children are at home watching a TV docudrama depicting the gang rape of a new inmate in the federal penitentiary. When teachers and the culture of school treat such children as if they know nothing of the adult world, the kids come to find school hopelessly archaic, out of touch with the times. This is why the postmodern subversive kinderculture always views school with a knowing wink and a smirk—how quaint school must look to our postmodern children.

There is nothing easy about the new childhood. Indeed, many teenagers and young adults speak of their stress and fatigue originating in childhood. If one has juggled the responsibilities of adulthood since the age of seven, physical and psychological manifestations of stress and fatigue during one's adolescence should surprise no one. Adolescent suicide did not exist as a category during the "old childhood"—by 1980 it was second only to accidents as the leading cause of death of teenagers. By the 1990s 400,000 young people were attempting suicide yearly and youth suicide was being described in the academic literature as an epidemic (Gaines, 1990). The covenant between children and adults has been broken by parental and clerical child abuse and the pathological behavior of other caretakers. Too often children of the late twentieth century have callously been deposited in inadequate child care institutions administered on the basis of cost-efficiency concerns, not on a larger commitment to the welfare of children. The tendency to segregate by age is well-established in late-twentieth-century America, and unless steps are taken to reverse the trend more generational alienation and antagonism will result (Gaines, 1994; Polakow, 1992).

In the context of this child segregation, cultural pathologies manifest themselves. Excluded from active participation in the social order, children find themselves both segregated and overregulated by institutional forms of social control. The overregulators pose as experts on child-raising, child development, child morality, and early childhood education with their psychodiscourse on the rigid phases of child development and the strict parameters of normality. In the name of "proper child-rearing techniques" experts tap into the larger ideology of personnel management that adjusts individuals to the demands of an orderly society. Like all strategies of personnel management, mainstream child psychology masks its emphasis on control. Intimidated by the scientific language of the experts, parents lose faith in their own instincts and surrender control to the authority figure on *Sally Jesse*. Play gives way to skill development as structure permeates all aspects of the child's life. Whereas middle- and upper-middle-class children suffer from the hyperstructure of skill development, poor children labeled "at-risk" are medicated and drilled in the misguided effort to reduce chaos and disorder in their lives. In the name of order the experience of poor children is further bureaucratized (Seiter, 1993; Polakow, 1992).

The Worldliness of Postmodern Childhood: The Wiseass as Prototype

The *Home Alone* movies can be understood only in the context of the postmodern childhood. Kevin McAlister is a worldly child—light-years separate Kevin from Chip, Ernie, and Robbie Douglas on *My Three Sons* of the late 1950s and early 1960s. As a black comedy for children, *Home Alone* struck an emotional chord with moviegoers that made it one of the most popular and profitable films of all time. Kevin, as kiddie-noir hero, is a smart kid with an attitude; Macauley Culkin's ability to portray that character turned him into an overnight celebrity—a role model for the prepubescent wiseass.

Kevin as postmodern wiseass could not tolerate children from the 1940s and 1950s, with their simpleminded the-policeman-is-our-friend view of the world. Bizarre in their innocence, such children are viewed by postmodern kids as antimatter reflections of themselves without responsibilities or cynicism. "What would we talk about?" Kevin might ask of a meeting with such kids. Unless Kevin had watched old movies or lived near a separatist group such as the Amish, he would have never seen such unworldly children. Almost every child depicted on TV in the contemporary era—Alex Keaton on *Family Ties*, Michele in *Full House*, Lisa and Bart Simpson on *The Simpsons*, Rudi on *The Cosby Show*—is worldly and wise. Bart Simpson may be an underachiever, but only in school—a place he finds boring, confining, and based on a childhood that no longer exists. Bart is not childish, the school is. The smart-ass child à la Culkin and Bart Simpson is the symbol for contemporary childhood. Imagine Bart's reaction to a "Yes, Virginia, there is a Santa Claus" adult monologue: "Right, daddy-o, now eat my shorts."

The wiseass is the hero of the subversive kinderculture. The appeal of *Home Alone* is connected to this insurgent response to middle-class propriety with its assumption of child helplessness and its worship of achievement. Child and adult are pitted against one another with the child as the sympathetic character. In the case of *Home Alone* no one could feel much sympathy for Kevin's parents with their lack of empathy for Kevin's position in the family and their lack of attention to his needs. Kevin's behavior is an act of righteous resistance to this unjust status quo. Like his kindred spirits, Bart Simpson and Beavis and Butt-Head, Kevin thrives on disorder—a chaos that undermines the social order constructed around bourgeois stability. As Beavis and Butt-Head might put it, order "sucks," disorder is "cool." The subversive kinderculture of the postmodern childhood thrives on this disorder.

Indeed, one of the subtexts running through the *Home Alone* movies involves the humorous juxtapositioning of comments of family members concerning poor, helpless little Kevin with the visual depiction of Kevin happy and in control of the disorder of his solitude. The appeal of the film revolves around Kevin's ability to tell his parents, "Even in the middle of all this exciting chaos, I don't need you." The self-sufficient boy-hero of the postmodern era—what a movie-marketing bonanza. He shows no remorse on learning that his parents have left him home alone: With eyebrows raised Kevin says to the camera, "I made my family disappear." Compare this postmodern reaction to parent-child separation to Dorothy's in *The Wizard of Oz*—Judy Garland's raison d'être is getting back home to Kansas. Kevin is self-actualized, living out the childhood fantasy of life without parental encumberment. Since he "can't trust anybody in this family," Kevin decides he would rather vacation alone than with "such a group of creeps." As a bellman scoops ice cream for him in his posh New York hotel room, it is obvious that Kevin's intuitions are correct. "*This* is a vacation," he sighs.

Confronting the Intensity of Youth in a Postmodern Childhood

As parties interested in the status of contemporary childhood, we ask: What does the popularity of the *Home Alone* movies tell us about the inner lives of children and their attempt to understand their relationship with the adult world? For a generation of home-aloners Culkin's Kevin is a character with whom they can identify, for he negotiates the cultural obstacles they also have had to confront. He offers them a sense of hope, a feeling that there is something heroic in their daily struggle. Once again, the corporate marketers are one step ahead of the rest of us, as they recognize the changing nature of childhood and colonize the psychological ramifications such changes produce. In retrospect it seems so easy: To canonize a child who is left home alone for Christmas is to flatter every postmodern child in the audience. Kevin's predicament validates a generation's lived experience, transforming unwanted children into pre-teen Ninja warriors. If nothing else, *Home Alone* is a rite-of-passage story about a boy home alone, endangered, besieged, who emerges victorious and transformed (Koch, December 27, 1990). "I'm no wimp," he proclaims as he marches off to battle, "I'm the man of the house."

In a postmodern era where children have already seen everything, have watched the media sell laundry detergent by exploiting a mother's love for her children, it is no surprise that kids of the 1990s experience difficulty with emotional investment. As a result, the interpersonal affect of postmodern children tends to be minimal—everything is kept at a distance and treated ironically (Grossberg, 1994). Kevin offers such children both something in which to invest and a sense that their desire for real experience is not pathological. This childhood and adolescent desire for extremes, for intense sensation, is typically viewed by the adult world as dangerous and misguided. Indeed, the very purpose of certain forms of traditional schooling and child rearing has been to tame such feelings. This visceral energy of the young—so central to Kevin in *Home Alone* and so enticing to young moviegoers—lays the foundation for a progressive postmodern child rearing and childhood education. Too often adults who are "in charge" of children forget the nature and power of this visceral energy/life force of young people. In their adult amnesia they fail to connect with the force and, as a result, relinquish the possibility of guiding it or being replenished by it. They often blame rock music, MTV videos, video games, communists, or satanists for creating the energy, forgetting that historically mediated forms of it have expressed themselves from ancient hunter-gatherer societies to modern and postmodern ones (Ventura, 1994; Rodriguez, 1994).

Its suppression in the postmodern North American culture at the end of the twentieth century undermines our civic, psychological, and intellectual growth. The very qualities adults fear most in our children—passion, visceral energy, and life force—can be used as the basis for a postmodern childhood education. In a sense the genie is out of the bottle and there is no way to get it back in. As the communication revolution has opened adult esoterica to children, we find there is no turning back. The endless debates over movie and record ratings are futile exercises; the question now revolves around how to provide children the type of emotional and intellectual supports that help them balance the interaction between their visceral energy and their newfound insights. Just as traditional forms of teaching and childhood curricular arrangements are passé given the "new times," forms of discipline and control strategies are obsolete. Can kids who hold Kevin's knowledge of the world in general and the anxieties and tribulations of adulthood in particular be domesticated and controlled (not to mention the question of *should* they) in the same ways as children of a different era of childhood were? Custodial schooling is no longer adequate for children of the 1990s—indeed, it was never adequate for children no matter what the era.

Education for domestication assumes that the information a child encounters can be regulated and sequentially ordered (Polakow, 1992; Gaines, 1990). Much schooling and child rearing is still based on such an archaic assumption, resulting in strategies that negate children's exploration, invention, and play. Indeed, the purpose of many of these strategies is to prevent the integration of acquired information from a variety of sources into the cognitive and emotional structures of an evolving personhood, that is, growth itself. Thus, child rearing insufficiently prepares children for adulthood or even postmodern childhood, as it ignores the world that surrounds children and shapes their lives. The lessons to be excavated from this quick analysis of the *Home Alone* movies are sobering in their urgency. The state of the family at the end of the twentieth century and the inability of the public conversation about it to transcend the most trivial forms of platitudes to the value of family in our "national character" is distressing. An effort to examine the nature of kinderculture and the forces that shape it simply does not exist in the surreal, image-based politics of the present era. The ambivalent adult relationship with children is a suppressed feature of the cultural landscape, rarely if ever addressed in even the professional schooling of child-welfare professionals, child psychologists, or elementary educators. These silences must end.

References

Aronowitz, S., and Giroux, H. (1991). *Post-modern education: Politics, culture, and social criticism*. Minneapolis: University of Minnesota Press.

Best, S., and Kellner, D. (1991). *Postmodern theory: Critical interrogations*. New York: Guilford Press.

Coontz, S. (1992). *The way we never were: American families and the nostalgia trap*. New York: Basic Books.

Ferguson, S. (1994). The comfort of being sad. *Utne Reader* 64 (July/August): 60–61.

Gaines, D. (1994). Border crossing in the USA. In A. Ross and T. Rose, eds., *Microphone fiends: Youth music, youth culture.* New York: Routledge.

Gaines, D. (1990). *Teenage wasteland: Suburbia's dead end kids.* New York: Harper Perennial.

Galston, W. (December 2, 1991). Home alone: What our policymakers should know about our children. *New Republic.*

Griffin, C. (1993). *Representations of youth: The study of youth and adolescence in Britain and America.* Cambridge, MA: Polity Press.

Grossberg, L. (1994). Is anybody listening? Does anybody care? On the state of rock. In A. Ross and T. Rose, eds., *Microphone fiends: Youth music, youth culture.* New York: Routledge.

James, C. (December 23, 1990). Scrooge pens the screenplay. *New York Times.*

Koch, J. (December 27, 1990). *Home Alone* hits home with a powerful, disturbing pop-culture potion. *Boston Globe.*

Lewis, J. (1992). *The road to romance and ruin: Teen films and youth culture.* New York: Routledge.

Lipsky, D., and A. Abrams. (1994). *Late bloomers.* New York: Times Books.

Morganthau, T., et al. (December 12, 1994). The orphanage. *Newsweek* 124 (24), 28–32.

Paul, W. (1994). *Laughing screaming: Modern Hollywood horror and comedy.* New York: Columbia University Press.

Polakow, V. (1992). *The erosion of childhood.* Chicago: University of Chicago Press.

Postman, N. (1994). *The disappearance of childhood.* New York: Vintage Books.

Rapping, E. (1994). *Mediations: Forays into the culture and gender wars.* Boston: South End Press.

Rodriguez, L. (1994). Rekindling the warrior. *Utne Reader* 64 (July/August): 58–59.

Rubin, L. (1994). *Families on the faultline: America's working class speaks about the family, the economy, race, and ethnicity.* New York: HarperCollins.

Seiter, E. (1993). *Sold separately: Parents and children in consumer culture.* New Brunswick, NJ: Rutgers University Press.

Seligman, K. (August 1, 1993). Poor kids often home alone. *San Francisco Examiner.*

Ventura, M. (1994). The age of endarkenment. *Utne Reader* 64 (July/August): 63–66.

Vogel, J. (1994). Throw away the key. *Utne Reader* 64 (July/August): 56–60.

2 *Are Disney Movies Good for Your Kids?*

Henry A. Giroux

ALTHOUGH IT APPEARS TO BE A commonplace assumption, the idea that culture provides the basis for persuasive forms of learning for children was impressed upon me with an abrupt urgency during the past few years. As a single father of three eight-year-old boys, I found myself somewhat reluctantly being introduced to the world of Hollywood animation films, in particular those produced by Disney. Before becoming an observer of this form of children's culture, I accepted the largely unquestioned assumptions that animated films stimulate imagination and fantasy, reproduce an aura of innocence, and, in general, are good for kids. In other words, such films appeared to be vehicles of amusement, a highly regarded and sought-after source of fun and joy for children. However, within a very short period of time, it became clear to me that the relevance of such films exceeded the boundaries of entertainment.

Needless to say, the significance of animated films operate on many registers, but one of the most persuasive is the role they play as the new "teaching machines," as producers of culture. I soon found out that for my children, and I suspect for many others, these films appear to inspire at least as much cultural authority and legitimacy for teaching specific roles, values, and ideals as do the more traditional sites of learning such as the public schools, religious institutions, and the family.

The significance of animated films as a site of learning is heightened by the widespread recognition that schools and other public sites are increasingly beset by a crisis of vision, meaning, and motivation. The mass media, especially the world of Hollywood films, on the contrary, constructs a dreamlike world of childhood innocence where kids increasingly find a place to situate themselves in their emotional lives. Unlike the often hard-nosed, joyless reality of schooling, children's films provide a high-tech visual space where adventure and pleasure meet in a fantasy world of possibilities and a commercial sphere of consumerism and commodification.

The educational relevance of animated films became especially clear to me as my kids experienced the vast entertainment and teaching machine embodied by Disney. Increasingly, as I watched a number of Disney films first in the movie theater and later on video, I became aware of how necessary it was to move beyond treating these films as transparent entertainment in order to question the messages behind them.

But at the same time, I recognized that any attempt to take up Disney films critically rubbed against the grain of American popular opinion. After all, "the happiest place on earth" has traditionally gained its popularity in part through a self-proclaimed image of trademark innocence that has protected it from the interrogating gaze of critics. Of course, there is more at work here than a public-relations department intent on protecting Disney's claim to fabled goodness and uncompromising reverence. There is also the reality of a powerful economic and political power that staunchly protects its mythical status as a purveyor of American innocence and moral virtue.[1] Quick to mobilize its monolith of legal institutions, public-relations spokespersons, and professional cultural critics to safeguard the borders of its "magic kingdom," Disney has aggressively prosecuted violations of its copyright laws, exercised control over who has access to the Disney archives, and has attempted to influence the uses of material researched in the archives. In its zeal to protect its image and extend its profits, Disney has gone so far as to take legal action against a small-time day care center that used Disney cartoon characters in its advertising. In this instance, Disney, as a self-proclaimed defender of family values, compromised its Dan Quayle philosophy for an aggressive endorsement of property rights. Similarly, Disney has a harsh reputation for applying pressure on authors critical of the Disney ideology and enterprise. But the power of Disney's mythological status comes from other sources as well.

Disney's image as an icon of American culture is consistently reinforced through the penetration of the Disney empire into every aspect of social life. Children experience Disney's cultural influence through a maze of representations and products found in home videos, shopping malls, classroom instructional films, box offices, popular television programs, and family restaurants. Through advertising, displays, and use of public visual space, Disney inserts itself into a network of commodities that lends itself to the construction of the world of enchantment as a closed and total category. Disney goes to great lengths to boost its civic image. Defining itself as a vehicle for education and civic responsibility,

Disney sponsors "Teacher of the Year Awards," provides scholarships to students, and, more recently, offers financial aid, internships, and educational programs to disadvantaged urban youth through its ice-skating program called Goals. In what can be seen as an extraordinary venture, Disney plans to construct in the next few years a prototype school that one of its brochures proclaims will "serve as a model for education into the next century." The school will be part of a 5,000-acre residential development called Celebration, which, according to Disney executives, will be designed after "the main streets of small-town America and reminiscent of Norman Rockwell images."[2]

What is interesting here is that Disney no longer simply provides the fantasies through which childhood innocence and adventure are produced, experienced, and affirmed. Disney now produces prototypes for model schools, families, identities, communities, and the way the future is to be understood through a particular construction of the past. From the seedy urban haunts of New York City to the spatial monuments of consumption shaping Florida, Disney takes full advantage of refiguring the social and cultural landscape while spreading the ideology of its Imagineers. For instance, not only is Disney taking over large properties on West 42nd Street in New York City in order to produce a musical a year, it has also begun building Celebration, which is designed to accommodate 20,000 citizens. According to Disney, this is a "typical American small town . . . designed to become an international prototype for communities."[3] What Disney leaves out of its upbeat promotional literature is the rather tenuous notion of democracy that informs its view of municipal government, since the model of Celebration is "premised upon citizens not having control over the people who plan for them and administer the policies of the city."[4] But Disney does more than provide prototypes for upscale communities; it also makes a claim on the future through its nostalgic view of the past and its construction of public memory as a metonym for the magical kingdom.

French theorist Jean Baudrillard has captured the scope and power of Disney's influence by arguing that Disneyland is more "real" than fantasy because it now provides the image on which America constructs itself. For example, Houston models its airport monorail after the one at Disneyland. Towns throughout America appropriate a piece of nostalgia by imitating the Victorian architecture of Disneyland's Main Street USA. It seems that the real policymakers are not those that reside in Washington, D.C., but those in California calling themselves the Disney Imagineers. The boundaries between entertainment, education, and commercialization collapse through the sheer omnipotence of Disney's reach into diverse spheres of everyday life. The scope of the Disney empire reveals both shrewd business practices as well as a sharp eye for providing dreams and products through forms of popular culture in which kids are willing to materially and emotionally invest.

Popular audiences tend to reject any link between ideology and the prolific entertainment world of Disney. And yet Disney's pretense to innocence appears to some critics as little more than a promotional mask that covers over its aggressive marketing techniques and influence in educating children to the virtues of becoming active consumers. Eric Smoodin, editor of *Disney Discourse*, a book critical of Disney's role in American culture, argues that "Disney constructs childhood so as to make it entirely compatible with consumerism."⁵ Even more disturbing is the widespread belief that Disney's trademark innocence renders it unaccountable for the diverse ways in which it shapes the sense of reality it provides for children as they take up particular and often sanitized notions of identity, culture, and history in the seemingly apolitical cultural universe of "the Magic Kingdom." For example, Jon Wiener, professor of history at the University of California at Irvine, argues that "Disneyland's version of Main Street America harks back to an image of small towns characterized by cheerful commerce, with barbershop quartets and ice cream sundaes and glorious parades." For Wiener this view not only fictionalizes and trivializes the history of real Main Streets at the turn of the century, it also represents an appropriation of the past to legitimate a present that portrays a world "without tenements or poverty or urban class conflict. . . . It's a native white Protestant dream of a world without blacks or immigrants."⁶

I want to venture into the contradictory world of Disney through an analysis of its more recent animated films. These films, all produced since 1989, are important because they have received enormous praise and have achieved blockbuster status. For many children they represent their first introduction into the world of Disney. Moreover, the success and popularity of these films, rivaling many adult features, do not engender the critical analyses often rendered on adult films. In short, popular audiences are more willing to suspend critical judgment about such children's films. Animated fantasy and entertainment appear to collapse into each other and as such fall outside of the world of values, meaning, and knowledge often associated with more pronounced educational forms such as documentaries, art films, or even wide-circulation adult films. Given the influence that the Disney ideology has on children, it is imperative for parents, teachers, and other adults to understand how such films attract the attention and shape the values of the children that view and buy them.

Below I argue that it is important to address Disney's animated films without either condemning Disney as an ideological reactionary deceptively promoting a conservative worldview under the guise of entertainment, or simply celebrating Disney as the Hollywood version of *Mr. Rogers' Neighborhood*, doing nothing more than providing sources of joy and happiness to children all over the world. In part, Disney does both. But the role that Disney plays in shaping individual identities and controlling the fields of social meaning through which children negotiate the world is far too complex to be reduced to either position. Disney inscribes itself in a commanding way upon the lives of children and powerfully shapes the way America's cultural landscape is imagined. Disney's commanding cultural authority is too powerful and far-reaching to simply be the object of reverence. What Disney deserves is respectful criticism, and one measure of such respect is to insert Disney's scripted view of childhood and society within a critical dialogue regarding the meanings it produces, the roles it legitimates, and the narratives it uses to define American life.

The question of whether Disney's animated films are good for kids has no easy answers, but at the same time it necessitates examining such films outside the traditional register of fun and entertainment. Disney's most recent films, which include *The Little Mermaid, Aladdin, Beauty and the Beast*, and *The Lion King*, provide ample opportunity to address how Disney constructs a culture of joy and innocence for children out of the intersection of entertainment, advocacy, pleasure, and consumerism. All of these films have been high-profile releases catering to massive audiences. Moreover, their commercial success is not limited to box-office profits. Successfully connecting the rituals of consumption and moviegoing, Disney's animated films provide a "marketplace of culture," a launching pad for an endless number of products and merchandise that include videocassettes, soundtracks, children's clothing, furniture, stuffed toys, and new rides at the theme parks.[7]

On a more positive note, the wide distribution and popular appeal of these films provide diverse audiences and viewers the opportunity to challenge those assumptions that allow people to suspend judgment regarding Disney's accountability for defining appropriate childhood entertainment. Critically analyzing how Disney films work to construct meanings, induce pleasures, and reproduce ideologically loaded fantasies is not meant as an exercise in disparagement. On the contrary, as a \$4.7 billion company, Disney's corporate and cultural influence is so enormous and far-reaching that it should go neither unchecked nor unmediated.

Disney's recent films embody structuring principles and themes that have become the trademark of Disney animation. As sites of entertainment, Disney's films work because they put children and adults alike in touch with joy and adventure. They present themselves as places to experience pleasure, even when we have to buy it. Hollywood glitz, colorful animation, and show-stopping musical scores combined with old-fashioned cheer create a celluloid zone of aesthetic and emotional comfort for children and adults alike. The rousing calypso number "Under the Sea," in *The Little Mermaid*, and "Be Our Guest," the Busby Berkeley–inspired musical sequence in *Beauty and the Beast*, are indicative of the musical talent at work in Disney's animated films. The four films draw upon the amazing talents of songwriters Howard Ashman and Alan Menken, and the result is a series of musical feasts that provide the emotional glue of the animation experience.

Fantasy abounds as Disney's animated films produce a host of exotic and stereotypical villains, heroes, and heroines. Whereas Ursula, the large, oozing, black-and-purple squid in *The Little Mermaid*, gushes with evil and irony, heroine-mermaid Ariel appears as a cross between a typical rebellious teenager and a fashion model from Southern California. Disney's representations of both evil and good women appear to have been fashioned in the editorial office of *Vogue*. The wolflike monster in *Beauty and the Beast* evokes a rare combination of terror and gentleness, whereas Scar, the suave and scheming feline, adds a contemporary touch to the meaning of evil and betrayal.

The array of animated objects and animals in these films is of the highest artistic standards. For example, the Beast's enchanted castle in *Beauty and the Beast* becomes magical as household objects are transformed into dancing teacups, a talking teapot, and dancing silverware. Such characters are part of larger narratives: Freedom, rites of passage, intolerance, choices, the injustice of male chauvinism, and the mobilization of passion and desire are just some of the many themes explored in these animated films. But enchantment is not without its price if it seduces its audience into suspending critical judgment on the messages produced by such films. Even though these messages can be read through a variety of interpretations and are sometimes contradictory, there are a number of assumptions that structure these films that represent the hidden face of Disney.

One of the most controversial messages that weave in and out of Disney's animated films concerns the portrayal of girls and women. In both *The Little Mermaid* and *The Lion King* female characters are constructed within narrowly defined gender roles. All of the women in these films are ultimately subordinate to men and define their sense of power and desire almost exclusively in terms of dominant male narratives. For instance, mermaid Ariel, modeled after a slightly anorexic Barbie Doll, at first glance appears to be engaged in a struggle against parental control, motivated by the desire to explore the human world and willing to take a risk in defining the subject and object of her desires. But in the end the struggle to gain independence from her father, Triton, and the sense of desperate striving that motivates her dissolves when Ariel makes a

Mephistophelean pact with Ursula: Ariel trades her voice to gain a pair of legs so that she can pursue handsome Prince Eric. Although children might be delighted by Ariel's teenage rebelliousness, they are positioned to believe in the end that desire, choice, and empowerment are closely linked to catching and loving handsome men. In *The Little Mermaid* Ariel becomes a metaphor for the traditional housewife-in-the-making narrative. When Ursula tells Ariel that taking away her voice is not so bad because men don't like women who talk, the message is dramatized when the Prince attempts to bestow the kiss of true love on Ariel even though she has never spoken to him. Within this rigidly defined narrative, womanhood offers Ariel the reward of marrying the right man and renouncing her former life under the sea—a telling cultural model for the nature of female choice and decisionmaking in Disney's worldview. It is difficult to see how a film such as this does more than reinforce negative stereotypes about women and girls. Unfortunately, this type of stereotyping is reproduced, to varying degrees, in all of Disney's animated films.

In *Aladdin* the issue of agency and power is centered strictly on the role of the young street tramp, Aladdin. Jasmine, the princess with whom he falls in love, is simply an object of his immediate desire as well as a stepping-stone to social mobility. Jasmine's life is almost completely defined by men, and in the end her happiness is ensured by Aladdin, who finally is given permission to marry her.

The gender theme becomes a bit more complicated in *Beauty and the Beast*. Belle, the heroine of the film, is portrayed as an independent woman stuck in a provincial village in eighteenth-century France. Seen as odd because she always has her nose in a book, she is pursued by Gaston, a vain, macho male typical of Hollywood films during the 1980s. To Belle's credit she rejects him, but in the end she gives her love to the Beast, who holds her captive in the hopes she will fall in love with him and break the evil spell cast upon him while a young man. Belle not only falls in love with the Beast, she "civilizes" him by instructing him to eat properly, control his temper, and dance. Belle becomes a model of etiquette and style as she turns this narcissistic, muscle-bound tyrant into a model of the "new" man, one who is sensitive, caring, and loving. Some critics have labeled Belle a Disney feminist because she rejects and vilifies Gaston, the ultimate macho man. Less obviously, *Beauty and the Beast* can also be read as a rejection of hypermasculinity and a struggle between the macho sensibilities of Gaston and the reformed sexist, the Beast. In this reading Belle is less the focus of the film than prop or "mechanism for solving the Beast's dilemma."[8]

Whatever subversive qualities Belle personifies in the film, they seem to dissolve when focused on humbling male vanity. In the end, Belle simply becomes another woman whose life is valued for solving a man's problems.

The issue of female subordination returns with a vengeance in *The Lion King*. All of the rulers of the kingdom are men, reinforcing the assumption that independence and leadership are tied to patriarchal entitlement and high social standing. The dependency that the beloved Mufasa engenders from the women of Pride Rock is unaltered after his death when the evil Scar assumes control of the kingdom. Lacking any sense of outrage, resistance, or independence, the women felines hang around to do his bidding. Given Disney's purported obsession with family values, especially as a consumer unit, it is curious as to why there are no mothers in these films. The mermaid has a domineering father; Jasmine's father is outwitted by his aides; and Belle has an airhead for a father. So much for strong mothers and resisting women.

Jack Zipes, professor of German at the University of Minnesota and a leading expert on fairy tales, claims that Disney's animated films celebrate a masculine type of power. More importantly, he believes that they reproduce "a type of gender stereotyping . . . that have an adverse effect on children in contrast to what parents think. . . . Parents think they're essentially harmless—and they're not harmless."[9] Disney films are seen by enormous numbers of children in the United States and abroad. As far as the issue of gender is concerned, Disney's view of the relationship between female agency and empowerment is not merely nostalgic—it borders on being overtly reactionary.

Racial stereotyping is another major issue that surfaces in many of the recent Disney animated films. But the legacy of racism does not begin with the films produced since 1989; on the contrary, a long history of racism associated with Disney's work can be traced back to denigrating images of people of color in films such as *Song of the South*, released in 1946, and *The Jungle Book*, which appeared in 1967.[10] Moreover, racist representations of Native Americans as violent "redskins" were featured in Frontierland in the 1950s. In addition, the main restaurant in Frontierland featured the real-life figure of a former slave, Aunt Jemima, who would sign autographs for the tourists outside of her "Pancake House." Eventually the exhibits and the Native Americans running them were eliminated by Disney executives because the "Indian" canoe guides wanted to unionize. They were displaced by robotic dancing bears. Complaints from civil rights groups got rid of the degrading Aunt Jemima spectacle.[11]

The most controversial example of racist stereotyping facing the Disney publicity machine occurred with the release of *Aladdin* in 1989, although such stereotyping reappeared in 1994 with the release of *The Lion King*. *Aladdin* represents a particularly important example because it was a high-profile release, the winner of two Academy Awards, and one of the most successful Disney films ever produced. Playing to massive audiences of children, the film's opening song, "Arabian Nights," begins its depiction of Arab culture with a decidedly racist tone. The song states: "Oh I come from a land / From a faraway place / Where the caravan camels roam. Where they cut off your ear / If they don't like your face. It's barbaric, but hey, it's home." In this characterization, a politics of identity and place associated with Arab culture magnifies popular stereotypes already primed by the media through its portrayal of the Gulf War. Such racist representations are further reproduced in a host of supporting characters who are portrayed as grotesque, violent, and cruel. Yousef Salem, a former spokesperson for the South Bay Islamic Association, characterized the film this way: "All of the bad guys have beards and large, bulbous noses, sinister eyes and heavy accents, and they're wielding swords constantly. Aladdin doesn't have a big nose; he has a small nose. He doesn't have a beard or a turban. He doesn't have an accent. What makes him nice is they've given him this American character. . . . I have a daughter who says she's ashamed to call herself an Arab, and it's because of things like this."[12]

Jack Shaheen, a professor of broadcast journalism at Southern Illinois University in Edwardsville, with radio personality Casey Kasem mobilized a public-relations campaign protesting the anti-Arab themes in *Aladdin*. At first the Disney executives ignored the protest but, due to the rising tide of public outrage, agreed to change one line of the stanza in the subsequent videocassette and worldwide film release; it is worth noting that Disney did change the lyrics on its popular CD release of *Aladdin*.[13] It is also worth noting that Disney executives were not unaware of the racist implications of the lyrics when they were first proposed. Howard Ashman, who wrote the title song, submitted an alternative set of lyrics when he delivered the original verse. The alternative set of lyrics, "Where it's flat and immense / And the heat is intense" eventually replaced the original verse, "Where they cut off your ear / If they don't like your face." Although the new lyrics appeared in the videocassette release of *Aladdin*, many Arab groups were disappointed because the verse "It's barbaric, but hey, it's home" was not altered. More importantly, the mispronunciation of Arab names in the film, the racial coding of accents, and the use of nonsensical scrawl as a substitute for an actual written Arabic language were not removed.

Racism is also a powerful but subtle structuring principle in Disney's more recent animated film, *Pocahontas*. In the Disney rendition of colonial history, Pocahontas is converted into a brown, Barbielike super model with an hourglass figure whose relationship with Aryan hunk John Smith transforms an historical act of colonial barbarism into a sentimental romance. In this romantic allegory, the rapacious and exploitative narrative of colonialism is rewritten as a multicultural love affair in which issues of human conflict, suffering, and exploitation are conveniently erased. Captain John Smith, whose historical reputation was founded on his unrelenting, murderous pursuit of "Indians," is mystified in Disney's *Pocahontas*. Rather than being portrayed accurately—as part of a colonial legacy that resulted in the genocide of millions of Native Americans—Disney turns Smith into a morally uplifted white male who ends up being Mr. Right for an ill-fated, brown-skinned version of Calvin Klein model Kate Moss. Although Disney's rendition of Pocahontas as a strong-willed woman may seem too politically correct for conservatives, the film is, in actuality, a deeply racist and sexist portrayal of Native Americans.

It is worth noting that racism in Disney's animated films does not simply appear in negative imagery or through historical misrepresentation; racist ideology also appears in racially coded language and accents. For example, *Aladdin* portrays the "bad" Arabs with thick, foreign accents, whereas the Anglicized Jasmine and Aladdin speak in standard, Americanized English. A hint of the unconscious racism that informs this depiction is provided by Peter Schneider, president of feature animation at Disney, who points out that Aladdin was modeled after Tom Cruise.[14] Racially coded language is also evident in *The Lion King*, where all of the members of the royal family speak with posh British accents whereas Shenzi and Banzai, the despicable hyena storm troopers, speak through the voices of Whoopi Goldberg and Cheech Marin in racially coded accents that take on the nuances of the discourse of a decidedly urban, black, and Latino youth. The use of racially coded language is not new in Disney's films and can be found in an early version of *The Three Little Pigs*, *Song of the South*, and *The Jungle Book*.[15] What is astonishing is that these films produce a host of representations and codes in which children are taught that cultural differences that do not bear the imprint of white, middle-class ethnicity are deviant, inferior, ignorant, and a threat to be overcome. There is nothing innocent in what kids learn about race as portrayed in the "magical world" of Disney. The race card has always been central to Disney's view of cultural and national identity, and yet the issue of race only seems to warrant public discussion when it appears allegedly in the discourse of civil rights to benefit black people either through affirmative action or in the outcry over the recent O.J. Simpson verdict. The fact of the matter is that when the race card is used to denigrate African Americans and other people of color, the issue of race as an act of racism seems to disappear from public discourse.

Another central feature common to all of Disney's recent animated films is the celebration of deeply antidemocratic social relations. Nature and the animal kingdom provide the mechanism for presenting and legitimating social hierarchy, royalty, and structural inequality as part of the natural order. The seemingly benign presentation of celluloid dramas in which men rule, strict discipline is imposed through social hierarchies, and leadership is a function of one's social status suggests a yearning for a return to a more rigidly stratified society, one modeled after the British monarchy of the eighteenth and nineteenth centuries. For children, the messages offered in Disney's animated films suggest that social problems such as the history of racism, the genocide of Native Americans, the prevailing sexism, and the crisis of democratic public life are simply willed through the laws of nature. Clearly, this is a dangerous lesson for powerlessness and is a highly conservative view of the social order and relations of the contemporary world.

Does this mean that Disney's children's films should be ignored or censored? I think a number of lessons are to be learned from recognizing the deeply ideological messages behind Disney's view of the world. First, it is crucial that the realm of popular culture that Disney increasingly uses to teach values and sell goods be taken seriously as a site of learning, especially for children. This means, at the very least, that it must be incorporated into schools as a serious object of social knowledge and critical analysis. Second, parents, community groups, educators, and other concerned individuals must be attentive to the messages in these films in order to both criticize them when necessary and, more importantly, to reclaim them for more productive ends. The roles assigned to women and people of color, along with ideas concerning a rigid view of family values, history, and national identity, need to be challenged and transformed. That is, such images and their claim to public memory need to be rewritten as part of the script of empowerment rather than be simply dismissed because they serve to undermine human agency and democratic possibilities.

Third, Disney's all-encompassing reach into the spheres of economics, consumption, and culture suggests that we analyze Disney within a range of relations of power. Eric Smoodin argues rightly that the American public needs to "gain a new sense of Disney's importance, because of the manner in which his work in film and television is connected to other projects in urban planning, ecological politics, product merchandising, United States domestic and global policy formation, technological innovation, and constructions of national character."[16] This suggests undertaking new analyses of Disney that connect rather than separate the various social and cultural formations in which the company actively engages. Clearly, such a dialectical position not only provides a more theoretically accurate understanding of Disney's power, it also contributes to forms of analysis that rupture the notion that Disney is primarily about the pedagogy of entertainment. Equally important, research about Disney must be at once historical, relational, and multifaceted.[17] Moreover, this type of study is perfectly suited for cultural studies, which can employ an interdisciplinary approach to such an undertaking, one that makes the popular the object of serious analysis, makes the pedagogical a defining principle of such work, and inserts the political into the center of the project.[18]

Fourth, if Disney's films are to be viewed as more than narratives of fantasy and escape, as sites of reclamation and imagination that affirm rather than deny the long-standing relationship between entertainment and pedagogy, cultural workers and educators need to insert the political and pedagogical back into the discourse of entertainment. In part, this suggests analyzing how entertainment can be rendered as a subject to work on rather than as something to be passively consumed. This suggests a pedagogical approach to popular culture that engages how a politics of the popular works to mobilize desire, stimulate imagination, and produce forms of identification that can become objects of dialogue and critical investigation. At one level, this suggests addressing the utopian possibilities in which children often find representations of their hopes and dreams. At another level, cultural workers need to combine a politics of representation with a discourse of political economy in order to understand how Disney films work within a broad network of production and distribution as teaching machines within and across different public cultures and social formations. Within this type of discourse, the messages, forms of emotional investment, and ideologies produced by Disney can be traced through the various circuits of power that both legitimate and insert "the culture of the Magic Kingdom" into multiple and overlapping public spheres.

Moreover, films such as these need to be analyzed not only for what they say but also for how they are used and taken up by adult audiences and groups of children within diverse national and international contexts. That is, cultural workers need to study these films intertextually and from a transnational perspective. Disney does not represent a cultural monolith ignorant of different contexts; on the contrary, its power in part rests with its ability to address different contexts and be read differently by transnational formations and audiences. Disney engenders what Inderpal Grewa and Caren Kaplan have called "scattered hegemonies."[19] It is precisely by addressing how these hegemonies operate in particular spaces of power, specific localities, and differentiated transnational locations that progressives will be able to understand more fully the specific agendas and politics at work as Disney is both constructed for and read by different audiences.

Fifth, pedagogically it is imperative that parents, educators, and cultural workers be attentive to how these Disney films and visual media are used and understood differently by diverse groups of kids. Not only does this provide the opportunity for parents and others to talk to children about popular culture, it also creates the basis for better understanding of how young people identify with these films, what issues need to be addressed, and how such discussions would open up a language of pleasure and criticism rather than simply shut such a conversation down. This suggests that we develop new forms of literacy, new ways of critically understanding and reading the electronically produced visual media. Teaching and learning the culture of the book is no longer the staple of what it means to be literate. Children learn from exposure to popular cultural forms, and these provide a new cultural register to what it means to be literate. This means that educators and cultural workers need to do more than recognize the need to take seriously the production of popular art forms in the schools; it also means there can be no cultural pedagogy without cultural practices that both explore the possibilities of different popular forms and bring out students' talents. The point here is that students should not merely analyze the representations of electronically mediated, popular culture—they must also be able to master the skills and technology to produce it. This means making films, videos, music, and other forms of cultural production. Needless to say, this suggests giving students more power over the conditions for the production of knowledge, but a cultural pedagogy also involves the struggle for more resources for schools and other sites of learning.

Finally, I believe that since the power and influence of Disney is so pervasive in American society, parents, educators, and others need to find ways to make Disney accountable for what it produces. The recent defeat of the proposed theme park in Virginia suggests that Disney can be challenged and held accountable for the so-called "Disneyfication" of American culture. Although it is indisputable that Disney provides both children and adults with the pleasure of being entertained, Disney's public responsibility does not end there. Rather than being viewed as a commercial public sphere innocently distributing pleasure to young people, the Disney empire must be seen as a pedagogical and policy-making enterprise actively engaged in the cultural landscaping of national identity and the "schooling" of the minds of young children. This is not to suggest that there is something sinister behind what Disney does as much as it points to the need to address the role of fantasy, desire, and innocence in securing particular ideological interests, legitimating specific social relations, and making a distinct claim on the meaning of public memory. Disney needs to be held accountable not only at the box office but also in political and ethical terms. And if such accountability is to be impressed upon the "magic kingdom," then parents, cultural workers, and others will have to challenge and disrupt the images, representations, and values offered by Disney's teaching machine. The stakes are too high to ignore such a challenge and struggle, even if it means reading Disney's animated films critically.

Notes

1. The reality of the Disney Company as a powerful economic and political empire can be seen in the record of its profits and its ever expanding corporate cultural reach. For instance, the Disney Company in 1994 took in nearly $5 billion at the box office, $3.5 billion from Disney theme parks, and almost $2 billion from Disney products. In addition, in the summer of 1995 the Walt Disney Company made the biggest deal of the American media industry by investing $19 billion to acquire Capital Cities/ABC. See, for example, Bruce Hovovitz, "Company Has Cradle-to-Grave Sway," *USA Today* (September 7, 1995), p. B1. On the specific properties involved in the merger between Disney and Capital Cities/ABC, see Jack Thomas, "For Viewers, Changes Not Expected to Be Big Deal," *Boston Globe* (August 1, 1995), pp. 33, 45, especially the chart on page 45.

2. Cited in Mark Walsh, "Disney Holds Up School as Model for Next Century," *Education Week* 13(39) (June 22, 1994): 1.

3. Cited in Tom Vanderbilt, "Mickey Goes to Town(s)," *Nation* 261(6) (August 28/September 4, 1995): 197.

4. Ibid., p. 199.

5. Eric Smoodin, "How to Read Walt Disney," in Smoodin, ed., *Disney Discourse: Producing the Magic Kingdom* (New York: Routledge, 1994), p. 18.

6. Jon Wiener, "Tall Tales and True," *Nation* (January 31, 1994), p. 134.

7. The term "marketplace of culture" comes from Richard de Cordova, "The Mickey in Macy's Window: Childhood Consumerism and Disney Animation," in Eric Smoodin, ed., *Disney Discourse: Producing the Magic Kingdom* (New York: Routledge, 1994), p. 209.

8. Susan Jefford develops this reading of *Beauty and the Beast* in Susan Jefford, *Hard Bodies: Hollywood Masculinity in the Reagan Era* (New Brunswick, NJ: Rutgers University Press, 1994), p. 150.

9. Cited in June Casagrande, "The Disney Agenda," *Creative Loafing* (March 17–23, 1994), pp. 6–7.

10. Upon its release in 1946, *Song of the South* was condemned by the NAACP for its racist representations.

11. These racist episodes are highlighted in Wiener, "Tall Tales and True," pp. 133–135.

12. Yousef Salem, cited in Richard Scheinin, "Angry Over 'Aladdin,'" *Washington Post* (January 10, 1993), p. G5.

13. Howard Green, a Disney spokesperson, dismissed the charges of racism as irrelevant, claiming that such criticisms were coming from a small minority and that "most people were happy with [the film]." *Washington Post* (January 10, 1993).

14. Cited in Rene Graham, "Can Disney Do It Again?" *Boston Globe* (June 11, 1995), p. 57.

15. See Susan Miller and Greg Rode, who do a rhetorical analysis of *The Jungle Book* and *Song of the South* in their chapter, "The Movie You See, the Movie You Don't: How Disney Does That Old Time Derision," in Elizabeth Bell, Lynda Haas, and Laura Sells, eds., *From Mouse to Mermaid* (Bloomington: Indiana University Press, 1995).

16. Smoodin, "How to Read Walt Disney," pp. 4–5.

17. Such work is already beginning to appear. For example, see the special issue of *South Atlantic Quarterly* 92(1) (Winter 1993), edited by Susan Willis, which takes as its theme "The World According to Disney." Also, see Smoodin, *Disney Discourse*; and Bell, Haas, and Sells, *From Mouse to Mermaid*.

18. For an example of such an analysis, see Stanley Aronowitz, *Roll Over Beethoven* (Middletown, CT: Wesleyan University Press, 1993); Henry A. Giroux, *Disturbing Pleasures: Learning Popular Culture* (New York: Routledge, 1994).

19. Inderpal Grewal and Caren Kaplan, "Introduction: Transnational Feminist Practices and Questions of Postmodernity," in Inderpal Grewal and Caren Kaplan, eds., *Scattered Hegemonies* (Minneapolis: University of Minnesota Press, 1994).

3

From Sesame Street *to* Barney and Friends: *Television as Teacher*

Eleanor Blair Hilty

Along with the family and the school, public television, by instructing out-of-school children, became the third education institution.

—Joel Spring, *The American School, 1642–1993*

PERHAPS I AM SIMPLY GROWING old and cynical, or maybe my skepticism about the value of educational television programs for children has grown in direct proportion to the number of hours that I have been subjected to this relatively new "educational institution." However, recently I have begun to have my doubts about television as teacher. I figure that during the past seven years I have watched approximately 1,000 hours of educational programs for children. Being a good mother I assumed that if it was on public television and, therefore, educational, it must be good for my children. Most importantly, if it was good for my children then I should share this experience with them. However, as much as I wanted to believe this vision, my skills of critical analysis could not be laid aside; so not only did I watch, I watched with a very critical eye, and I was amazed by what I heard and saw. In this chapter I attempt to capture what I learned, and even what I did not learn, from watching these shows. I've tried to describe my thoughts from both the perspective of a parent and that of a professional educator—two roles that for me are often inseparable.

Television and American Life

The Spindlers (1982) urged us to "make the familiar strange and the strange familiar" when seeking to understand the commonplace in our culture. For the baby boomers and their children, television has been commonplace in their lives almost from birth, as commonplace as any other accoutrement of modernity. Few of us can remember a time in our homes when the television was not turned on; many of us ate dinner against the backdrop of the evening news. Childhood memories are often marked by remembrances of those children's programs that were most popular during a particular time period. In retrospect, it is amazing to consider how quickly television became an intimate part of American life. For many families, watching television was the *only* activity they did as a family. Television was both entertainment and social phenomenon, a familiar guest in one's home. Within this context, it is easy to see how we as a culture would quite naturally accept the idea that television could (and should) function as both entertainment *and* education. As a nation, our anxieties and fears about educational excellence and equality of opportunity were quelled by the belief that television might provide a means to boost school readiness among "disadvantaged" children. It was a simple solution to a complex problem.

The Birth of Children's
Educational Programming

The concept of educational programs for children arrived with television, but it was the Carnegie Commission on Educational Television that recommended in 1967 the use of children's television as a "means of social reform" (Spring, 1994, 332). The report stated that "Public Television programs should give great attention to the informal educational needs of preschool children, particularly to interest and help children whose intellectual and cultural preparation might otherwise be less than adequate" (Spring, 1992, 95). These recommendations eventually led to the establishment of the Children's Television Workshop in 1968, "and on November 10, 1969, the first production of *Sesame Street* was broadcast" (Spring, 1994, 333). It was the birth of *Sesame Street* that marked the beginning of a revolution in children's programming. From the beginning, the characters portrayed on children's educational programs were an important dimension of these programs. Identification with these characters provided a consistent element that defined the major themes and social interactions within individual programs. These characters ranged from the benevolent father figure best represented by Mr. Rogers and

Captain Kangaroo to the large, articulate animals found in Big Bird and Barney to even the sort of mother-teacher role exemplified by Shari Lewis with her puppets.

Educational programs for children that were once the mainstay of public television offerings for children quickly appeared on both public and commercial television stations, and the differences were often negligible. The more popular programs like *Sesame Street* and, more recently, *Barney and Friends* are favorites with both children and adults. However, there is no consensus that this is necessarily a good thing. J. Healy (1990) expressed concern about this widespread acceptance: "The worst thing about *Sesame Street* is that people believe it is educationally valuable. It stands as a symbol of 'good' programming, an institutionalized excuse for 'boob tube' as baby-sitter. Well-intentioned parents earnestly swallow the dictum: 'It helps children learn'" (220). Parents believe these programs are educational and therefore preferable to other children's programs, and children actually seem to enjoy the wide array of characters and experiences they encounter in these programs, but the most essential question remains unanswered: What do kids really get from these programs?

Barney and Friends: Boom or Bust?

Consider one of the most popular offerings on PBS in the form of *Barney and Friends*. A collaborative effort of The Lyons Group and Connecticut Public Television, *Barney and Friends* ran during the 1992–1993 television season in the form of thirty half-hour episodes (Singer and Singer, 1993, 1). As a typical educational program for a young audience, this series "included elements that were potentially relevant to a general program of preparing preschoolers for effective school readiness" (Singer and Singer, 1993, 22). Young children, in particular, love Barney and all it represents: whimsy, fantasy, unconditional love, and, perhaps most important, an element of goodness and rightness absent in our everyday lives. These qualities are most clearly represented in the theme song that Barney and friends sing at the end of each program: "I love you. You love me. We're a happy family . . ." and so forth.

Of course there's nothing wrong with this song, but it is almost too, too sweet. On the surface, the words are simple; it's a simple song with a comforting message. Perhaps I spend too much time thinking about these matters, but when I hear this song I simultaneously hear another level of meaning. I also hear a child's plaintive plea for reciprocal love and affection, a plea that I find discomfitting. Unconditional love—

shouldn't this be a given in children's lives? And if it's not, what does this song represent to those who hear it?

My doubts were further fueled when I began to regularly read newspaper accounts of "Barney bashings." Consider the college student in Worcester, Massachusetts, who "jumped from a car, shouted obscenities and assaulted a woman dressed as Barney the dinosaur. 'Why are you doing this to me?' said the woman, who was dressed as Barney to celebrate the opening of a drugstore. And he said, 'Because we . . . hate Barney'" (Woman in Barney Costume, 1994, 3A). Perhaps the most humorous and, yes, even disturbing examples of "Barney bashing" on the Internet were recently discussed in two of Mike Royko's columns:

> Something new and shocking has been brought to my attention by a man who is the father of young children. . . . Believe it or not, there are many people who go on-line to talk about how much they hate Barney. . . . It goes beyond hatred. They talk about how they would like him to die. And they even compete with each other to see who can come up with the most grotesque idea for putting him to death. One person wrote that Barney should be ground up and turned into little meat patties to be served as burgers to innocent children in the school lunchroom (Royko, 1995a, 4A).

And another Royko quote:

> An Internet jockey named Jamie monitors the Barney haters closely, and he has passed along what he says is the real reason for their campaign to kill the big, cheerful dinosaur that is loved by millions of little children. . . . According to many of the Barney haters, the government of the United States is in touch with aliens from outer space who are reptilian in nature. . . . Many of them believe that TV shows like Barney that show reptiles in a good light are the government's attempt to brainwash our children out of their innate human repugnance toward anything that is reptilian. . . . These people take this business really seriously. Some even attribute a religious significance to it, believing that the biblical references to serpents was God's warning about these things (Royko, 1995a, 4A).

It is shocking to consider that there are people out there who feel passionately enough about Barney to exert time and energy lambasting this large, purple dinosaur on the Internet. Royko is shocked also, albeit tongue-in-cheek, but what is it about Barney that evokes this type of response?

Consider the six-year-old child I know who, when asked about her feelings toward Barney, delighted in teaching me her version of the Barney song:

> I hate you.
> You hate me.

We're a dysfunctional family.
Take a great big gun,
fire a shot from me to you.
Won't you say you hate me too.

Cute—at least she's verbally precocious, but is Barney responsible? I feel compelled to consider the source of this anger. What is the relationship between this type of response and the characters that evoke simultaneous love and contempt? One explanation is offered in a study conducted by J. Singer and D. Singer (1993) for the Yale University Family Television Research and Consultation Center. They suggest:

> The fad of "Barney-bashing" evident in comments by television critics reflects a cynical lack of awareness by some adults of the urgency with which infants and preschool children require consistent periods of exposure to expressions of love and comfort and a sense of security. Such experiences may provide the child with a sense of personal worth and strength that may help in later confrontations with the inevitable disappointments, dangers, fears and even betrayals of later life (13).

The study concluded that "something very basic is being met here—a loving, caring, predictably benign presence for the child, once a role played by grandparents or uncles or aunts when extended families lived in close proximity but now are much less available because of family fractionalization and mobility" (Singer and Singer, 1993, 21). So there—but I am still uncomfortable. Are we now expecting television executives to simultaneously concern themselves with making a profit *and* accepting a moral responsibility for meeting the educational and emotional needs of our children? Has television become both teacher and agent of social reform? I can see the newspaper headline: "Large purple dinosaur solves problems of family fractionalization and mobility." I can almost hear the collective sigh of relief; one more social problem can be checked off our lists.

Is it possible that the anger directed at Barney—from both children and adults alike—is a response to a sickeningly sweet message that ignores the complex realities of life for a significant number of children and adults? Realistically, a large purple dinosaur cannot replace the presence of a "real" family or "real" people who are caring and compassionate. And stereotypical role models of "ideal" children from appropriately diverse racial and ethnic backgrounds cannot begin to emulate the cultural and economic differences between children who do not live in families that reflect "appropriate" middle-class ideals in behavior, attitudes, and beliefs. Could it be that we unconsciously attempt to subjugate *all* children and fail to recognize that they are insulted by attempts to ceaselessly amuse and entertain without engaging them in substantive issues or real-life vignettes? Or perhaps we have missed the "real" issue altogether: Hating Barney may be a rite of passage, a developmentally appropriate stage where children and young adults assert themselves as separate, mature, and even cynical beings in much the same way that children regularly reject their parent's values, beliefs, and attitudes. Obviously, there is no one explanation for this hostility toward Barney; however, it is thought-provoking. Why do people hate Barney and not Big Bird or Bert and Ernie? They seem equally offensive, but in the minds of young people there must be subtle differences.

Of course, it is not entirely accurate to suggest that Barney is the only character that children and adults love to hate. Mention *Mr. Rogers' Neighborhood*, another popular children's program, and one will usually evoke a wide range of emotions, most of which are negative. He is often ridiculed as too slow or redundant. Even his character is assaulted as "too effeminate" and "too white and middle-class." Most of my college students have seen Eddie Murphy's parody of the show on *Saturday Night Live* from the 1980s. He doesn't appeal to many adult viewers who want something flashier, faster, action-packed, and, of course, more multicultural, but, personally, I like Mr. Rogers. His program represents a much sounder approach to the teaching and learning of young children. The pace and rhythm of the show are slower and more methodical, yet the host deals with some very complex issues in a manner that will often appeal to those children who are "put off" by the pace of more contemporary programs. But once again I am forced to consider another, and perhaps more likely, explanation for the negativism: Mr. Rogers does not conform to stereotypical conceptions of masculinity. Middle-class values, beliefs, and attitudes shape the form and content of these programs in lieu of an emphasis on pedagogical style and content.

The Sanctity of Children's Educational Programs

You may still assume that I am the only one with an overactive imagination and intellectual predilections that prevent me from accepting that most children find *Barney and Friends* and *Sesame Street* very entertaining. Those who do not probably recognize that these programs are for preschoolers and, thus, not "cool" for older groups of children. And perhaps college students are even more cynical and "jaded" with this media-centered culture of consumerism and are simply saying "no" to these overprocessed and idealized images of goodness in a youthful, aggressive fashion. Nevertheless, a central question remains unanswered: What do these programs really represent for the larger viewing audience? Does this group simply accept with complacency the notion that children's educational programs are "educational" and thus "good" for children, parents, and society at large?

It is the commonly accepted assumption that children's educational programs are good, and to the average adult children's programs that are educational *do* look good—and perhaps this is the problem. Children's programs represent an adult conception of "good" education for children. But then what do most adults know and believe about children? Are they really unique and special or are they simply little adults "revving up their engines" to enter adolescence and adulthood at full throttle? As dramatic as this may seem, this latter view of childhood dominates and shapes adult visions of what is good and appropriate for young children and, thus, what is good and appropriate for children's programs. These programs are most often fast-paced and colorful, and all the big ideas are there (e.g., the alphabet, numbers, sight words, multiculturalism, and so on). What could be wrong here? Why is it that when I watch these programs I feel assaulted by the dizzying array of bright lights and colors and even the occasional "educational" concept? Here is Healy (1990) describing her encounter with children's educational programming:

> From across the room I am stunned by *Sesame Street*'s sensory assault. . . . We are all, in fact, overwhelmed as we sit, silent, engulfed by a cacophony of vignettes that change, literally, by the minute; *Sesame Street* segments run anywhere from thirty or forty-five seconds up to a rare maximum of three minutes. Muppets, people, objects, cartoons, cascade inexorably—each scene arrestingly novel and removed both visually and contextually from the last. . . . "*One, two, three,*" shouts a disembodied voice. *H* floats by, suddenly experiencing an explosion of parts that transform it to *h.* "*H,*" the voice intones, but immediately *h* is gone and we are on a street in London were cartoon characters shout a slapstick routine that features rhyming sounds, unrelated in any discernible way to the previous "teaching" (218–219).

It's possible that these programs have *no* impact on the learning experiences of children. But then we must also consider the possibility that there may be deleterious effects associated with the viewing of these programs. Healy (1990) is convinced that the impact is negative:

> I am convinced it is not merely a coincidence that our faith in [*Sesame Street*] has coincided with a major decline in reading and learning skills. Uncritical acceptance of *Sesame Street* as a model for "learning" has been part of a larger infatuation with expedient, product-oriented approaches that denigrate the essence of the educational enterprise. Its substitution of surface glitz for substance has started a generation of children in the seduc-

tive school of organized silliness, where their first lesson is that learning is something adults can be expected to make happen for them as quickly and pleasantly as possible. Thus prepared, they can hardly be blamed if they fail to discover for themselves the personal joys—time consuming as they are—or serious learning, mental effort, and mastery (221).

Once again, I am struck by how much we do know about the teaching and learning of young children, and by how little of that information impacts what we actually do when we interact with children in a teaching/learning context.

There is another issue. Why are the voices of children absent from our discussions and decisions regarding their teaching and learning? During the past forty years, youth in America have been introduced to an increasingly large number of TV characters whose aims and purposes seem to be innocent enough: the preparation of children for academic and social success. According to Healy (1990), "*Sesame Street*'s raison d'être has been to improve the educational prognosis for the disadvantaged" (220). Just as we have regularly attempted to find just the "right" educational institution that meets the needs of all children—rich and poor alike—we assume that the "right" television program will redress the inequities faced by poor children and children of color in our culture—a paternalistic role, at best, but one that also begs a question: How do these programs intersect with the cultures of a diverse range of students, many of whom find the hegemony of white, middle-class norms and mores offensive and detrimental to their experience of success and achievement? Where are the voices of these children and their parents in discussions of "disadvantaged" children and their "failure" to benefit from the vast array of children's educational programs offered daily on television? Of course, we cannot ignore the reality that the middle-class peers of these children also watch these programs—in addition to the other enriching activities that they often experience as part of their preschool preparation. Thus, "disadvantaged" children don't really benefit from children's educational programs; they remain "disadvantaged" despite the best efforts of these programs. Once again, simple solutions cannot address complex social problems.

Outrageous as it may seem, is it possible that our placid acceptance of the "goodness" and "rightness" of children's educational programming is related to the corresponding lack of power and status of its target group—young children? Surely many of these kids have powerful, well-educated parents, and we all know and recognize the tremendous buying power of children, but as a group do children have a voice? Are their needs and concerns represented by adult needs and concerns? Are young children important enough to cause vigilant adults to fight for their "best" interests; to compel us to seriously consider their needs and desires; to make sure that the educational programs they watch are truly effective in producing a lifelong desire to learn?

Do we as adults "need" to believe that when we "park" our children in front of an electronic baby-sitter that it addresses the real or perceived educational needs of children? We want to believe that educational programs for children are educational and, therefore, good. And on a very superficial level it "looks" good to adult viewers. Bright lights, lots of information, excitement, and all the rest. It's almost like "preschool-in-a-can"—everything kids are supposed to learn in thirty- to sixty-minute blocks. These programs may completely ignore everything we know about child development and developmentally appropriate teaching and learning—but hey, who cares? The kids seem to love it. They will sit still through hours of this media blitz. And those who don't do this, well, *they* are a problem—short attention span, hyperactive, behavior-disordered. Complacency in learning may begin in front of the TV. Is it any surprise that children come to school unprepared to take responsibility for their own learning as active participants in the teaching-learning process? It isn't, as many teachers suspect, that we have to seek to entertain in the same way that children's programs do but rather that children have already been indoctrinated to passive learning—somebody else makes the decisions; somebody else takes the responsibility of making learning exciting. If one accepts that years two through six are critical periods of cognitive growth, what happens when we regularly place children in front of the TV for hours at a time during this period of development? Is it really surprising that children come to school lethargic and unmotivated to learn?

Finally, should we pity the child who has not had the opportunity to watch Big Bird and Barney—a child who is not conversant on the lives and activities of these characters? Children's educational programs permeate and define every dimension of a child's life. At the very least these children must be confused when they encounter everything from groceries, clothes, videos, toys, party invitations, and the like that are engraved with the familiar (or to the novice television watcher, unfamiliar) characters from the programs that most children watch. Previous generations of children learned the familiar rhythms of American life through families and schools. The familiar rhythms of postmodern America pulsate with the themes, music, and characters from these television programs.

PBS in Critical Perspective

The goodness and worth of public television's efforts to educate and serve public interests have seldom been questioned; it is right up there with God, family, and country. At least this was true until recently. In an attempt to cut government funding, some Republicans have cast a critical eye toward federal funding for public television. Federal funds make up approximately 14 percent of the budget for the Corporation for Public Broadcasting (Zoglin, 1995, 56). This fact has caused PBS's most vocal opponents to support Newt Gingrich's concerns "that public television is elitist and just a 'sandbox for the rich,' and that Joe Taxpayer should not have to pickup the tab anymore." However, "'elitism' is really a code word for a more virulent complaint made by conservative critics: that PBS programming has a liberal bias" (Zoglin, 1995, 56).

Although this controversy can be characterized as merely one part of a much broader conservative agenda, I was taken aback at the unanimous response of my colleagues to this assault on the integrity of public television and its use of federal moneys. This response was an unequivocal outpouring of support and affirmation for the integrity of public television programming. The uncontested conclusion was that public television is superior to commercial television offerings, and that it should therefore not have to "prostitute" itself in the marketplace in an attempt to be financially self-sustaining. These feelings are consistent with those from the 1960s when Spring (1994) found that

> there seemed to be a general acceptance of the fact that commercial programming was shaped by a combination of influences by advocacy groups, government officials, advertisers, industry standards, and the production process. If commercial television shaped mass culture, then mass culture was indirectly shaped by these influences on commercial broadcasting. From this perspective, public television was given influence over high culture, while commercial television was allotted low culture (339).

For many, the mandate of public television continues to be the same: "to provide a place where high-quality programming can flourish without the commercial pressures that dog the networks" (Zoglin, 1995, 56). Public television is perceived as the place where the integrity of the mind is placed above profit.

Whether or not public television is a bastion of liberal values and beliefs could be debated ad nauseam. However, the real issue has to be whether public television is functioning for the public good. Is it really a foregone conclusion that children's educational programs are good and therefore must also be good for society—and should be paid for by society? Isn't it apparent that public television *is* the exemplar of what television can be and, perhaps, should be under the best circumstances? Perhaps it is not as apparent as we once believed. Lewis H. Lapham (1993) argues that the issue is not about money and PBS. Instead the real issue is that "PBS had nothing to say that wasn't being said by somebody else. Maybe the system never had anything to say, but in the context of the changes that have reshaped the means of communications over the last ten years, and as one of many instruments in what has become an entirely new media orchestra, PBS no longer can be heard to be making a distinctive sound" (43).

Oops. I guess the sanctity of PBS offerings can no longer be taken for granted, but perhaps these questions will lead to other questions about the goodness and worth of educational programs generally.

Conclusion

Children's programs have become an all-too-frequent guest in our homes—a guest whose intentions may not be entirely honorable. The role of television, particularly children's programming, is seldom subjected to the scrutiny and critical analysis warranted by more "serious" popular commercial programming. Programs in this latter genre are looked at carefully for content: violence, inappropriate language, or explicit sexuality. Yet the producers of children's programs frequently claim that the programs are educational and deal in appropriate ways with sensitive issues such as divorce, multiculturalism, handicaps, and the like.

Before assuming that children's television programming is benign and not worthy of critical consideration, however, I would argue that it is worthy of the same critical consideration as children's literature, textbooks, toys, and so on. The messages are powerful and long-lasting. I will ask you to consider who determines the goodness and worth of these programs. In March 1994, a Nickelodeon official was quoted as "taking aim at the preschool set, and backing up its plans with a $30 million programming investment." Geraldine Laybourne, president of Nickelodeon/Nick at Nite, said, "With all the negative messages that bombard kids today, television has consistently failed to serve their needs—with the exception of a few bright spots on the dial." Furthermore, she proposed that Nick Jr. will be "the safe and imaginative place where young kids can learn and play" (Nickelodeon Developing Programming, 1994, 6C). Granted, this is not public television, but it's a beautiful vision; these people aren't making a profit; they've become morally responsible and committed to the healthy development of children in America. So why do I feel like I'm still on the set of Barney—all saccharine and no substance? Of course, Nickelodeon is the network that brings us *Xuxa* on a daily basis during the week. Xuxa, with her seductive dress and suggestive lyrics, seems to inspire the children to almost maniacal levels of excitement. Although the program does deal with selective, and unrelated, issues that are educational, I am confounded by the thought that someone somewhere in "TV-Producer Land" thinks Xuxa is a good role model for young children or even that this program is educational in any serious sense of the word.

Should I also accept at face value the finding of the 20th Century Fund Task Force on Public Television in 1992? They found the following: "Inherent in that mission [of public television] is its role as an alternative to commercial television, which is driven by concern for the marketplace, and therefore fails to capture many of the values we hold dear, such as excellence, creativity, tolerance, generosity, responsibility, community, diversity, concern for others, and intellectual achievement" (Lapham, 1993, 35).

The task force, of course, "endorsed each of these fine values, regretted their temporary absence, and took note of the several obstacles that cruel fate had placed in the way of their joyful expression. . . . They didn't dwell on public television's abject dependence on its corporate sponsors or its eagerness to hustle toys to children through the friendly offices of Barney and Big Bird" (Lapham, 1993, 36). My cynicism continues as I now note that the Yale University study (Singer and Singer, 1993) that overwhelmingly supported the value and worth of *Barney and Friends* as well as other public television formats for children was *entirely* financed by a "gift" from Connecticut Public Television. Of course, this redefines the battle as public television (high culture that is sacred and "above" commercial concerns) versus commercial television (low culture that is committed to the bottom line and therefore blameless if it puts profits above children).

So where does this go? Several points need to be made. Research has not clearly documented the educational benefits or detriments of children's educational programs. What do we know about the interaction and effects of television on a very young population? Who watches these shows? For how long? What is the short- or long-term effect—psychologically, sociologically, economically, and philosophically? Also, how have we utilized the knowledge we have about teaching and learning to shape what goes on in these programs? Research into the teaching/learning process consistently supports the notion that meaningful knowledge is socially constructed (Abbott, 1995, 8). Why do we continue to reject these findings by producing children's educational programs that ignore contemporary issues regarding the nature and quality of effective teaching and learning? Has public television simply become one more attempt to accelerate the learning potential of young children without clearly identifying and understanding the real detriments to their overall readiness to begin school at five or six?

Despite its tremendous growth and influence as a "third education institution," television has not been held accountable for its outcomes as an educator of young children. Shouldn't we attempt to link aims and purposes with outcomes? Just as it is impossible to clearly articulate the *one* best vision for all schools in America, it may be equally difficult to achieve any degree of consensus about the aims and purposes of educational programs for children. However, it would seem a worthy goal to educate the public concerning the pros and cons of this type of programming. Additionally, those responsible for programming decisions should be held accountable for their efforts to educate and, thus, impact the lives of a very young and vulnerable viewing audience. If one accepts that television has become the "third education institution" in America, then one must seriously examine the powerful academic and social messages being transmitted to children through these programs.

Stephen R. Covey (1989), in *The Seven Habits of Highly Effective People*, discusses a principle: "Begin with the end in mind." This means "to start with a clear understanding of your destination. It means to know where you're going so that you better understand where you are now and so that the steps you take are always in the right direction" (98). This ideal is most meaningful to me as I think about the attempts we make to educate and better facilitate the healthy development of young people. What is the impact of the unidimensional, undeveloped characters portrayed in these shows? Why do we try so hard to present token representatives of every race, ethnicity, and gender without consideration of the equally important variables of social class and geographic or demographic differences? As Lapham (1993) describes it, "the sponsoring corporations have filled the PBS with programs that are best understood as advertisements for a preferred reality" (39). It is interesting to note that although most teachers of young children are female, a majority of the main characters assuming instructional roles on children's educational programs are male; and although a rapidly increasing number of children are poor children of color, this group is still underrepresented on children's educational programs—a preferred reality, perhaps.

Should there not be more recognition of the role played by corporate sponsors who dictate the content of most programs? Once again, Lapham (1993) describes quite eloquently "the expectant PBS courtier [who] is constantly bowing and smiling in eight or nine directions, forever turning, like a compass needle into the glare of new money" (42). The public has falsely assumed that children's educational programs are indeed educational and thus good for children. Healy (1990) is equally disappointed: "If *Sesame Street* did not purport to be seriously educational, it might pass as clever and colorful light entertainment. But lauded as our major media effort to educate children, I believe it has failed and misled us at a time when we desperately need better models"

(234). We have naively assumed that corporate *and* public interests could be simultaneously served by children's educational programs.

As a parent, I know that raising a child is exhausting, and my frustration was great when I had a child that would not sit and watch television for extended periods like other children. I needed a break, and I wanted to believe that I could both educate and amuse my child with the "right" educational program. Fortunately, my frustration was short-lived. She is growing up all too quickly, and I have learned to appreciate those qualities in her that caused her to refuse to watch television for long periods of time. She still doesn't like children's educational programs, and I am relieved, because I now see how few benefits can be associated with the viewing of these programs.

We cannot assume that educational programs are a substitute for "real" families or "real" teachers, but we can assume that they are teaching "real" values, beliefs, and attitudes. It would seem to be a worthy endeavor to engage others in a critical discussion of the value and worth of these programs. Surely this process may be as important as the outcome, because although profit ultimately is the "real" focus of these programs, our children's lives and minds are the "real" issue. Are there not more meaningful ways that we can simultaneously attend to both these issues and perhaps improve the net outcome of our efforts? We are guardians of our children's future, and the impact of these programs on this future is a serious concern. An honest examination of how truly "strange" children's educational programs have become is long overdue. If television is to function as both entertainment *and* teacher, it is time to reframe the conversation to reflect the needs and interests of the larger community. Those populations of children who have the most to gain from these programs must be acknowledged and involved in the articulation of reasonable and effective strategies that will make this innovation truly work for the good of all.

References

Abbott, J. (1995). Children need communities. *Educational Leadership* 52 (May): 6–10.

Covey, S. R. (1989). *The seven habits of highly effective people: Restoring the character ethic.* New York: Simon and Schuster.

Healy, J. M. (1990). *Endangered minds: Why children don't think and what we can do about it.* New York: Touchstone.

Lapham, L. H. (1993, December). Adieu, Big Bird: On the terminal irrelevance of public television. *Harper's* 287, 35–43.

Nickelodeon developing programming for preschool kids. (1994, March 24). *Asheville Citizen-Times*, 6C.

Royko, M. (1995a, March 1). For Barney, it's a cyberjungle out there. *Asheville Citizen-Times*, 4A.

_____. (1995b, March 15). Watch out for those cunning reptiles. *Asheville Citizen-Times*, 4A.

Singer, J. L., and Singer, D. G. (1993, August 8). Progress Report for Research Project Series "100" *Barney and Friends as Education and Entertainment*. New Haven, Connecticut: Yale University Family Television Research and Consultation Center.

Spindler, G., and Spindler, L. (1982). Roger Harker and Schonhausen: From the familiar to the strange and back again. In G. Spindler, ed., *Doing the ethnography of schooling: Educational anthropology in action*. New York: Holt, Rinehart, and Winston.

Spring, J. (1992). *Images of American life: A history of ideological management in schools, movies, radio, and television*. Albany: State University of New York Press.

_____. (1994). *The American school, 1642–1993*. 3rd ed. New York: McGraw-Hill.

Woman in Barney costume attacked at drugstore opening. (1994, April 11). *Asheville Citizen-Times*, 3A.

Zoglin, R. (1995, January 23). Mom, apple pie, and PBS. *Time* 145, 56.

4 Beavis and Butt-Head: *No Future for Postmodern Youth*

Douglas Kellner

TRADITIONALLY, YOUNG PEOPLE were educated through fairy tales, folk traditions, and children's literature, as well as through institutions like family, school, and church. In our times, media culture has replaced traditional institutions as major instruments of socialization, and young people often receive role models and materials for identity from media corporations rather than their parents or teachers (Kellner 1995). Moreover, a commercially produced and dominated youth culture has replaced traditional artifacts of children's culture. In this media youth culture, popular music, television, film, and video and computer games create new idols, aspirations, and artifacts that profoundly influence the thought and behavior of contemporary youth.

MTV's animated cartoon series *Beavis and Butt-Head* has emerged as one of the most popular and controversial artifacts of youth culture in recent years. Since its release in 1993 the series has attracted a diverse audience of fervent fans and has elicited intense controversy concerning its messages and effects. In the following discussion I provide a reading of what the series tells us about the condition of contemporary youth, discuss the controversies over its effects, and conclude with some remarks on how to deal with media culture and the need for a critical media pedagogy to develop media literacy to empower young and old audiences.

Beavis and Butt-Head, Media Culture, and Contemporary Youth

Animated cartoon characters Beavis and Butt-Head sit in a shabby house much of the day watching television, especially music videos, which they criticize (they are either "cool" or they "suck"). When they leave the house for school, for their work in a fast-food joint, or for adventure, they often engage in destructive and criminal behavior. Developed for MTV by animated cartoonist Mike Judge, the series spoofs precisely the sort of music videos played by the network itself.[1] *Beavis and Butt-Head* quickly became a cult favorite, loved by youth, yet it elicited spirited controversy when some young fans of the show imitated typical *Beavis and Butt-Head* activity, such as burning down houses and torturing and killing animals.[2]

The series provides a critical vision of the current generation of youth raised primarily on media culture. This generation was conceived in the sights and sounds of media culture, was weaned on it, and was socialized by the glass teat of television used as pacifier, baby-sitter, and educator by a generation of parents for whom media culture, especially television, was a natural part of everyday life. Beavis and Butt-Head are purely a product of media culture and reveal the extent to which contemporary youth are totally immersed and socialized by media culture—often with destructive consequences.

In a sense, *Beavis and Butt-Head* depicts the dissolution of a rational subject and perhaps the end of the Enlightenment in today's media culture. Beavis and Butt-Head react viscerally to the videos, snickering at the images, finding representations of violence and sex "cool" (anything complex that requires interpretation "sucks"). Bereft of any cultivated taste, judgment, or rationality, and without ethical or political values, the characters act mindlessly toward their culture and society and appear to lack almost all cognitive and communicative skills—victims of undereducation and excessive media socialization.

The intense alienation of Beavis and Butt-Head, their love for heavy metal music culture and media images of sex and violence, and their violent cartoon activity soon elicited heated controversy, producing *Beavis and Butt-Head* effects reflected in thousands of articles and heated debates; the U.S. Senate even condemned the show for promoting mindless violence and stupid behavior.[3] From the show's first airing the media focused intensely on the show, and there were strongly opposed opinions of it. In a cover story on the show, *Rolling Stone* declared the duo "The Voice of a New Generation" (August 19, 1993), and *Newsweek* also put them on its cover, both praising them and damning them by concluding: "The downward spiral of the living white male surely ends here: in a little pimple named Butt-Head whose idea of an idea is, 'Hey, Beavis, let's go over to Stuart's house and light one in his cat's butt'" (October 11, 1993). "Stupid, lazy, cruel; without ambitions, without values, without futures"—these are some of the other terms used by the media to describe the characters and the series (*Dallas Morning News*, August 29, 1993), and there have been countless calls to ban the show.

Indeed, a lottery prizewinner in California began a crusade against the series after hearing about a cat that was killed when kids put a firecracker in its mouth, imitating Beavis and Butt-Head's violence against animals and a suggestion in one episode that they stick a firecracker in a neighbor's cat (*Hollywood Reporter*, July 16, 1993). Librarians in Westchester, New York, ranked *Beavis and Butt-Head* high "on a list of movies and television shows that they think negatively influence youngsters' reading habits" because of the characters' attacks on books and frequent remarks that books, or even words, "suck" (*New York Times*, July 11, 1993). Prison officials in Oklahoma banned the show; schools in South Dakota banned clothing and other items bearing the characters' likenesses (*Times Newspapers Limited*, October 11, 1993); and a group of Missouri fourth-graders started a petition drive to get the program off the air (*Radio TV Reports*, October 25, 1993).

Yet the series continues to be highly popular into the mid-1990s, and it has spawned a best-selling album of heavy metal rock, a popular book, countless consumer items, and movie contracts that are in the works. *Time* critic Kurt Anderson praised the series as "the bravest show ever run on national television" (*New York Times*, July 11, 1993), and there is no question but that it has pushed the boundaries of the permissible on mainstream television to new extremes (some critics would say to new lows).

Beavis and Butt-Head is interesting for analyzing the effects of contemporary media, because the main characters get all of their ideas and images concerning life from media culture, from which they also derive their entire view of history and the world. When the characters see a costumed rapper wearing an eighteenth-century-style white wig on a music video, Butt-Head remarks, "He's dressed up like that dude on the dollar." To them, the 1960s is the time of hippies, Woodstock, and rock 'n' roll; Vietnam is ancient history, collapsed into other American wars. Even the 1950s is nothing but a series of mangled media clichés: On the pop duo Nelson, formed by the twins of 1950s teen idol Ricky Nelson, Butt-Head remarks, "These chicks look like guys." Beavis responds: "I heard that these chicks' grandpa was Ozzy Osbourne." And Butt-Head rejoins: "No way. They're Elvis's kids."

The figures of history are collapsed for Beavis and Butt-Head into media culture and provide material for salacious jokes, which require detailed knowledge of media culture:

BUTT-HEAD: What happened when Napoleon went to Mount Olive?

BEAVIS: I don't know. What?

BUTT-HEAD: Popeye got pissed.

Beavis and Butt-Head is "postmodern" in the sense that it is purely a product of media culture, with its characters, style, and content almost solely derived from TV shows. The characters are a spinoff of Wayne and Garth in *Wayne's World*, a popular *Saturday Night Live* feature that spun off into popular movies. They also resemble SCTV characters Bob and Doug McKenzie, who sit around on a couch and make lewd and crude remarks while watching TV and drinking beer. Beavis and Butt-Head also take the asocial behavior of cartoon character Bart Simpson to a more intense extreme. Their comments on the music videos replicate the popular Comedy Central Channel's *Mystery Science Theater 3000*, which features two cartoon stick figures making irreverent comments on god-awful, old Hollywood movies and network television shows. And, of course, the music videos are a direct replication of MTV's basic fare.

Moreover, Beavis and Butt-Head seem to have no family, living alone in a shabby house, getting enculturated solely by television and media culture. There are some references to their mothers, and in one episode there is a suggestion that Butt-Head is not even certain who his father is; thus the series presents a world without fathers.[4] School is totally alienating for the two, as is their working in a fast-food restaurant. Adult figures they encounter are largely white conservative males or liberal yuppies, with whom they often come into violent conflict and whose property or goods they inevitability destroy.

Such images reveal the breakdown of the family in contemporary society and the systematic deprivation of working-class youth. Beavis and Butt-Head are, of course, young white boys, so the oppressiveness of their situation is nothing in comparison to the racial oppression and violence on display in films like *Boyz N the Hood*, or *Menace 2 Society*. Yet the series puts on display the inchoate social violence that permeates media culture and everyday life and shows both how Beavis and Butt-Head's lack of education and life opportunities drive them to violence *and* render them victims of an uncaring and oppressive society.

There is a fantasy-fulfillment aspect to Beavis and Butt-Head that perhaps helps account for its popularity: Kids often wish that they had no parents and that they could just sit and watch music videos and go out and do whatever they wanted to (sometimes we *all* feel this way). Kids are also naturally disrespectful of authority and love to see defiance of social forces that they find oppressive. Indeed, Beavis and Butt-Head's much maligned, discussed, and imitated laughter ("Heh, heh, heh . . ." and "Huh, huh . . . ") may signify that in their space *they rule*, that Beavis and Butt-Head are sovereign, that they control the television and can do any damn thing that they want. Notably, they get in trouble in school and other sites of authority with their laugh, but at home they can laugh and snicker to the max.

And so the series has a utopian dimension: the utopia of no parental authority and unlimited freedom to do whatever they want when they want to. "Dude, we're there . . ." is a favorite phrase they use when they decide to see or do something—and they never have to ask their (absent) parents' permission. Yet they represent the consequences of totally unsocialized adolescent behavior driven by aggressive instincts.[5] Indeed, their "utopia" is highly solipsistic and narcissistic, with no community, no consensual norms or morality to bind them, and no concern for other people. The vision of the teenagers alone in their house watching TV and then wreaking havoc on their neighborhood presents a vision of a society of broken families, disintegrating communities, and anomic individuals without values or goals.

Beavis and Butt-Head are thus left alone with TV and become couch-potato critics, especially of their beloved music videos. In a sense, they are the first media critics to become cult heroes of media culture, though there are contradictions in their media criticism. Many of the videos that they attack are stupid and pretentious, and in general it is good to cultivate a critical attitude toward cultural forms and to promote cultural criticism—an attitude that can indeed be applied to much of what appears on *Beavis and Butt-Head.* They have their moments as media critics, mooning *The Brady Bunch* and making sarcastic remarks about Madonna or insufferable *60 Minutes* commentator Andy Rooney. Such critique distances the audience from music video and media culture and calls for making critical judgments on its products. Yet many of Beavis and Butt-Head's own judgments are highly questionable, praising images of violence, fire, naked women, and heavy metal noise while declaring that "college music," words, and any complexity in the videos "suck."

Yet the series does provide some sharp social satire and critique of culture and society in America. The episodes constantly make fun of television, especially music videos, and other forms of media culture. They criticize conservative authority figures and wishy-washy liberals. They satirize authoritarian institutions like the workplace, schools, and military recruitment centers and provide critical commentary on many features of contemporary life. They make fun of authoritarians in many institutions and attack the hypocrisy of Rush Limbaugh and the Right and various hypocrites who come into their classroom to teach them manners or salesmanship.

But the series undercuts some of its social critique by reproducing the worst sexist, violent, and narcissistic elements of contemporary life, which are made amusing and even likable in the figures of Beavis and Butt-Head. The series is aggressively "politically incorrect," making fun of feminism, environmentalism, and do-gooders of all sorts—even while it consistently satirizes conservative and authoritarian figures.

Beavis and Butt-Head's almost instinctive sexism, however, allows a di-
agnostic critique—as I argue below—of the infantile roots of sexism, just
as their narcissism and violence allows a critique of a society that fails to
educate and provide opportunities for self-development for much of its
youth.

Consequently, *Beavis and Butt-Head* is surprisingly complex and requires sustained critique to analyze its contradictory text and effects.
There is no denying, however, that the *Beavis and Butt-Head* effects are
among the most significant media phenomena of recent years.[6] Like director Rick Linklater (*Slacker* and *Dazed and Confused*), Judge has obviously tapped into a highly responsive chord and created a media sensation, with Beavis and Butt-Head serving as powerfully resonant images.
In 1993, while I was lecturing on cultural studies, wherever I would go
audiences would ask me what I thought of *Beavis and Butt-Head*, and so
I eventually began to watch it and to incorporate remarks on the series
into my lectures.[7] If I was critical or disparaging, young members of the
audience would attack me, and after a lecture at the University of Kansas
a young man approached, incredulous that I would dare criticize the series and certain that Mike Judge was a great genius who understood exactly how it was for contemporary youth, having no prospects for a job
or career and little prospect for even marriage and family and a meaningful life. In this situation, I was told, what else can young people do except watch MTV and occasionally go out and destroy something?

In a sense, the series enacts youth and class revenge against older,
middle-class, conservative adults, who invariably are portrayed as oppressive authority figures. Their neighbor, Tom Anderson—depicted as a
conservative World War II and Korean War veteran—is a special butt of
their escapades, and they cut down trees in his yard with a chain saw,
which, of course, causes the tree to demolish his house, assorted fences,
power lines, and cars. They put his dog in a Laundromat washing machine to clean it; they steal his credit card to buy animals at the mall;
they lob mud baseballs into his yard, one of which hits his barbecue;
they destroy a swimming pool that they are supposed to help him build;
and otherwise they torment him. Beavis and Butt-Head also blow up an
army recruiting station with a grenade as the officer attempts to recruit
them; they steal the car of a wealthy man, Billy Bob, who has a heart attack when he sees them riding off in his vehicle; and they love to put
worms, rats, and other animals in the fast food that they are shown giving to obnoxious white male customers in the burger joint where they
work.

Beavis and Butt-Head also love to trash the house of their "friend,"
Stewart, whose yuppie parents indulgently pamper their son and his
playmates. Stewart's permissive liberal parents are shown to be silly and

ineffectual, as when his father complains that Stewart violated his parents' trust when he let Beavis and Butt-Head in the house after they caused an explosion that blew the wall out. The mother gushes about how cute they are and offers them lemonade—in fact, few women authority figures are depicted, and most women, like men, are presented as ineffectual or ridiculously authoritarian.

The characters also torment and make fun of their liberal hippie teacher, Mr. Van Driessen, who tries to teach them to be politically correct. They destroy his irreplaceable eight-track music collection when he offers to let them clean his house to learn the value of work and money. When he takes them camping to get in touch with their feelings and nature, they fight and torment animals. In fact, they rebel against all their teachers and authority figures and are thus presented in opposition to everyone, ranging from conservative males to liberal yuppies to hippie radicals.

Moreover, the series presents the revenge of youth and those who are terminally downwardly mobile against more privileged classes and individuals. Like the punk generation before them typified by the Sex Pistols, Beavis and Butt-Head have no future. Thus, although their behavior is undeniably juvenile, offensive, sexist, and politically incorrect, it allows diagnosis of underclass and downwardly mobile youth who have nothing to do but destroy things and engage in asocial behavior.

From this perspective, *Beavis and Butt-Head* is an example of media culture as popular revenge:[8] Beavis and Butt-Head avenge youth and the downwardly mobile against the oppressive authority figures they confront daily. Most of the conservative men have vaguely Texan or southwestern accents, so perhaps the male authority figures represent oppressive males experienced by Judge in his own youth in San Diego, New Mexico, and Texas. Moreover, Beavis and Butt-Head's violence is that of a violent society in which the media present endless images of the sort of violent activities that the two characters regularly engage in. The series thus points to the existence of a large teenage underclass with no future and that is undereducated and potentially violent. The Beavis and Butt-Heads of society (that is, the young underclass) have nothing to look forward to in life save a job at the local 7-Eleven, where if they work long enough they get robbed at gunpoint. Consequently, the series is a social hieroglyph that allows us to decode the attitudes, behavior, and situation of large segments of youth in contemporary U.S. society.

For a critical theory of media culture, then, it is wrong to simply excuse the antics of Beavis and Butt-Head as typical behavior of the young. Likewise, it is not enough simply to condemn them as pathological.[9] Rather, the series reveals how violent society is becoming and the dead-end futures of downwardly mobile youth from broken homes who are undereducated and have no real job possibilities or future. Indeed, the heavy metal culture in which Beavis and Butt-Head immerse themselves is a way for those caught up in dead-end lives to blot everything out, to escape in a world of pure noise and aggression, and in turn to express their own aggression and frustrations through heavy metal "headbanging." Thus, when Beavis and Butt-Head play the "air guitar," imitating heavy metal playing during the music videos, they are signaling both their aggression and the hopelessness of their situation.

Beavis and Butt-Head's narcissism and sociopathic behavior are symptoms of a society that is not providing adequate nurture or support to its citizens. It is indeed curious that many of the most popular media culture figures could easily be clinically diagnosed and analyzed as narcissistic: Rush Limbaugh, Andrew Dice Clay, Howard Stern, and other popular media figures are examples of empty, insecure, and hostile individuals who resort to extreme behavior and assertions to call attention to themselves. Popular media figures, and we count Beavis and Butt-Head among that group, tap into audience aggressions and frustrations and become popular precisely because of their ability to articulate inchoate social anger. Indeed, compared to a Rush Limbaugh, Beavis and Butt-Head are relatively modest and restrained in their narcissism.

Beavis and Butt-Head, Rush Limbaugh, and other figures of contemporary U.S. media culture also think they know things but in fact are know-nothings in the tradition of American anti-intellectualism. These figures are essentially buffoons—sometimes entertaining and often offensive—who in the classical syndrome of narcissism are empty, insecure, and aggressive. They masquerade their emptiness and insecurity in verbal bravado and aggressiveness and attention-seeking action. They also display classic symptoms of fear of women, whom they continually objectify, and engage in puerile and infantile sexual jokes and gestures. Beavis and Butt-Head are classic teenagers whose hormones are out of control and who cannot control their elders; Howard Stern and Andrew Dice Clay exhibit similar symptoms. These figures of popular entertainment are all white boys incapable of taking the position of the Other, of empathizing with individuals and groups different from their own, and of respecting differences. They are all extremely homophobic, though Beavis and Butt-Head are obviously repressing homosexual proclivities signaled in all the "butt" jokes, "suck" references, and Butt-Head's injunction: "Hey Beavis, pull my finger."

In a sense, *Beavis and Butt-Head* is an example of what has been called "loser television," surely a new phenomenon in television history. Previous television series tended to depict wealthy or secure middle-class individuals and families who often led highly glamorous lives. It was believed that advertisers preferred affluent environments to sell their products, and so the working class and underclass were excluded from network television for decades. Indeed, during the Reagan era in the 1980s, programs like *Dallas, Dynasty,* and *Lifestyles of the Rich and Famous* celebrated wealth and affluence and represented the antithesis of loser TV. This dream has been punctured by the reality of everyday life in a downsliding economy, and so a large and growing audience is attracted to programs that articulate their own frustration and anger in experiencing downward mobility and a sense of no future. Hence, we have witnessed the recent popularity of loser TV, including *The Simpsons, Roseanne,* and *Beavis and Butt-Head.*

During the 1994 and 1995 seasons Beavis and Butt-Head's social mayhem receded somewhat—perhaps under pressure of network censorship when the show became a hotbed of controversy—and they were often shown to be victims as much as victimizers. In episodes from the 1994 season such as "The Great Cornholio" Beavis is the victim of excessive sugar consumption; in "Pipe of Doom" first Butt-Head and then Beavis get stuck in a construction-site pipe; in "Patients, Patients" a dentist messes up work on Butt-Head's braces, and an eye doctor misprescribes glasses for Beavis, harming his eyesight; in "Pumping Iron" they are attacked in a health club by weightlifters as well as the equipment they don't know how to use; and in "Liar! Liar!" they are victims of job discrimination and lie-detector tests. Indeed, almost all of the episodes from 1994 and 1995 show Beavis and Butt-Head as victims of their undereducation and underclass situation, and these episodes can almost be read as cautionary morality tales showing the harmful effects of ignorance.

Moreover, they are constantly victimized by women: In "Date Bait" they buy women movie tickets, give them money, and wait outside the back door of the theater for the women to let them in, but when the women leave the theater with tough dudes (whom they picked up inside), Beavis and Butt-Head are brushed aside by their "dates" and then attacked by a macho usher when they try to sneak in the back door; in another episode they leave a pay-for-play phone-sex line connected for hours; in "Beard Boys" they cut off their hair and paste it on their faces to try to attract girls after seeing a TV scene where a bearded dude was popular with women; and in many episodes they meet women only to get rejected.

In one poignant episode, the boys are watching Nirvana's video of "Heart-Shaped Box," and Beavis says that he'd like to have a cool room, like in the video, so he could "get chicks"; Butt-Head responds, "You're never going to fix up your room like that. You're just going to hang around this dump spanking your monkey and you're never going to score." Indeed, occasionally the characters break out in despair, recognizing their hopelessness and that they will never "score"—or have any kind of future at all. In the 1994 episode titled "Madame Blavatsky," Beavis and Butt-Head are shown walking through a slum, and they fantasize about having a car and getting chicks; they see a fortune teller's sign, and after painfully decoding the language Butt-Head wants to go up and have his fortune told.

BEAVIS asks: What's that?

BUTT-HEAD: You know, your future.

BEAVIS: What's that?

BUTT-HEAD: I don't know.

Thus, *Beavis and Butt-Head* allows a critique of the plight of contemporary youth facing disintegrating families, little education, and no job possibilities. Beavis and Butt-Head's destructiveness can be seen in part as an expression of their hopelessness and alienation and shows the dead-end prospects for many working-class and middle-class youths. Moreover, the series also replicates the sort of violence that is so widespread in the media—from heavy metal rock videos to TV entertainment to the evening news. Thus, the characters' violence simply mirrors growing youth violence in a disintegrating society and allows the possibility of gaining critical insights into the social situation of contemporary youth.

The *Beavis and Butt-Head* Effects

Yet the show *is* highly violent and has already had spectacular violence effects. In *Liquid Television*, the animated short that preceded the series, Judge shows Beavis and Butt-Head playing "frog baseball," splattering frogs and bashing each other with baseball bats—am image memorialized on one of the many Beavis and Butt-Head T-shirts. In other shows during the first season they use lighters to start fires, blow up a neighbor's house by sniffing gas from the stove and then lighting it, and engage in multifarious other acts of mayhem and violence. A Los Angeles–area schoolteacher discovered that about 90 percent of her class watched the show, and so she invited a local fire department official to speak to her class after several students wrote about playing with fire and explosives in their autobiographical sketches. Some examples: "A major 'Beavis and Butt-Head' fan, Jarrod Metchikoff, 12, used to 'line them [firecrackers] up in a tube and shoot them in the sewer pipe' until his mother found out. Brett Heimstra, 12, said he set off firecrackers in manholes and sewers until his mother discovered them and he 'heard some stuff about how it's dangerous.' Elizabeth Hastings, 12, said she knows a boy who lights firecrackers in portable toilets" (*Los Angeles Times*, October 16, 1993).

The fire official told the students "about a 10-year-old Orange County boy who lost use of his hand after an explosion caused by WD-40 and a cigarette lighter" (*Los Angeles Times*, October 16, 1993). After the initial reports of cruelty to animals and of fans of the show starting fires, many more such reports came in. The fire chief in Sidney, Ohio, "blamed MTV's cartoon for a house fire started by three girls" (*Plain Dealer*, October 14, 1993). Further: "Austin, Texas, investigators say three fires started by kids may have some connection to the show" (*USA Today*, October 15, 1993). And teenage fans of the show were blamed for setting fires near Houston's Galleria mall (*Radio TV Reports*, October 25, 1993).

Intense criticism of the show's violence—and congressional threats to regulate TV violence—led MTV to move its slot to later in the evening (there was also a promise not to replay the more violent episodes or to show Beavis and Butt-Head setting fires or Beavis shouting "Fire! Fire!"), but the series had already become part of a national mythology, and its popularity continued apace.[10] Indeed, media culture is drawn to violence and taboo-breaking action to draw audiences in an ever more competitive field. Thus, the program's excesses are directly related to a competitive situation in which commercial media are driven to show ever more violent and extreme behavior in the intense pressures for high profits—a trend that many believe will accelerate as the number of TV channels grows and as competition becomes fiercer.

Yet one of the differences between the violence shown on *Beavis and Butt-Head* and that of the Warner Brothers cartoons (Bugs Bunny et al.) is that unlike much classical cartoon violence, which was totally unreal—characters blown up, pulverized, and then miraculously returned to life—when Beavis and Butt-Head suffer or inflict violence one sees pain and destruction that is irreparable and for all time (with the possible exception of a program where Beavis cut off Butt-Head's finger with a chain saw). Their bodies are depicted as vulnerable, and the consequences of the violence are shown to be significant. Arguably, the show can thus be interpreted as providing warnings against violence rather than merely depicting its trivialization or glorification, as in much media culture.

Nevertheless, MTV was probably right to cut out the most violent episodes after the first season and to play the program later at night, for the show was definitely fostering violent behavior against animals and influencing children to start fires, engage in destructive behavior, and the like. Media culture can have powerful effects when it taps into audience concerns and in turn becomes part of a circuit of culture with distinctive effects. Media cultural texts articulate social experiences, transcoding them into the medium of forms like television, film, and popular music. The texts are then appropriated by audiences, which use certain resonant texts, images, and figures to articulate their own sense of style, look, and identity. Media culture provides resources to make meanings, pleasure, and identity, but it also shapes and forms specific identities and circulates material whose appropriation may insert audiences into specific positions (for example, macho Rambo, sexy Madonna, disaffected slackers, violent Beavis and Butt-Head, and so on) (Kellner 1995).

The *Beavis and Butt-Head* effects have been particularly striking. Not only did the show promote acts of violence and copious discussion of media effects, but the characters became a model for youth behavior, with young people imitating their antics and behavior patterns. Even if children and youth do not imitate Beavis and Butt-Head's violence, they may imitate their language and antics. Their laugh has become infamous, and many a parent or friend has gone into despair from imitation of their distinctive laughter ("Heh, heh, heh . . ." or "Huh, huh . . . ").[11] Other language and phrases like "X rules!" or "Whoah!" have been circulated and imitated endlessly, as have more dubious terms such as "buttmunch," "ass-wipe," "bunghole," "fart-knocker," "wussie," or "dillweed"—in addition to the famous dichotomous judgment that things are either "cool" or they "suck."

Moreover, the obsessive focus on genital and anal functions is one of the distinctive features of the series that distinguishes it from previous cartoon series. In older series sexuality was expunged from the cartoons, as were bodily functions. In contrast, *Beavis and Butt-Head* is full of references to excrement as well as nose-picking, farting, and other activities previously taboo on television. Obviously, a young audience delights in such transgressions, although the obsessiveness and repetitiveness of genital and anal references becomes a bit trying for cultural critics, and it probably drives parents crazy when they hear such language and references repeated by their children.

The characters' behavioral gestures, such as playing the air guitar to music videos and mooning TV figures to display contempt, may also be the sort of behavior that circulates via imitation of the figures of media culture. Thus, whereas it is only in extreme cases that audiences imitate the violence of Beavis and Butt-Head or Rambo, it is often the figures of language or behavior through which media culture shapes the thought and behavior of its audiences. For these reasons it is important to en-

gage in serious critical scrutiny of a media culture phenomenon like
Beavis and Butt-Head.

In addition, the series generated a large consumer market of Beavis
and Butt-Head products, which in turn proliferated its images and effects. For example: "Mask-maker Ed Edmunds of Distortions Unlimited
says he's sold 40,000 Beavis and Butt-Head masks, his top sellers for this
Halloween season" (*USA Today,* October 26, 1993). Beavis and Butt-
Head T-shirts are everywhere, and the characters' images adorn many
products, webpages, and advertisements in addition to the MTV cartoons. The show also has strongly influenced musical tastes and sales,
providing a boon for heavy metal rock. Studies showed that sales
jumped for every video that appeared in the show—including the ones
that were panned.[12] The *Beavis and Butt-Head* effects even became part
of political contestation:

> It was only a matter of time before "Beavis Clinton" and "Butt-Head Gore"
> T-shirts began appearing on the streets of Washington. The hapless, ugly,
> dumb cartoon characters have been altered to look like the leaders of the
> free world, thanks to local political entrepreneurs and T-shirt creators Kath-
> leen Patten, Beth Loudy and Chris Tremblay. On the shirts, Beavis is sport-
> ing a Fleetwood Mac T-shirt and is seen asking Butt-Head, "Eh, do you
> think we'll get re-elected?" To which the veep, wearing the Greenpeace
> whale logo, says: "Huh . . . nope" (*Washington Times,* October 26, 1993).[13]

Previous studies of media effects seem blind to the sort of complex effects of media-culture texts I have discussed in analyzing the *Beavis and
Butt-Head* effects. Dominant paradigms either theorize media effects as
direct and manipulative or privilege the role of the audience in constructing meaning. In fact, some figures and material of media culture—
young stars of TV and film, Rambo, Madonna, rap music, heavy metal,
Beavis and Butt-Head, and so on—provide powerful, resonant images
that are used to produce meaning, identities, discourse, and behavior.
The media provide symbolic environments in which people live and
strongly influence their thought, behavior, and style. When a media sensation like *Beavis and Butt-Head* appears, it becomes part of that environment and in turn becomes a new resource for pleasures, identities,
and contestation.

Thus, it is totally idiotic to claim that media culture has no discernible
effects, as in the dominant paradigm from the 1950s, which lasted several decades.[14] Yet it is equally idiotic to blindly claim that audiences
simply produce their own meanings from texts and that the texts do not
have their own effectivity. As the discussions in my book *Media Culture*
(Kellner 1995) show, media culture has very powerful effects, although

its meanings are mediated by audiences, and even figures like Beavis and Butt-Head—or even a Rambo or a rapper—become contested terrain in which different groups inflect meanings in different ways.

Conclusion

The *Beavis and Butt-Head* effects that I have just discussed crystallize the experiences and feelings of alienation and hopelessness produced by a disintegrating society and shape these experiences into identification with slackers, heavy metal rock music, and nihilistic violence. Popular media texts tap into and articulate feelings and experiences of their audiences and in turn circulate material effects that shape thought and behavior. Thus, rather than condemn shows like *Beavis and Butt-Head* out of hand, one could view them as a wake-up call, as signs of a disintegrating social order, as signs of the need for education and opportunities for undereducated working-class youth, and as signs that parents should pay more attention to their children and their children's culture.

Yet one should also carefully and critically review *Beavis and Butt-Head*, for the texts of media culture have very powerful and distinctive effects that should be subject to critique and debate. How, then, should parents, educators, and concerned citizens respond to the *Beavis and Butt-Head* phenomenon? One response by parents and educators has been to attempt to censor and police children's viewing of the program and to protect tender young minds from its allegedly harmful contents. Some parents and teachers may indeed find the program without redeeming social value and want to protect their children from the show.

Another approach, one that I recommend, is to use the program as an opportunity to teach children media literacy and criticism. This involves watching the show with children, discussing its images and messages and its potential effects on the audience. Such an exercise might well grasp young viewers' imaginations and help to cultivate critical media literacy, thus empowering young people to critically analyze their culture. If our culture is increasingly a media culture, then media education should be an important part of general education—not to mention children's socialization. In this case, popular programs like *Beavis and Butt-Head* can be a positive opportunity for media education rather than an opportunity for ineffectual handwringing and bemoaning of the decline of American culture.

If we watch closely, *Beavis and Butt-Head* and other popular artifacts of media culture can tell us much about our culture. What they suggest may not be pretty and may be quite disturbing. Critical analysis of *Beavis and Butt-Head* may suggest the need to develop alternative cultures for children and youth. Yet cultivating critical media pedagogy through the reading of popular media artifacts may provide critical literacy that empowers the young. In any case, we need to take media culture seriously, study its artifacts and effects, and cultivate media literacy as well as alternatives. Media culture *is* a form of pedagogy, and we must accordingly develop counterpedagogies. Such is the challenge of *Beavis and Butt-Head* in the age of media culture.

Notes

1. *Beavis and Butt-Head* was based on an animated short by Mike Judge in which the two characters play "frog baseball"; it was shown at the Sick and Twisted Animation festival and was taken up by MTV's animated series *Liquid Television*. The series *Beavis and Butt-Head* premiered in March 1993, but because there were only four episodes the show went on hiatus, returning May 17 after Judge and his team of creative assistants put together thirty-two new episodes (*San Francisco Chronicle*, June 29, 1993). The series tripled MTV's ratings, and MTV ordered 130 more episodes for 1994 (*New York Times*, October 17, 1993); it has continued into 1995, now telecast to a worldwide audience on MTV international.

2. An October 9, 1993, story in the *Dayton Daily News* reported that a five-year-old boy in Dayton, Ohio, ignited his bedclothes with a cigarette lighter after watching the pyromaniac antics of Beavis and Butt-Head, according to his mother. The boy's younger sister, two, died in the ensuing blaze. The mother said her five-year-old son had become "obsessed" with Beavis and Butt-Head and imitated their destructive behavior.

3. On October 23, 1993, a U.S. Senate hearing on TV violence focused media attention on the show, though Senator Ernest Hollings botched references to it, saying: "We've got this—what is it—Buffcoat and Beaver or Beaver and something else. . . . I haven't seen it; I don't watch it; it was at 7 o'clock—Buffcoat—and they put it on now at 10:30, I think" (*Hartford Courant*, October 26, 1993). Such ignorance of media culture is often found in some of its harshest critics.

4. Their family genealogy in a book on the series puts a question mark in the place of both of their fathers (Johnson and Marcil 1993). So far, their mothers have not been shown, though there are some references to them—usually as "sluts." It is also unclear exactly whose house they live in, or are shown watching TV in, and whether they do or do not live together. One episode suggests that they are in Butt-Head's house and that his mother is (as always) out with her boyfriend, but other episodes show two beds together in what appears to be their highly messy bedroom, and as of fall 1995 their parents have never been shown.

5. Psychoanalysts like to identity Beavis and Butt-Head with the Freudian id, with uncontrolled aggression and sexual impulses that they cannot understand or control (they were often shown masturbating, or talking about it, and Beavis uncontrollably "moons" attractive female singers while watching music videos).

There is also a barely repressed homoerotic element to their relationship, expressed in the endless "butt" jokes and references, their constant use of "sucks," and other verbal and visual behavior ("Hey Beavis, pull my finger!").

6. "Margot Emery was taking a midterm examination in a mass communications theory course for master's degree candidates at the University of Tennessee at Knoxville when she found, on the last page, a question about . . . Beavis and Butt-head. Novelist Gloria Naylor, Hartford Stage Company artistic director Mark Lamos and other distinguished panelists were discussing stereotypes in art, especially the depiction of Jews in *The Merchant of Venice*, when unexpectedly the talk swung around to . . . Beavis and Butt-head. Fred Rogers of 'Mister Rogers' Neighborhood' was being honored for his work by the Pittsburgh Presbytery and wound up discoursing upon . . . Beavis and Butt-head. Thomas Grasso, a prisoner whose main problem these days is deciding whether he'd rather have the state of Oklahoma execute him or the state of New York imprison him for a very long time, recently wrote a poem comparing Gov. Mario Cuomo and a New York corrections official to . . . Beavis and Butt-head.

"In fact, it has become so rare to read 10 pages of a magazine, to browse one section of a newspaper or to endure 30 minutes of television or radio talk without bumping into some knowing reference to the animated MTV dullards" (*Hartford Courant*, October 26, 1993).

7. Via MTV marathons of the series in summer and fall 1993, January and November 1994, and Steve Best's collection of 1995 episodes, I was able to see almost every episode of the series. I also did extensive Nexis database searches for mainstream media references to and debates over the series from its debut in 1993, and there were literally hundreds of references to the series. There also appeared a best-selling album of the heavy metal that Beavis and Butt-Head celebrate, a best-selling book, movie deals in the works, and many websites that I perused. Consequently, one can also easily speak of the "Beavis and Butt-Head" effects.

8. On this concept and a wealth of examples, see Kellner 1978.

9. After a Washington, D.C., psychologist said that Beavis and Butt-Head's humor sounded like the antics of normal youth, she frantically called back the reporter after seeing that night's episode, which led her to comment: "I totally condemn this program. I do not see any shred of normal adolescent behavior here. It's one of the most sadistic, pathological programs I've ever seen. I would not recommend it to anyone of any age" (*Washington Times*, October 17, 1993). The same story noted that an advocate of People for the Ethical Treatment of Animals stated: "Psychiatrists will tell you that almost every major serial killer has animal abuse in their background. Beavis and Butt-Head not only torture animals, but they are preoccupied with fire, and those are two of the three predictors of adult criminal behavior."

10. MTV's parent company, Viacom, was engaged at the time in a much-publicized battle to merge with Paramount, and the conglomerate obviously did not want bad publicity. Thus, MTV had to walk the line between preserving its most profitful and popular product and avoiding excessive media criticism. The result was compromises that softened the edge of *Beavis and Butt-Head* while attempting to preserve the show's popularity. As of fall 1995 the MTV strategy has

worked, with the show continuing to be highly popular with controversy diminishing.

11. For example: "Tiffany Martin, an area nursing student, loves her boyfriend. But lately he has been imitating that 'Beavis and Butt-head' heh-heh-heh laugh so much that it has worked her nerves to the point where she's flirted with breakup thoughts. 'People who watch that show, their intelligence is so lacking. I think that's what's getting to me about him,' she surmises. And sometimes that's all it takes. A certain facial expression. A bizarre habit. Even a tiny phrase uttered one too many times." *Buffalo News* (October 22, 1993).

12. The group White Zombie's album *La Sexorcisto: Devil Music, Vol. 1*, for example, "wasn't selling enough to make the nation's Top 100 charts, averaging only about 2,000 copies a week. But the group's video has been a fixture on 'Beavis and Butt-Head' since the summer, and the exposure—along with the bratty teens' words of praise—have propelled the album into the national Top 30. Estimated sales now: more than 500,000 copies. . . . Rick Krim, MTV's vice president of talent and artists relations, explains the response to the 'Beavis and Butt-Head' exposure. 'We had liked the "Thunder" video and supported it with play on the various specialty shows,' he says. 'That never really sparked significant album sales, the "Beavis and Butt-Head" exposure sure did. The sales response was pretty immediate. . . . Almost everything that gets played on the show gets some sort of sales bump from it" (*Billboard*, September 4, 1993).

13. Such an anti-Clinton move could backfire as younger voters might interpret the association to suggest that Clinton and Gore are "cool" and thus come to support them.

14. I am speaking of Lazarsfeld's "two step flow" model, which claimed that media culture had no direct effects, that its effects were modest and minimal, and mediated by "opinion leaders" who had the more important effects on consumer and political behavior, social attitudes, and the like (see Katz and Lazarsfeld 1955 and the critical discussion of its effects in Gitlin 1978).

References

Gitlin, Todd. (1978). "Media Sociology: The Dominant Paradigm." *Theory and Society* 6: 205–253.

Johnson, Sam, and Chris Marcil. (1993). *Beavis and Butt-Head: This Book Sucks.* New York: Pocket Books.

Katz, Elihu, and Paul F. Lazarsfeld. (1955). *Personal Influence.* New York: Free Press.

Kellner, Douglas. (1979). "TV, Ideology, and Emancipatory Popular Culture." *Socialist Review* 45 (May-June): 13–53.

_____. (1995). *Media Culture.* London and New York: Routledge.

5 Video Games and the Emergence of Interactive Media for Children

Eugene F. Provenzo Jr.

AS I FIRST WROTE THIS ESSAY the film *Mortal Kombat* was premiering across America. It joined several other recent movies based on video games, including *The Adventures of Super Mario Brothers*, *Double Dragon*, and *StreetFighter II*. The fact that a large number of recent movies are based on video games suggests an important shift in the nature and influence of media in our culture. Until recently, video games as media forms stood by themselves. They did not create other forms of media. If anything they were derivative or supplementary. Thus, the movie *RoboCop* spawned the video game of the same name. Now video games create the foundation for new films. This shift is an extremely important one. It suggests that video games have a greater narrative authority than was the case a few years ago—one that is primary rather than derivative compared to other competing media such as film.

This raises a number of important questions. To what extent do the narratives found in video games shape the content of the films that they are derived from? If the games are violent, does this mean in turn that the narratives that evolve out of them and are transferred to the cinematic world are equally violent? In looking at films such as those mentioned above, this would indeed seem to be the case.

I argue here that video games represent a new frontier for media in our culture. Video games are a complex and rapidly evolving form—one that most parents and adults pay relatively little attention to. Few realize how sophisticated the games have become in recent years, how they have evolved and adapted new technologies that make them increasingly realistic and interactive.

In fact, the evolution and increasing technical sophistication of these games have been quite remarkable. Beginning in the mid-1970s there was *Pong*, Atari's simple electronic table-tennis game. Pong was followed by *Space Invaders*, in which row upon row of alien spacecraft descend toward earth and are shot at by the player, whose mission is to stop the alien invaders from taking over the planet. *Space Invaders* was followed by *Missile Command*, in which the player destroys incoming nuclear missiles before they annihilate civilization. From *Space Invaders* and *Missile Command* video games evolved into *Pac-Man*, with its obsessive "munching" and consumption of every object in sight. More recently we have seen the introduction of home machines by companies such as Nintendo and Sega with games like *Super Mario Brothers*, *Double Dragon II*, and *Mega Man*.

Each successive generation of video games has become more technologically sophisticated, more realistic, and more violent. The newest wave of video games, based on CD-ROM technology (the same technology people use for music recordings and computer software), is in fact becoming more like film and television than what we traditionally expect of a video game. This is a major evolutionary step beyond the simple graphics of the classic *Space Invaders* arcade game so popular fifteen or twenty years ago, or the tiny animated cartoon figures of the Nintendo system that have dominated the video game market in recent years.

In addition, new virtual reality technologies already on the market make it possible to participate physically in what takes place on a television or computer screen. Input devices like Sega's *Activator!* put you even more literally into the game. With Sega's *Activator!* you lay a track of sensors in a circle around your feet; when you jump your character jumps, when you punch your character punches, when you kick your character kicks. Imagine using the *Activator!* with a program such as *Streets of Rage*, which is also manufactured by Sega. The game is marketed with suggestions on its packaging: "Jab 'em. Slam 'em. Kick or throw 'em. Whatever it takes. . . . All with your barehanded martial moves. . . . Amazingly realistic street fighting action."

Now consider this same technology being used to create pornography. It doesn't take too much imagination to come up with a program in which you touch and feel while watching a figure on the computer screen do the same. Choose the sex, the hair color, the costume (or lack of costume) of the computer-generated figure in front of you. There are already names in computer circles for this new use of the technology—dildonics and cybersex.

CD-ROM games such as *Virtual Valerie*, for example, allow you to enter a voluptuous young woman's apartment. Once inside you can look through her things, including her purse, her books, and even her personal copy of the game *Virtual Valerie*. The point of the game is to eventually interact with Valerie herself. In one scene Valerie appears on the computer screen wearing a see-through brassiere, panties, and hose while lying on a couch. With her legs spread apart, she asks the player to remove her brassiere, which she finds "a little snug." The object of the program is to eventually remove all of Valerie's clothes and get her into bed with you. If you don't answer certain questions correctly, Valerie won't take her clothes off. Give her the right answers and she's yours.

The CD-ROM program *Penthouse Interactive* extends the possibilities suggested by *Virtual Valerie* and its successor, *Virtual Valerie II*, by offering the user three Penthouse Pets from which to choose. Essentially, the program allows you to pose the Pets that you want. You're the photographer, the person in charge. One of the Pets, Dominique St. Croix, begins the program by smiling at you from the screen, licking her lips, and breathing heavily as she suggests, "Let's get interactive."

Examples such as these, combined with increasingly sophisticated virtual reality devices, suggest that we are at the point where we can begin to wire people into computer consoles and experience something close to Aldous Huxley's "Feelies": Interactive media becomes an alternative to reality.

This is the real significance of video game technology for contemporary childhood. It represents the first stages in the creation of a new type of television—an interactive medium as different from traditional television as television is from radio. The remaining years of this decade will see the emergence and definition of this new media form in much the same way that the late 1940s and early 1950s saw television emerge as a powerful social and cultural force.

At the present time, video game systems are found in more than one-third of all households in the United States. In 1992, the video game industry grossed $5.3 billion. This represents more money than all of the tickets sales at movie theaters for the same period. Some analysts estimate that by the end of the century interactive entertainment software could be a $35 billion industry. Much of this industry will involve the types of participatory/game-based technology described above. The largest single target audience will no doubt be children.

If the video game industry is going to provide the foundation for the development of interactive television, then concerned parents and educators have cause for considerable alarm. During the past decade, the video game industry has developed games whose social content has been overwhelmingly violent, sexist, and even racist.

In my book *Video Kids: Making Sense of Nintendo*, I scrutinized the social content of video games produced by the Nintendo Corporation.[1] Assuming that video games are social texts that can be "read" and deciphered, using content-analysis techniques I examined the forty-seven most popular video games in the United States manufactured for the Nintendo Entertainment System. Of the ten most popular games, which included titles such as *Bad Dudes*, *RoboCop*, *Double Dragon*, and *Double Dragon II*, all had violence and fighting as their main theme. To be sure, in some cases it was in the relatively benign form of games such as *Super Mario Bros. 2*, in which Mario and sidekick Luigi rescue the Princess. Other games were much more graphic. In *RoboCop*, for example, the instructions explain that:

> What's going on in old Detroit isn't pretty. An epidemic of crime, violence, and death has turned it into the most lethal spot on earth—especially if you are a cop. The government has thrown up its hands in despair and turned over the police department to O.C.P.—a private corporation that isn't as squeamish about individual rights as elected officials are.
>
> You're about to find yourself face to face with the malevolent Clarence Boddicker, who kills cops slowly, as a hobby; the savage and relentless robot ED-209; and ultimately Dick Jones, the mastermind who set all the wheels in motion.
>
> No flesh-and-blood-cop has a chance against these odds. Once upon a time you didn't either. But that was before you became ROBOCOP. [2]

RoboCop is played on the graphically limited 16-bit Nintendo Entertainment System. Imagine this game, or a similar game scenario, being used with live action clips from the original *RoboCop* movies. The technology required is, in fact, part of the new CD-ROM technology that is sweeping through the video game industry and that represents the first stages in the development of interactive television.

One of the most popular CD-ROM games currently available in arcades and in home-player systems is *Mortal Kombat*. As I mentioned, it has become so popular that a major motion picture based on the game has just been released. *Mortal Kombat* has a scenario in which the player enters the Shaolin Tournament for Martial Arts. The tournament was corrupted long ago by Shang Tsung, an evil demon with supernatural powers. The player takes on a series of opponents who are henchmen for Shang Tsung. The player can select different characters to fight. The player can also choose a persona, playing the game as different martial arts fighters with different skills. In the end, in order to win, the player must defeat Shang Tsung.

Mortal Kombat is different from earlier Nintendo games with violent content, such as *Streets of Rage* and *Street Fighter II*, in that its highly detailed graphics are based on human actors being filmed in a wide range of martial arts poses. The result is that the program is much more realistic than earlier martial arts video games since its graphic content is digitized film. Sound effects are combined with highly realistic pictures as limbs are torn off the bodies of the losers and blood spatters across the game screen. Admittedly, some versions of the game that have been released include less blood and gore, but extreme violence and physical harm is the main theme of the game.

Mortal Kombat is by no means the only digitized film currently on the market. Sega Corporation created a major controversy in Australia during the summer of 1993 when it introduced the video game *Night Trap*. Like *Mortal Kombat, Night Trap* is very violent and uses film clips with live actors to depict the action. But *Night Trap* is much more sophisticated than *Mortal Kombat*. In *Night Trap* the player or "viewer" becomes a major character in the story that unfolds. The scenario for the story explains how "five beautiful co-eds are being stalked in an eerie estate." Mysterious black-hooded figures are pursuing the co-eds and it's the player's job to rescue them.

The player is given orders by Commander Simms, who heads the Sega Control Attack Team (S.C.A.T.). He explains, "If you don't have the brains or guts for this mission, then give the control to someone who does." Cameras have been set up by an advanced team in eight of the rooms in the house. Your job is to trap the hooded figures before they get to the girls.

The use of Commander Simms to spur the players on is extremely disturbing. A respected Canadian children's media critic and educator, Sandra Campbell, expressed concern to the author over the Simms character, whom she saw as "militaristic and fascist." His behavior, according to her, encourages children to blindly and unthinkingly follow commands—in this case his orders lead to extremely violent consequences.

In *Night Trap*, it turns out that the black-hooded figures are some type of mysterious aliens who hold their captives still with a giant claw and drill into their necks with a giant motorized drill. When captives pass out after much screaming and carrying on, they are taken away to the basement of the house, where their blood is drained into wine bottles.

Night Trap is sexist, violent, and at times just plain silly. It would not be that important except that it is an interactive game and its animated characters are digitized movie actors rather than cartoon figures. As mentioned earlier, there has been considerable debate about *Night Trap* in Australia. After numerous complaints, followed by hearings before the Australian Senate's Select Committee on Community Standards and Electronic Technology, the game was withdrawn from the Australian market.

Kevin Bermeister, managing director of Sega-Ozisoft (the Australian distributor for Sega), in a brief to the Select Committee clearly recognized the implications of his company's new product, explaining:

> The rapid growth in technology over the past five years has meant a significant improvement in the depiction of violence in video games to the point where the latest product releases utilize live actors to play roles within a video game environment. These technologies will continue to improve bringing with them an even greater ability for publishers and developers of video games to release products which bring the fantasy experience of a video game much closer to reality. [3]

According to Bermeister: "Technologies such as CD Rom/Multimedia, Virtual Reality and Holograms will spread quickly into homes around the western world during the balance of this decade and will take many people by surprise as to the nature of these systems and the power of the new entertainment forms which they provide."

Unlike movies, videos, TV, pay-TV, or any form of passive entertainment, this form is *interactive*, requiring the user to participate in the actions and activities of the software, thereby making the experience far more realistic and intense. In the case of current technology such as interactive video games (e.g., Sega/Nintendo games consoles), it is quite apparent when watching players that their concentration and involvement in the product (participation levels) are far greater than those for other passive entertainment forms.[4]

In a recent interview for the British television program *World in Action*, Tom Kalinske, president of Sega of America, explained his company's programs: "All we are really doing is interpreting what one sees in the world today and making some game play out of it."[5] According to Kalinske, the games should be encouraged and embraced by educators and the general public since they expand the fantasy experience of the child. "I would think that teachers would think that it's a positive that a child can expand his fantasy, expand his horizons and enter into a fantasy world where he's thinking about all sorts of things he's never seen before."[6] For a child playing Sega's *Night Trap*, this fantasy world would include torturing women with machines and murdering them so that their blood can be sucked out and decanted into wine bottles.

Tom Kalinske is a businessman. He is proud of the fact that *Sonic the Hedgehog II*, his recent hit video game, had over $28 million in sales on its first day of release and that its gross thus far has been larger than that of any motion picture movie in history.[7] He also believes that companies like Sega "can't police every aspect of human behavior." Yet despite this statement, Sega has recently announced that it will impose a voluntary rating system on its games. Similar to the codes developed by the movie industry during the 1960s, the system includes the categories GA (for general audience), MA-13 (for mature audiences thirteen years and older), and MA-17 (for audiences over seventeen years of age).

Why is Sega imposing a rating system on itself? Is Kalinske contradicting himself? Some argue that it's a clever marketing strategy that allows the company to bring attention to their most violent products—thus making them stand out in the marketplace for teenagers and adults particularly interested in such products. I believe that Sega's adoption of a rating system demonstrates a realization that its video games are becoming more and more like film and television and that very soon it will be difficult to differentiate between the two. By self-imposing a rating system, Sega heads off a problem that it would eventually have to address. Sega has recently announced a partnership with Time Warner Entertainment and Tele-Communications Inc. to start delivering video games to homes in the United States next year via cable. The service will cost between $10 and $20 per month and actually represents the beginning of a new interactive television industry—delivered by cable—that, if typical of most video games currently available, will probably be extremely violent.

I suspect that Tom Kalinske is a well-meaning man. Watching him in television interviews, he appears to be pleasant enough and certainly enthusiastic about his company's products and about entertaining children. He also reminds me of Steve Martin's character in the film *Grand Canyon*, who makes violent B-grade action films. In the film, Martin's character is shot by an armed robber. Traumatized by the violence committed against him, Martin's character declares, "I can't make another piece of art that glorifies violence and bloodshed and brutality. . . . No more exploding bodies, exploding buildings, exploding anything. I'm going to make the world a better place."[8] When asked several months later by a friend how his "new direction" is working out, Martin replies, "Fuck that. That's over. I must have been delirious for a few weeks there."[9] Having said this, Martin then uses the same defense Kalinske does for Sega's games: "My movies reflect what's going on; they don't make what's going on."[10]

The fact is we don't really know whether or not media such as video games—particularly in their emerging format as interactive and participatory television—"make what's going on." The research simply doesn't exist to tell us whether or not the games—particularly in their increasingly realistic and interactive modes—have a long-term effect on children.

Yet one cannot help but be both concerned and questioning. In addition to the violence of video games, media violence in television, film, and popular music is already a major part of the experience of American childhood. In the case of television, for example, by the end of elementary school the average child will have viewed 5,000 murders.[11]

Deborah Prothrow-Stith maintains that media sources teach our children that "violence is funny, is entertaining, is successful, is the hero's first choice, is painless, is guiltless, is rewarded. . . . If you watch little children watch their first cartoon, they literally learn when to laugh. It's not a natural response to violence to laugh. But they learn, because the other children around them laugh. Because there's a laugh track, because there's music that tells them when to laugh."[12]

The connection between media violence and violence in our culture and among our youth population is consistently denied by members of the film and television industry as being a problem. For example, Barbara Hall, a TV writer and producer, argues that "theories linking violence to television watching are very specious. They don't prove anything."[13]

Despite arguments such as those by Hall and others to the contrary, there is a significant research literature that connects violence to media exposure. To cite several representative examples: L. A. Joy et al. investigated the impact of introducing television for the first time to an isolated Canadian community. The community, which was called "Notel" by the researchers, had never had television before because of signal problems. Using a double-blind research design, forty-five first- and second-graders were observed during a two-year period in order to see if aggressive behavior such as hitting, biting, and shoving increased. In the two control groups aggressive behavior did not increase significantly. In Notel, during the same two-year period, such behavior increased by 160 percent.[14]

L. R. Huesmann, in a twenty-two-year study of 875 men in a semirural setting, studied whether or not the viewing of violent television predicted the seriousness of criminal acts committed by the time the subjects were thirty years old. After controlling for the subjects' baseline aggressiveness, socioeconomic status, and intelligence, Huesmann found that violent television viewing was a significant predictor for criminal behavior.[15]

In a June 1992 article in the *Journal of the American Medical Association,* Dr. Brandon Centrewall of the University of Washington Department of Epidemiology and Psychiatry looked at violence in the United States from an epidemiological point of view.[16] Centrewall compared homicide rates in the United States and Canada, where television was introduced in the mid-1940s, with the Republic of South Africa, where television was introduced thirty years later. Canada, which had not gone through political and social unrest during the 1960s, provided a control model for the United States. In order to rule out the effect of racial con-flict in South Africa, only the white homicide rate was considered by Centrewall.

Centrewall found that the homicide rate in both Canada and the United States increased by almost 100 percent between 1945 and 1970. Television ownership increased at almost the same percentage as the homicide rate for the same period. In South Africa, the white homicide rate gradually declined between 1945 and 1970. When television was in-troduced in 1975, the white homicide rate exploded, increasing 130 per-cent by 1983. Centrewall concludes from his research that in the United States and Canada "the introduction of television in the 1950s caused a subsequent doubling of the homicide rate, i.e., long-term childhood ex-posure to television is a causal factor behind approximately one half of the homicides committed in the United States, or approximately 10,000 homicides annually."[17] Centrewall goes on to conclude that despite other factors such as poverty, crime, alcohol, drug abuse, and stress, the epidemiological evidence suggests that "if hypothetically television technology had never been developed, there would be 10,000 fewer homicides each year in the United States, 70,000 fewer rapes and 700,000 fewer injurious assaults."[18]

How does television violence relate to the new media forms that are evolving out of the fusion of video games and television? In *Video Kids: Making Sense of Nintendo*, I argue that the impact of video games on children needs to be much better understood than it is at this time. Early research on arcade games, for example, suggests that children probably do not become more violent or aggressive by playing a game such as *Space Invaders* or *Pac-Man*. *Space Invaders* and *Pac-Man*, however, are a very different experience for players than *Double Dragon II* and *Streets of Rage*, both in widespread use on the Nintendo and Sega systems, or the new games that are coming into use as CD-ROM and online technology becomes more widespread and as interactive television becomes a real-ity. In the new games, the potential to participate in violence is much greater. The video game model turns television—which up until this time has been a largely passive and receptive experience—into an inter-active and participatory experience.

This fact is particularly disturbing if programming for video games and television remains as violent as it has been up until now. Video games are highly structured and programmed universes. Either you play the game according to a fairly rigid set of rules or you lose. Thus, if the game is about kicking, punching, and killing your opponent, then in order to win you must do exactly that. In the relatively benign context of a Pac-Man munching dots, violence probably is not a serious problem.

But when the reality of the game escalates through the use of powerful movie-based formats and virtual reality devices that put the player in the middle of the action, then there is serious cause for concern.

What happens when a child can step inside the violence of television, where that child watches RoboCop blow away Detroit, controlling the movements of RoboCop by moving hands and feet? What happens when children can literally participate in television? No one knows, but for the welfare and betterment of our children we had better find out.

We are now at the threshold of a new generation of interactive television and video games. Although this technology has wonderful potential, I am also convinced that if we continue to use this technology without realizing and addressing the full ramifications and significance of the social content of video games then we will be doing a serious disservice to both ourselves and to our children.

I would like to suggest that Tom Kalinske at Sega of America and his company consider alternatives to much of the programming that they are currently producing. The video game medium has remarkable potential for entertainment and enlightenment. Companies such as Sega need to understand what it is their products may or may not be doing to our children and to our culture. They may also find that providing more constructive programming is highly profitable.

Sega understands the new medium of interactive television and the brave new world we are entering. But we, as parents and educators, cannot just leave it up to the multinational corporations like Sega and Nintendo to be concerned about this new medium. The emerging world of interactive television and video games is, in the end, ultimately much more than just "child's play"!

Notes

1. Eugene F. Provenzo Jr., *Video Kids: Making Sense of Nintendo* (Cambridge: Harvard University Press, 1991).

2. *RoboCop: Instruction Manual* (San Jose, California: Data East, 1988).

3. Brief from Kevin Bermeister (Sega-Ozisoft) to the Chairperson, Australian Senate Select Committee on Community Standards and Electronic Technology, May 14, 1993.

4. Ibid.

5. Tom Kalinske, as quoted on the program "Welcome to the Danger Zone," *The World in Action*, Granada Television, first broadcast in March 1993.

6. Ibid.

7. Ibid.

8. Quoted from Michael Krasny, "Honey, I Warped the Kids," *Mother Jones*, July/August 1993, p. 17.

9. Ibid.

10. Ibid.

11. Barry, David, "Screen Violence: It's Killing Us," *Harvard Magazine*, November–December 1993, p. 40.

12. Ibid., p. 41.

13. Ibid., p. 40.

14. L. A. Joy, M. M. Kimball, and M. L. Zabrack, "Television and Children's Aggressive Behavior," in T. M. Williams, ed., *The Impact of Television: A Natural Experiment in Three Communities* (Orlando, Florida: Academic Press, 1986), pp. 303–360.

15. L. R. Huesmann, "Psychological Processes Promoting the Relation Between Exposure to Media Violence and Aggressive Behavior by the Viewer," *Journal of Social Issues* 42(3) (1986), pp. 125–129.

16. Brandon S. Centrewall, "Television and Violence: The Scale and Problem and Where to Go From Here," *Journal of the American Medical Association* 267(22) (June 10, 1992), pp. 3059–3063.

17. Ibid., p. 3061.

18. Ibid.

6 Mighty Morphin Power Rangers: *The Aesthetics of Phallo-Militaristic Justice*

Peter McLaren and Janet Morris

ONE OF THIS CENTURY'S best-kept secrets is the way in which technology has transformed violence into a spectacle of stunning beauty. Violence, when it's stylized, when it's choreographed and hyper-accelerated or played in slow motion, when it is set to the strains of a poignant Beethoven sonata, the minimalist pulses of a Philip Glass creation, or the tremulous strains and corrosive screams of a Diamanda Galas vocal, can be thrillingly sublime and breathtakingly beautiful. Since the advent of cinema and television we've been blessed with endless variation: severed heads floating through the air in all the splendor only freeze-frame decapitation can convey; severed arms gliding down elevator shafts while still pulsing huge arcs of blood; hideously dislocated jaws and cheekbones shattering beyond recognition; noses crumpling like beer cans; eyes gouged by lightning-swift fingers trained by Shaolin priests; skin ceremoniously flayed, revealing, as the victim screams, shiny bone laced with blood vessels; intestines greedily gobbled up by lip-smacking zombies who look like your Uncle Roger after a night out on the town; mutants giving birth to talking heads; and aliens thrusting about chest cavities like restless adolescents trapped in a small town, finally shooting through jagged rib cages, snarling giddily past their first few gulps of oxygen. Can't you just imagine a video of, say, Courtney Love in her kinderwhore clothes singing "Doll Parts" to exploding torsos and exposed spinal columns? That's real Americana. We delight in all of it, in the sheer art of simulating violence.

I (Peter McLaren) remember my delight at the soft-core violence of my youth, a violence born of my addiction to American TV shows: Roy

Rogers cracking the bad guy in the jaw; Gene Autry snapping out a right to the cheek of the guy in the black hat; and the same all over again with minor variations in the fight scenes of the Cisco Kid, Bat Masterson, Davy Crockett, Wyatt Earp, Marshall Dillon, the Rifleman, the Lone Ranger, Zorro, Sky King. Back then, it was considered cheating to use your feet, and you never hit a man who was down. Bruce Lee and Jackie Chan changed all of that—and so did Sam Peckinpah and even Oliver Stone, for that matter—and eventually screen villains became so loathsome that you could rationalize and perhaps even justify almost any torturous method to eliminate them and still be considered cool.

Our point is not to trace the history of the way violence has been choreographed but rather to point out the fact that violence has been naturalized and aestheticized in film (as, for instance, in the anticipated fight scenes of adventure features) to such an extent that it now functions much the same way as nature. Youths are prepared along the way to see violence as something that is not only inevitable but necessary in order to bring the world back to a state of happy equilibrium. Our observations suggest that choreographed techno-violence is now part of the perpetual pedagogy of TV shows and subsequently participates informally in the act of child rearing by the state. Such video violence needs to be seen in terms of the formation of what we call a "kinship imaginary" that, through the consolidation of the family unit–school culture–entertainment industry triad, is able to scaffold those discourses necessary for the reproduction of an ideological community compatible with that of the nation-state. Of course, a semiautonomy necessarily exists among all three elements of the triad—what we would also refer to as bourgeois social formations—and consequently each one has to be seen in terms of its combinatory function as ideological apparatuses that complement the linguistic and ethnic community we identify as "American." The family unit, the culture of the school, and the entertainment industry are all formally egalitarian apparatuses that weave together what might be considered the hegemonic ideologies of state citizenship. We wish in this chapter merely to consider the role of media violence in the *Mighty Morphin Power Rangers* (*MMPR*)as an articulatory practice that helps to impose violence as the uniform cultural language within a multicultural society through its patriarchal idealization as a means of subduing the evil "Other." Violence is constructed as a means of instituting social norms of community that ultimately support the status quo. In the sense articulated by Walter Benjamin in "The Work of Art in the Age of Mechanical Reproduction," *MMPR* elevates violence to a new level of aesthetic pleasure. In effect, it has become liberated from any meaning other than its own surface effect; it becomes, in other words, its own justification.

At a time in which the serial killer in contemporary American culture "is represented as the last, albeit psychotic, frontiersperson . . . the last person who can act" (Gange and Johnstone, 1993, 60), is it any wonder that *MMPR* is currently so popular in American kinderculture? *MMPR*—whose recently spawned stepchildren include V.R. Troopers, SuperHuman Samurai Syber-Squad, and Tattooed Teenage Alien Fighters from Beverly Hills—appears to represent the next, graduated step up from *Teenage Mutant Ninja Turtles* (*TMNT*) for the adolescent action-adventure audience. However, as younger children have come to consider *MMPR* as the "coolest" series, the demographic for this show has widened to take in preschool as well as adolescent audiences (Doyle, 1994). Today, *MMPR* is the most highly rated children's television program (Bellafante, 1993). It currently captures 99 percent of the 2- to 11-year-old audience, as do the sales of matching toys (Warrick, 1994). It ranks number one among all children's programs in the United States. In the United Kingdom it holds five out of the top ten children's program slots; in Italy it holds a 60–70 percent share of young viewers; in France, its debut episode attracted a 75 percent share of the children's audience, and it holds ten of the top eleven best-selling children's home videos in the United States, with sales exceeding 8 million units. Executive producer Shuki Levy hopes that the late-afternoon time slot will broaden the core audience of *MMPR* to include young teens and the rest of their families (Saban Press Book, 4).

Recently the *Los Angeles Times* ran a story on Mafia involvement in high-level counterfeiting that helps to produce and distribute Mighty Morphin look-alikes. Burbank-based Saban Entertainment is using private investigators, armed marshals, and undercover operatives to track down the counterfeiters and to, in the words of Angie Small, vice president of legal affairs, "protect the good name and the goodwill" of the Power Rangers. About 10 million units of counterfeit material have already been seized, and Saban Entertainment has a toll-free number for boys and girls if they suspect an impostor: 800-MORPHER. Saban Entertainment is currently putting together some major "sting" operations against the mob in cooperation with the FBI. In a promotional, accelerated society of the spectacle, it is not surprising that organized crime is playing a key role in the tabooed behavior we can now identify as Morphin trafficking. It has occurred to us that if the same level of corporate energy spent on reducing Morphin trafficking was spent on the economic infrastructure of U.S. inner cities, the drug problem would be greatly lessened.

We readily acknowledge that the surrealistic forms of violence we depicted to introduce this chapter cannot be applied to *MMPR*. We do suggest, however, that such a show prepares youth to abstract the consequences of real violence from the spectacle of video violence itself. As such the show prepares the groundwork for transforming violence into aestheticized commodity forms that are perhaps more associated with "upmarket" cultural formations—the art films and "quality" television dramas. The frequent and consistent reports on correlations between the high levels of violence portrayed on *MMPR* and violent behavior in children may lead automatically to the conclusion that *MMPR* is most popular (and problematic) simply because of frequent violent sequences. The difference between cartoon portrayals of violence as portrayed on *TMNT*, however, and real-life character portrayals of violence portrayed on *MMPR* seems to be at issue. Much of the martial arts fighting in *MMPR* takes place on grassy fields, making school yards, backyards, and parks an authentic "re-creation" environment. A study from California State University found that "the children who had watched Power Rangers imitated the martial arts sequences down to specific kicks, somersaults, and arm movements—even echoing the sounds the characters made during the show's fight scenes" (Power Rangers Spark Violence, 1994).

Various studies around the world concluded that *MMPR* had aggressive affects on children in more than seventy-two countries (Cody, 1994). Although representatives of Saban Entertainment (the licensed producer of *MMPR*), may argue that "kids recognize the looniness of this [program], the outrageousness" (Cody, 1994), this fact in no way suggests that the show cannot influence real violence in real settings. This is true even when the show features a short concluding section that attempts to convince viewers that the violence is really "made-up" entertainment where nobody gets injured. Most young viewers already know the show is fiction and that the violence is manufactured; in fact, they can point to the phoniness of the show in ways more sophisticated than many adults. That the show is recognized as unrealistic does not really make an impact on how viewers affectively invest in such a program. As Larry Grossberg (1992) and other media scholars have pointed out, television programs can help to produce specific economies of affect-mattering maps that need to be understood conjuncturally, in relation to the social and cultural settings where the viewers watch the show, the individual subjectivities of the viewers and the ways in which their subjective formations mediate, engage, or resist the show's many competing discourses (and this may involve the race, class, sexual orientation, and other characteristics of the viewers), and the specific articulations that are made among the structures of violence in the show and family violence, schoolyard violence, violence in organized sports, and so on. In others words, to what extent do the values and representations of *MMPR* confirm preexisting categories in the lives of the viewers? What are the contiguities between family values and those represented in the TV show? There may be no causal relationship between youth behaviors and viewing *MMPR*, but the show, in our mind, certainly is a major contributing determinant to reproducing the larger discourse of violence as a preferred means of solving problems in everyday life. Imitating violence often leads to an identification with violence, to incorporating violence, to unconsciously locating violence as a central activity around which subjectivity pivots. Recently, *MMPR* was removed from broadcast schedules in both Scandinavia and Canada. The show was canceled in Scandinavia after a brutal school yard slaying of a five-year-old girl by three boy playmates. However, the show was reinstated after a few days because a causal relationship between the show and that tragedy could not be proven. In fact, it was reported that none of the boys had ever seen the show, although the boys did mention *Teenage Mutant Ninja Turtles* to police investigators (Warrick, 1994). In November 1994, the Canadian Broadcast Standards Council (a self-regulatory trade association) determined that fighting constituted between 25 percent and 35 percent of each *MMPR* episode (Doyle, 1994). This evaluation led to the removal of *MMPR* from one network and from YTV (the cable channel for youth); as of this writing, the show had not been reinstated.[1]

There is little doubt that the frequent portrayals of violent confrontation are an important part of the show's appeal. (We refer to some changes in the characters of the show and some thematic adjustments. Three of the original actors have been replaced. Recent changes seem to be motivated by a desire to cover various racial representations, thereby avoiding charges of racism. Most of the analysis of this show was undertaken when the show had its original cast.) The live-action scenes of superheroes wearing metallic spandex suits and what look like spray-painted riot-gear helmets that have been totemized into fearsome creatures are actually purchased from a Japanese show called *Zyu Rangers*. These live-action scenes (called *sentai*) are very staged and add to the cartoon-like atmosphere of the show. However, it is suggested here that the show's portrayals of females and nonwhite ethnic groups in Ranger roles have both broadened the demographic and provided an "equity-conscious" image for the show. This allows *MMPR*'s producer to sidestep more direct criticism while legitimating and valorizing violence under the guise of clean-cut righteousness.

In addressing the issue of violence in *MMPR*, the *Globe and Mail*, a Canadian national newspaper, exhibits this kind of confusion, stating,

> *Power Rangers* doesn't appear to be guilty of sexual stereotyping. *Though its themes of action, adventure and destruction might suggest a limited appeal to female viewers, there are two girls among the six Power Rangers. The role-*

model qualities don't stop there. A racially mixed group, the Rangers also attend school, protect young kids and do their homework, when not protecting the world from evil and fighting ugly monsters with virtuoso martial arts skills (Doyle, 1994, emphasis added).

This statement exhibits the common logical error that many people tend to make: Equality is based on the extent to which females and people of color have the opportunity to adopt the dominant Euro-American ideology. Show after show demonstrates that the equity image is not played out through representations of different ideological perspectives; rather, it is clear that cultural and gender differences are articulated into a racist, patriarchal, militarist ideology—through the production of a kinship imaginary that is both reflective and constitutive of white-supremacist, patriarchal, capitalist social relations. White supremacy is not a hegemonic bloc reserved only for people with white skin.

Hegemonic reproduction of dominant gender and racial relations effectively parrots real life hegemonic transactions in that they tend to be conveyed through both deep structure and nuanced relations rather than through concrete, linear narratives. The Power Rangers themselves were originally made up of six teenagers: two females (one Asian, one white) and four males (three white, one African American). Currently there are three white males, one African American female, one white female, and one Korean/Anglo male. Although the uniformity (and gender and race neutrality) of their buttocks-hugging spandex fighting suits lends a sense of power equity within the group that overcomes their different body types, they are color-coded to reveal traditionally racialized and genderized identity markers: pink for the Caucasian female; yellow for the Asian female (now African American); black for the African American male (now Korean/Anglo); and red, white, and blue for the white males. The color-coding obviously signifies a hierarchy based on white-supremacist patriotism: Only the white males are worthy of bearing the national colors— "red, white, and blue"—and so are the only "real" or authentic Americans. To be an American in *MMPR* does not really mean portraying a diversity of cultural, social, or political viewpoints, as it is predicated on emptying oneself of difference and eliminating specificity, a process that enables one to be overcoded by the ideological and affective appeal of red, white, and blue. Those who are worthy to "wear" such colors are those that are the most trusted to be free from the possible contaminating influence of ethnic difference: the white male Rangers. The multicultural diversity that is championed by the show's producer actually works against diversity, subtending rather than unsettling dominant systems of meaning.

In the Power Rangers press kit distributed by Saban Entertainment, Adam, the new Black Ranger, is described as "half-Korean and half-American" and as practicing "Zen-like meditation" (the meditation described as Zen-*like* because it's probably hard to get the authentic thing in his hometown of Garland, Texas, where the actor was born) and Shaolin kung fu (the actor reportedly holds an authentic purple sash in this martial art). When I (Peter McLaren) asked a promotion representative during a telephone conversation if "half-Korean and half-American" meant Adam was Korean and possibly African she said, "No—he's American." Asked if Adam could be Korean and perhaps Latino, I was given the same response. Apparently if you are Korean you are not American and if you are half-American that excludes you from being either African or Latino. American means one thing: being white.

The main plot of each half-hour program revolves around the traditional good-versus-evil battles, with directives communicated to the Power Rangers through their creator-leader, the wizard Zordon, an elderly Caucasian male. Zordon has been permanently trapped by Rita Repulsa—a female character who embodies the forces of evil—in a phalliclike shaft of green light at his command center located in another dimension, causing the wizard to appear at times as a postmodern, soap opera–like rendition of his historical counterpart from Oz. Rita, who has escaped from an intergalactic prison with henchcreatures Baboo, Squatt, Goldar, and Finster, is coordinating a takeover of Earth. Zordon responds to Rita's threat with a call to Alpha 5, the robot running his Earth command center, by asking for "five of the wildest, most willful humans in the area"—who, not surprisingly, turn out to be teenagers. The Power Rangers themselves are superhuman, extraterrestrial beings capable of "morphing" into mechanical dinosaurs or "Dinozords" (the Rangers' original vehicles, these were later upgraded to "Thunderzords"). In their original incarnation (before the latest round of character changes), only four of the six Rangers—all white—derived their strength from the power (and no doubt the recent preteen popularity) of the dinosaur; the original Trini and Zack (respectively, the Asian female and African American male Rangers who have been replaced by Aisha, an African American female, and Adam, the Korean/Anglo male) received their power from the Saber-toothed Tiger (with Power Dagger weapon and Griffin Thunderzord vehicle) and the Mastodon (with Power Axe and Lion Thunderzord). Whereas the other female—Kimberly, the Pink Ranger—derived her strength from the more graceful flying dinosaur, the Pterodactyl (with Power Bow and Firebird Thunderzord), Jason (now Rocky) and Billy—respectively, the Red and Blue Rangers—received their strength from the two most powerful dinosaurs: the Tyrannosaurus Rex (with Power Sword and Red Dragon Thunderzord) and the Triceratops (with Power Lance and Unicorn Thunderzord).

This strategy of "morphing" into prehistoric creatures presented a convenient way of dealing with battle death scenarios in a vicarious, unreal manner while keeping with the dominant, militarist ideology of deference to authority, sacrifice, and martyrdom. This is especially true when these towering machines known as the Thunderzords combine into the Megazord—a samurai-like mechanical transformer that holds the Rangers in the command center (the fact that the females are seated behind the males can be read as a sign that they belong at the back of the bus). Rita creates the Green Ranger in order to serve her, but the Rangers are able to break Rita's spell. Tommy (the Green Ranger) gives up his powers to Jason rather than lose them to Rita after the other Rangers are abducted and their Power Coins taken for ransom. However, Tommy seeks help from Zordon and is able to challenge Rita, free the Rangers, and return the Power Coins to the Rangers. Rita Repulsa's boss, Lord Zedd, returns Rita to her space dumpster and challenges the Rangers himself. The Rangers are given new powers by Zordon as well as new vehicles. The new Thunderzords are modeled after the Red Dragon, Griffin, Unicorn, Firebird, Tiger, and Lion—real and mythological creatures—although their source of strength still comes from the dinosaurs.

Determining leadership among the Rangers is communicated in the show in much the same way that it is on the playground. Until the leadership recently fell into the hands of the White Ranger, the leadership of the Red Ranger was communicated mainly through deference of decisionmaking by others to him and his physical stature, most notably, his always bare and oversized biceps. However, in a recent change, which can only be interpreted as a reenactment of the resurrection of Jesus Christ, the Green Ranger was "born again" as the White Ranger and was granted extraordinary powers (from the white tiger) that can never be drained. According to Zordon, it was the Green Ranger's "devotion" and "sacrifice" on the battlefield (which completely drained his powers—or killed him) that earned him immortality, although some industry insiders suggest that the appearance of the White Ranger is related to the fact that Saban Entertainment had run out of Green Ranger *sentai*. This was confirmed informally by one of our (Peter McLaren's) students who during an airplane flight reportedly met somebody who worked on the show. This individual admitted that although *MMPR* was the most successful program he was likely to ever be associated with, it was, in everybody's mind who worked on it, "a piece of shit."

That the acting in the show at its best approaches rigor mortis really makes no difference to its viewers. The symbolic or archetypal aura surrounding the characters is what invests the show with such symbolic potency. When the White Ranger (whose weapon is the enchanted white saber known as Saba and whose vehicle is the White Tigerzord) first enters the picture, he is seen descending from the heavens through a bright-white light. Clearly, children can transfer the positive messages received from early religious education (which in Christianity tends to focus on the wonder of Jesus and his love for children) to militarism: sacrifice results in the ultimate reward for becoming God's warrior—"angeldom." At this point the show breaks with the dominant ideology as the Red Ranger atypically accepts his demotion with enthusiasm and grace. Falling back into routine, the Red, White, and Blue Rangers issue directives and man the controls in the Mega Tigerzord battleship while the Pink, Yellow, and Black Rangers take on subordinate positions.

The female Rangers are the "worriers" of the group, constantly needing reassurance from the males and concerned that another Ranger might need assistance. They routinely look for approval of their actions from the male Rangers. During one scene Trini is standing between Jason and Billy when they learn that the world is in mortal danger. Paralyzed by anxiety, she grabs her partners' shirts, bends her knees, and screams: "What should we do?" Male Rangers never ask female Rangers for advice about strategic action in fighting evil but occasionally consult them about issues that have to do with "love interest" or male-female relationships, such as when the Black Ranger asks a female Ranger's advice on how to win the heart of Angelica. Kimberly is described in Saban's promotion package as somebody who "loves mirrors, shopping malls, and gymnastics" and who "is always the most popular girl and loves the attention she receives." Included in the promotional package is what can be described as the most absurd and illogical rationalization for a consumer ethics that could be mustered by a media corporation: "Kimberly does exhibit one 'spoilt' trait, she loves to shop! But for her it isn't about what she buys, it is about going somewhere and having fun looking at things. In others words, she is not spoilt; it's just her way of being nice to herself!" Aisha, the new Yellow Ranger, is described as a party-loving girl who indulges in "cool hip-hop dancing" and as "strongly opinionated."

In contrast, the male characters are described as reflecting characteristics that are much more admirable and virtuous: Adam, the new Black Ranger, is "focused and disciplined, possessing great inner strength"; Rocky, the new Red Ranger, is "open and giving"; Tommy, formerly the Green Ranger and now the White Ranger leader, exhibits "courage, strength, and honor"; Billy, the Blue Ranger, is described as "ultra-intelligent" and "a sweet, good-hearted super-genius."

These appear to be the gender stereotypes that feminists have been struggling against in adult movies for decades. The male Rangers rarely, if ever, doubt their actions or seek approval from the female Rangers. The male Rangers are composed of "true grit": irreducible essences untainted by doubt or moral uncertainty—commodity fetishes in the service of further disciplining everyday life for young viewers in the sense of rationalizing, valorizing, legitimating, and naturalizing capitalist social relations centered around the will to power. The image of *MMPR* is constructed out of socially and historically specific social relations and assists youthful viewers in negotiating their lifeworlds, usually through violence as a form of engineered necessity.

Each Power Ranger, regardless of gender or ethnicity, interprets and reacts to Zordon's instructions with an unquestioning acceptance of presumably life-threatening missions. It's the perfect image of melting-pot consensus leading to coordinated action on behalf of social justice and the "American way of life." The extraterrestrial nature of Zordon, who is often revealed as a computer-generated image imposed on the sky above, conveys a pure, righteous, godlike status. By comparison, Lord Zedd, also an extraterrestrial, is a "towering, well-muscled creature with blood-red exterior and razor-sharp body armor" (Saban Press Book, 1994, 3) and is more evil than Rita Repulsa (and replaces Rita after her retreat to her space dumpster) and appears as a devil incarnate, complete with hellfire surrounding him. In keeping with basic militarist ideology, the enemy must be dehumanized in order for murder to appear legitimate and righteous. Lord Zedd's army of "putties," which engaged in martial arts battles with the Rangers, are real-life figures like the Rangers but cannot be distinguished from one another, as they dress identically and wear helmets. The only evil force to have a face and personality is Lord Zedd disciple Rita Repulsa, a middle-aged Asian woman dressed in Kabuki-style garb. However, Rita is not so much "evil" as she is childish, exhibiting foolish, "spoiled-brat" behavior. It is interesting to note that this female villain is not intimidating but is "repulsive," which seems to play on the kind of school-yard harassment to which unpopular girls are subjected. Such girls have "cooties" and are "stinky" but never possess power that is potentially threatening. By contrast, the female Rangers, who embody the "popular" female, are physically attractive, obedient, and masters of martial arts and appear to possess upper-middle-class backgrounds. Being popular and equal to the boys means relinquishing feminine characteristics and embracing militarism. Although these girls are superhuman, extraterrestrial beings, they are subject to the stereotypical female plagues such as fainting at the sight of a boyfriend and jealous rivalry between each other. Yet the male Rangers are not subject to such in-fighting—just a kind of bonzo team camaraderie and American Gladiator, jock-sniffing solidarity.

Mothers may look on with pride as their perky little daughters don Power Rangers outfits, conjure up glandular attitudes, and "kick male butt," but they might not realize that it is the daily economy of lowbrow, chest-beating masculinity that is being celebrated instead of a more critically minded feminine ethics that would make Carol Gilligan proud. To be a successful female Power Ranger one must relinquish the feminist standpoints of critique and transformation. This bogus representation of gender equality is also noted in analyses of action-based films such as the testosterone-fueled *Rambo* series (see Kellner, 1994). Similarly, some minorities may be satisfied that they are finally represented as equals to their Caucasian counterparts simply because of *appearances,* not realizing that the show obscures subject positions that are context-dependent on racialized experiences and that deny oppositional or counterhegemonic perspectives. The characters in *MMPR* rely on pregiven, stereotypical categories of race, ethnicity, class, and sexual orientation and prefabricated emotions and desires—all of which reflect a total engineering of desire through the power of image-value.

What is missing, however, is not simply a proliferation of cultural differences, such as the inclusion of subjects who are self-divided and lacking coherence as a unified subject of history (although this, admittedly, would be welcomed); absent are those differences that could make a real difference. Such differences might speak from a standard epistemology of the oppressed that would be willing to critically engage and challenge the world of patriarchal capitalist social relations and provide alternative and oppositional perspectives, not just on the sexism or racism of *MMPR* but in relation to the show's unquestioning articulations of neoimperialist ideology that sees the forces of good in the guise of a federation of freedom-fighters with white male leadership supposedly leading a NATO-like battalion of warriors against universal evil.

Alarmingly absent also is any substantial evidence that a subject does not have to relinquish critical self-reflexivity and political agency in the service of fighting evil. *MMPR* prepares viewers for the kind of one-dimensional morality that films such as *Love and a .45, Natural Born Killers,* and *Pulp Fiction* try to parody, the generalized commodity forms of shopping-mall values that characterize the Christian Right's menu for salvation and the "repressive desublimation" of the Washington political scene and politicians such as Jesse Helms and Pat Buchanan. Youth appear to be caught between their demonization in the media as responsible for the "moral panics" of nihilistic, random violence brought on by boredom, lack of ambition, or lack of economic opportunity—the "accident scene" of "youth in crisis" (Ackland, 1995)—and their positioning within the discourse of a simpleminded, flag-waving patriotism such as that exhibited in *MMPR.* This show would seem to support the idea that in times of economic scarcity the best solution for potential "Dead-End Kids" is to join the military, where you can "be all you can be" and get paid to do in real life what the Power Rangers can only accomplish in fiction. In this way *MMPR* provides a discursive space for the nascent formation of the phallo-military warrior citizen, a formation fully realized only after the hazing rites of boot camp.

Naturally, the mainstream media exhibit a kind of "regulation phobia" in responding to the barrage of criticism currently being directed toward the show. Arguments such as "children know the difference between fantasy and reality" or "*Power Rangers* is just a small part of what children learn every day" have been featured (Doyle, 1994). However, those who are against media regulation also tend to be against adding the subject of media literacy to the core curriculum. Unfortunately, it is often the teachers that end up having to cope with the effects of *MMPR*. According to one teacher, Laurie Bethune, it is an uphill battle:

> When kids write in their journals, they usually have the freedom to write about anything. However, it got to the point where they were writing about the same thing; hurting, hitting, knocking, and killing ruled their stories. There was no more creativity and no more innocence that children (4–7 years old) usually have. When I banned the *Power Rangers* as a subject, they had a real problem thinking about other subjects to write about.

As it stands, teachers are left talking to each other about coping strategies rather than pedagogical strategies, about taking on the role of "recess police" outside the classroom and "image salespeople" inside, trying in vain to pitch their counterlessons on critical citizenship to children who are already so infused by the absolutism that characterizes Morphin identity that possibilities for unsettling or subverting Morphin consciousness is not very promising in the near future.

Notes

Thanks to Shirley Steinberg, Miki Cohen, Ana Cura, Bibiana Carlos, Miles Collyer, and Hillary Erlich for some of the ideas discussed in this paper.

1. The decision of the Broadcast Standards Council was based on Article 2 of the "Voluntary Code Regarding Violence in Television Programming." Subsection 2 or the Article states, "In children's programming portrayed by real-life characters, violence shall only be portrayed when it is essential to the development of the character and plot." It should be noted, too, that any home that subscribes to cable can receive the show via an American network. This may be one of the reasons why the cancelling of the show on Canadian stations has not met with more resistance.

References

Ackland, Charles. (1995). *Youth, Murder, Spectacle: The Cultural Politics of "Youth in Crisis."* Boulder: Westview Press.

Bellafante, Gina. Mighty Raters. *Time*. December 6, 1993, p. 88.

Benjamin, Walter. The Work of Art in the Age of Mechanical Reproduction, in *Illuminations*. Trans. Harry Zohn. London: Fontana, 1973.

Cody, Jennifer. Power Rangers Take on the Whole World. *Wall Street Journal*. March 23, 1994, p. C7.

Doyle, John. Why Their Plug Was Pulled. *Globe and Mail*. November 7, 1994, p. A11.

Grossberg, Lawrence. (1992). *We Gotta Get Out of This Place: Popular Conservatism and Popular Culture*. New York: Routledge.

Kellner, Douglas (1994). *Media Culture*. Unpublished manuscript.

Mighty Morphin Power Rangers Press Book. Saban Entertainment, 1994.

Power Rangers Spark Violence, Study Says. *Toronto Star*. April 12, 1994, p. B1.

Warrick, Pamela. Morphin Madness. *Los Angeles Times*. November 24, 1994, pp. E1, E16.

7

"Mom, It's Not Real!" Children Constructing Childhood Through Reading Horror Fiction

Linda K. Christian-Smith and Jean I. Erdman

SWAMP MONSTERS, WEREWOLVES, nightmarish summer camps, sinister theme parks, and the things in the basement—these are the dark entities and places of many childhoods. They take on life through the media and horror fiction written especially for children. Horror, once the province of adult fiction, is rapidly becoming an established genre in children's and adolescent literature through Christopher Pike's novels and R. L. Stine's Goosebumps series written for second- through fourth-graders. (R. L. Stine also writes Fear Street, the horror series for adolescent readers.) Hardly noticeable a few years ago, horror fiction for young readers represented three of the top four best-sellers on the *Publishers Weekly* list of children's trade books in 1992 (Gray, 1993).

In this chapter we examine the Goosebumps horror series. We first explore the larger socioeconomic and political context of childhood and children's publishing. Then we present four readings of selected books in the Goosebumps series, two readings from the writers of this chapter, two readings from young boys. In this regard we examine how the two boys make meanings from Goosebumps and reveal how their interpretations construct and are constructed by their understandings of what it means to be a male child.

Our Stories

According to G. L. Anderson (1989) researchers need to account for the background and biases they bring to their inquiry and delineate the social and political forces shaping the social universe studied. Who is the "we" mentioned in the foregoing? We are white women, university teachers, and researchers of curriculum and instruction working from the perspectives of feminism, critical theory, postmodernism, and antiracism. Both of us also incorporate insights from poststructuralism in our teaching and research. The following assumptions and positions inform our study of the Goosebumps children's horror series.

Jean's Story

I am an adult who had systematically avoided horror as harmfully scary and leading to bad dreams, irrational fears, and a distorted sense of fearfulness of the world, and so my decision to permit my eldest son, John, to read and buy Goosebumps was indeed a big step. As a white working-class girl in a small city in Wisconsin in the late 1950s, I lived in a sheltered world of home, school, church, and public library. I read several library books weekly, but book purchases were a rare Christmas present. Now, as an upper-class parent married to an attorney, I had little practice from my childhood in buying books—it was given that books came from the library. Buying books for myself and my two sons, John and Jimmy, ages eight and four, is a great joy to me, something somewhat out-of-control. I am not frugal and buy more adult books than I can read. I think about these books and my social class and white privilege and read them hurriedly within the triple burden of homemaker, parent, and employed professional. As a working mother, I keep the house organized, know where the gift-wrapping paper is, check whether fingernails are clipped, note the children's shoe sizes, and so forth. Gendered work is lightened considerably by my social-class privilege.

Noticeably lacking are any adult or children's horror books—until the recent addition of Goosebumps. I had never differentiated horror as "not real," and I viewed it as depraved and a bad influence on people—a view in accord with my protective stance toward childhood (Berlak and Berlak, 1981; Elkind, 1984, 1988), which I have carried from my upbringing first to elementary school teaching and later to teaching teachers and parenting. Most recently I have begun to examine children's horror fiction as it develops children's reading fluency. I am also beginning to differentiate reading responses by whether readers are children, young adults, or adults.

Linda's Story

Reading several of the Goosebumps books for this study transported me back to my childhood as a working-class girl of Eastern European background residing in a small city in northern Minnesota during the 1950s. I found much in these books I could identify with and yet much that was different than the experiences of my childhood. I have always been fascinated by the strange, macabre, and unexplained. Stine's *Say Cheese and Die* reminded me of my visits to the remains of a reputedly haunted, burned-out house near the school where I attended kindergarten. Leading to the old house was a boardwalk, under which trolls were thought to live. This was the quintessential dare of my childhood. My early home-alone fears were fed by and made sense of through horror fiction. Yet there were family members available to comfort and care for me, which is seldom the case in Goosebumps. Alongside my reading of Nancy Drew and Jane Austen were H. P. Lovecraft's and Edgar Allan Poe's stories and the Saturday monster movies such as *I Was a Teenage Werewolf.* In high school I graduated to Mary Shelley's *Frankenstein,* Robert Louis Stevenson's *The Strange Case of Dr. Jekyll and Mr. Hyde,* and Bram Stoker's *Dracula.* I was hooked on the older versions of films loosely based on these novels.

Today I read little contemporary horror fiction except for the latest installment of Anne Rice's *Vampire Chronicles.* I remain a fan of vintage horror films such as *Night of the Living Dead* and contemporary thrillers like *Alien.* However, as a feminist critical educator, I am horrified by the general violence and women's mutilation in the "slice-and-dice" scenes prevalent in contemporary horror fiction and films. As one who subscribes to critical literacy frameworks, I am well aware of the utopian and socially incorporated aspects of popular fiction. Reconciling my intellectual frameworks with my feelings of revulsion and my interest in horror is an ongoing process.

The Social Construction of Childhood and Masculinities

Childhood often assumes a natural status in psychological discourse, although it is a social construct varying across different historical and cultural sites (Steedman, Urwin, and Walkerdine, 1985). The form that childhood takes in a society is closely related to the ways work and leisure are organized as well as school, family, and peer relationships. According to Carmen Luke (1990), social, political, and economic relations shape concepts of childhood. In Western societies, children are often regarded as low-status, economically dependent, incompetent individuals who achieve competency and normality through their interactions with adults who initiate children into larger cultural values. Adult society is constructed as the norm and the desirable state, whereas children's society seems to be different and often aberrant. These notions of childhood are of recent origin.

According to P. Aries (1962), children in Western societies historically participated freely in everyday events with adults and acquired the knowledge of living from these interactions. During the late Middle Ages childhood as an historical construct and discourse developed as children were increasingly regarded as separate and different from adults. Luke (1989) identifies the large social, economic, and political changes brought on by the printing press, the Reformation, the social rebellion of peasants, and the rise of the mercantile class as key moments in this shift in thinking. By the sixteenth century, a discourse on childhood was systematized through the printing and disseminating of information on family life, child rearing, and education by pastors and itinerant evangelists. Gradually the school and family were constituted as "disciplinary sites" where children were defined as needing moral guidance and protection. Valerie Walkerdine (1984) suggests that the "normalization" of the child continues to underlie today's schools and families, which endeavor to produce self-regulated individuals who fit into the dominant social structure.

Luke (1991) suggests that these dominant notions of childhood actually mask assumptions that the "normal" child is a white, middle-class, heterosexual boy. How do boys acquire a sense of themselves from which masculinities are constructed? What "normalizing" processes do boys experience? S. Askew and C. Ross (1988, 2) suggest that there exists a dominant construction of masculinity in the press and media, representing men as tough, strong, aggressive, independent, brave, sexually active, intelligent, and so forth. R. W. Connell (1987) notes that configurations of masculinities are hierarchically ordered on the basis of physical size and strength. Individual men also occupy positions along the continuum of action—emotion, sexual experience-inexperience, sport-art, and manual/sporting orientations. These locations are mediated by race, ethnicity, class, sexuality, and age. For example, white middle-class men are expected to use their minds and be independent and competitive as well as physically strong. The masculinities of white working-class men and those of color are constructed around toughness, roughness, physical strength, and actions.

Connell (1987, 184) refers to these configurations as "hegemonic masculinity," defined as "a social ascendance achieved in a play of forces that extends beyond contests of brute power into the organization of private life and cultural processes." Hegemonic masculinities are constructed in the public sphere in relation to women and to subordinated masculinities. However, "hegemony" does not imply a totalizing process without alternatives and resistances to dominant masculinities. For many men, personal and social difficulties often arise from the pressures to prove their masculinity and hide their vulnerability. Hegemonic masculinity especially creates conflicts for the youngest men, because children in general are not expected to manifest such characteristics. Yet boys' gendered subjectivities are the object of intense regulation through subtle and overt pressures on them to start taking up miniature versions of hegemonic masculinities beginning early on. (These are generalities and cultural stereotypes that do not indicate the many ways men and boys rework dominant masculinities.) Literacy, particularly popular children's horror fiction, is a part of this regulation process. However, through the reading of this genre boys may make sense of their life worries and resist this regulation of their gendered subjectivities, as will be shown in the following readings of Goosebumps.

Chills and Thrills: The Horror Genre

We are all living amid a large-scale revival of horror in films, television, videos, and video games but especially in fiction. Recall the tremendous success of Michael Jackson's 1984 *Thriller* disc heralded by a video linking sex with zombies, vampires, and wolfmen. Fox's *X-Files* has gone beyond cult status as more and more viewers grit their teeth at the weekly horrors confronting Agents Scully and Mulder. Stephen King now boasts an adolescent readership in addition to his strong following among adults. And then there is R. L. Stine's aptly named Goosebumps series for children. Although horror has social, economic, political, and psychological aspects, it is first physiological. The word itself stems from the Latin *horrere*, meaning "to bristle," as when the hair stands on end during excitement. The flesh also becomes bumpy in an attempt to increase body temperature during a chilling experience (Twitchell, 1985, 10). These "goosebumps" represent the frightful encounter with the strange and horrible.

J. B. Twitchell (1985) notes that horror has always been present in English literary tradition—from Grendel in *Beowulf*. Then, monsters were the vehicle for promoting the protagonist's heroism. Once the monster was destroyed, readers would value the protagonist all the more. The notion of the monster changed during the eighteenth century, when William Hogarth produced social commentaries in the form of engravings of humans becoming monsters through alcoholism, drug addiction, cruelty, and murder as responses to the social transformation brought on by urbanization and capitalism. At the end of the nineteenth century horror classics such as *Dracula, Frankenstein,* and *The Strange Case of Dr. Jekyll and Mr. Hyde* became the sites for extended commentaries on social changes wrought by the rise of technology and the scientific mentality. In the United States Poe and Lovecraft mingled themes of forbidden desires with horror. In today's horror genres fictional monsters more frequently take center stage, with the victims and protagonists in the back rows.

What accounts for the enduring attraction of horror? Twitchell (1985) suggests three scenarios: satisfaction with overcoming fears; imaginative consideration of objects of sublimated desire; and rites of passage to reproductive sexuality. (Twitchell's suggestions that the horror genre involves a rite of passage to reproductive sexualities do not apply to Goosebumps. Since sexual tensions are absent in the series, it conforms to social beliefs regarding the asexual child. The kinds of sexual themes found in Stine's Fear Street and Christopher Pike's adolescent horror novels do not appear in Goosebumps.) Horror depends on not knowing enough and being kept from complete knowledge. The revelation constitutes the moment of supreme horror. During horror scenes one is cut off from ordinary comforts. Only individual efforts allow one to deal with the threat. Horror monsters frighten by acting out desires, usually sexual, that are feared or taboo and are in turn punished for doing so. Horror is a mode of incorporation into the existing economic structure through buying and collecting books and memorabilia. Horror's socially regulative aspects may be glimpsed in the current stalk-and-slash horror films, where women are routinely mutilated and/or murdered when they move beyond traditional notions of femininity and where men such as Michael Meyers and Freddie Kruger do the mutilating and murdering. Horror regulates men's actions—but in ways that are different, which will be explored in this chapter.

Tales from the Dark Side:
Popular Children's Horror Fiction

J. Rose (1984) indicates that children's literature is a contradictory term because children figure mainly as objects of an essentially adult enterprise. Adults control all aspects of book preparation and economically benefit from the increasingly lucrative children's publishing industry. Children are positioned as consumers of versions of childhood provided by adults.

Profiting from childhood is a more recent development in the larger children's culture. In publishing, this most likely originated in children's series books like best-sellers Tom Swift, Nancy Drew, and the Hardy Boys published by the Stratemeyer Syndicate earlier in the century (Christian-Smith, 1991). The era of quick, multimillion-dollar sales from children's series books was ushered in in 1979, when Scholastic Books developed the first teen-romance series, Wildfire (Christian-Smith, 1990). Seeing Wildfire's sales reach $2.25 million in the first year, other publishers raced to develop their own romance series. Scholastic has remained a strong contender in the field through its popular Baby-Sitters Club, Goosebumps, and other series. In a little more than ten years Scholastic has grown from a small educational publisher on the verge of bankruptcy to an international employer of 3,300 with annual revenue of $554.28 million in 1995 from subsidiaries in the United States, Canada, England, Australia, and New Zealand (Standard & Poor's, 1995, 2292; Directory of Corporate Affiliation, 1993, 962). Responsible for this growth are Scholastic's numerous school and home book clubs, trade book series, educational magazines, textbooks, and software divisions. Scholastic is making inroads into television, video, and film productions through its popular teen program *Charles in Charge,* Baby-Sitters Club home videos, and the current film versions of *The Indian in the Cupboard* and *Baby-Sitters Club* (Nathan, 1995).

R. L. Stine's Goosebumps books represent Scholastic's latest foray into the series market and another first in publishing—a horror fiction series just for children. Stine's professional relation with scholastic books began in 1966 as assistant editor of *Junior Scholastic Magazine* and the humor magazines *Bananas* and *Maniac,* each aimed at middle school readers (Very, 1994). Stine is a prolific writer of more than 100 adolescent and children's fiction and information books, including some horror titles for Scholastic and Archway's best-selling Fear Street horror series for young adults. Parachute Press, a book-packaging company owned and managed by Jane Waldhorn, Stine's spouse and former editor of Scholastic's *Dynamite* magazine, holds the copyright on Goosebumps and Fear Street. Part of Goosebumps's success is owed to the savvy packaging and marketing aimed at child consumers and their parents.

Creating Desire: "Mama, I Just Can't Seem to Stop [Reading Goosebumps]!"

By the time children read Goosebumps they may be very familiar with the series format. Today's children are bombarded with series books from the Cooper Kids Adventure Series (Crossway Books) to Sleepover Friends (Scholastic). Many children may also have had experiences in their earliest years with picture books marketed as series. The back covers of Berenstain Bear books depict the front covers of all the previous series books, making it easy for even prereaders to check which ones they have read or own. Jean's youngest son, Jimmy, has commented: "I am collecting Berenstain Bear books." He studies the back covers, exclaiming: "That many books! Read me some of the [titles]" during reading aloud while potty training. Despite owning numerous Curious George titles and a set of Beatrix Potter books, Jimmy "collects" Berenstein Bear books through studying the inside and outside back covers.

Goosebumps uses the back cover to pique interest in the current title, similar to the old inside front cover book jacket blurb but distinctive for emphasis on the reader's physiological and emotional response with minimal attention to character and plot development. Predicted reader responses are often in pun form ("A chilling preview" for the announcement of *Phantom of the Auditorium* in which it is cold in the auditorium), rather than providing a description of the narrative. The page(s) announcing the new title and the back cover highlight the name of the next title.

The Goosebumps series provides increasingly intense marketing between covers, beginning with a one-page entry after the last page of the final chapter, such as:

Add more
Goosebumps
to your collection . . .
A chilling preview of
what's next from
R. L. STINE
PHANTOM OF THE
AUDITORIUM

One to three unpaginated, excerpted chapters from that upcoming title are inserted after the final chapter. Next follows an About the Author page and many other inclusions, such as:

- order blanks for Goosebumps (in every book) and other series titles (#1, #7, #15, #22)
- a Goosebumps calendar ad (#24, #25, #27, #28, #33, $9.95)
- a Goosebumps backpack ad (#32)—$5.00 plus purchase proofs from #32, #33, #34, and Goosebumps Official Collector's Caps Book "WITH 16 COMPLETELY COOL CAPS AND A HEAVY-DUTY GOOSEBUMPS SLAMMER" at $5.99
- Book and Light Set #2 (#31, $12.95)
- three Monster Blood Books (#3, #18, #29) and "slime" (#34, $11.95)
- a Goosebumps fan club (#23, #30, #31, $9.95) including a "Goosebumps" baseball cap, a shoe box–sized cardboard coffin labeled "Goosebumps," a newsletter, and doorknob paper proclaiming "Goosebumps Keep Out"

- a Goosebumps Contest (#20, #21, #22) query, "What gives you Goosebumps?" Winning entries appeared on inside back covers of #28, #29, #30, #31

The Excerpted Chapters—Tantalizing the Reader

The excerpted chapters include one to three of the first eight chapters (consecutive chapters if more than one), unpaginated. As is the case with many Goosebumps chapters, the excerpted chapters tantalize the reader to find out how a main character will handle a dangerous and somewhat mysteriously vague, frightening situation. The chapters typify the multiple miniclimaxes throughout Goosebumps books, which the readers I interviewed refer to as "taking a wide turn" and as "mysterious."

Stine indicates that he often starts with a title, decides on an ending, creates an outline, and then writes. He states: "I get ideas from all kinds of places. People know how desperate I am for ideas, because I'm doing so many books, so they try to help me. . . . You sit down and think until you have one. . . . I have no choice—I have to have the ideas" (Verney, 1994, 213).

The Goosebumps market is viewed as having agency and driving Stine: "With two best-selling series going full speed, Stine really doesn't have a choice. For his popular 'Fear Street' series and his newer 'Goosebumps' series, Stine writes 24 novels a year" (Verney, 1994, 213). He is credited with writing more than 100 books in four years (1991–1995) and is reported to receive 400 letters weekly (Verney, 1994) and, more recently, 500 daily (Verney, 1994). The market "demands" that he come up with ideas.

For many years, Stine's specialty "was making younger kids laugh, not giving teens the shivers" (*The Scream*, 1994, 213). In this issue of *The Scream*, the official newsletter of the Goosebumps Fan Club (1994), Stine says about humor and horror: "Someone once called me the Jekyll and Hyde of kids' books, and I guess that's about right. I wrote about 30 or 40 joke books and humor books before I slipped into my horror identity." Stine watches MTV and has edited and still reads humor magazines for ideas. *The Scream* retains many elements of elementary school culture dominant in recent decades but now imbued with horror, including: a spooky word unscramble; a parts-of-speech feature ("If you were a zombie when you studied grammar, here are a few hints: NOUN: person, place, or thing [astronaut, graveyard, snake]"); and a fill-in-the-blank story ("School Cafeteria Surprise!"). The marketing is omnipresent as well: a Goosebumps Fan Club bookstore party photo; an ad for

Goosebumps novels and Book and Light Set #2; an ad for the Monster
Blood Pack; a query to "fans" to name the Goosebumps book they would
like to see made into a sequel and another that asks, "If you could have
anything with 'Goosebumps' on it, what would it be?" To enclose and
further solidify product interrelationships, Curly, the skeleton-narrator-
"slammer" image from the Goosebumps Official Collectors Caps Book,
has a letters column in *The Scream*. Finally, author Stine is honored in
The Scream as "Author of the Year" and the "official" #1 author in the
United States; Stine also "sends an exclusive monster-sized 'thank you'
to fan club members—Keep reading Goosebumps!"

A related spin on creating the Goosebumps market is the Goosebumps Kids Club events at bookstores across the country. I (Jean) just
attended such an event with my son John. The clerk, wearing a Goosebumps Fan Club cap, provided name tags on which children were to
identify their favorite Goosebumps title. The two activity leaders (store
employees) used handwritten notes and materials set up in advance.
Children sat on the carpet in haphazard rows while customers shopped
or listened. The leaders competed for children's attention with occasional noise from customer checkouts. There was no shushing of children or others and little communication among the children.

Adults accompanying the kids sat at the edges of the group of children
or shopped. White children and one black child arrived with adults and,
often, with siblings—one of whom appeared more interested in Goosebumps. The fourteen children present on time were joined by nine late
arrivals, but there were no reprimands for tardiness. Sweatshirts and
caps promoting the Green Bay Packers, Pocahontas, and Mickey Mouse
were in evidence. One child was about fourteen, ten were ten to thirteen, eight were seven or eight, and four were six or younger.

A leader made brief announcements of Kids Club events for Goosebumps, American Girl Dolls, and the Boxcar Children. A leader read
aloud excerpts from *Phantom of the Auditorium* for thirty minutes. The
"right answer," fast-paced questions that followed ("Who was in charge
of the play?") elicited animated short answers that were rewarded with
small prizes (pencils). A fast, repetitive, rhythmic, exciting video-plat-
form game atmosphere was evident, with kids performing the role of
platform characters, jumping up for rewards (Provenzo, 1991).

A leader mixed dough ingredients for "Pimples on Gangrene"—purple
and green cookies made with butter ("slime"), sugar ("kidney stones"),
and the like. Soon, already-baked cookies were brought out; kids deposited their name tags with their favorite Goosebumps title and helped
themselves. They then moved to tables to create masks with craft sup-
plies (paper plates, feathers).

By the title favorites on the name tags and the activities, Goosebumps is once again, this time via the bookstore, examining and intensifying the market—our kids. This market, intensively created by Goosebumps books, products, and events, is a striking example of the market-driven nature of children's literature today. Goosebumps demonstrates how children's literature interplays with and promotes a consumer-oriented (instead of critical or reflective) and possessive-individualistic view of reading and childhood. Owning the books becomes a necessary status symbol by providing a common discussion ground with other children at school. It also provides a source of security and escape—something to do when bored, when there is "nothing to do."

The increased pressure on children and parents to buy Goosebumps stems from the reluctance and refusal of school and public libraries to purchase Goosebumps. Reluctance and refusal are related to library budget cuts/constraints and self-censorship by libraries and schools for fear of parental/community criticism. Goosebumps's limited availability at libraries heightens the pressure on parents and children to buy them.

Goosebumps certainly engages with many of the fears children have today regarding lack of control, violence, and isolation. It subverts children's expectations of support from friends and family. Goosebumps presents the world as a dangerous place where there are few safe havens for children. However, these children are not passive victims of the fearful aspects of life. With little support and understanding from adults, especially parents, these children are forced to solve their own problems individually or with a few friends. Although achieving self-reliance is a traditional theme in books for children, Goosebumps does not incorporate the power of the social collective in this process.

Goosebumps may also be thought of as a series of cultural narratives representing the regulation of masculinities. In the novels, boys are pressured to take up miniature versions of hegemonic masculinities—they desire physical strength and control but not to be bullies. Yet in Goosebumps boys' fears and their sensitive sides are repressed as important parts of their masculinities. These competing masculinities represent the multiple gender subjectivities offered to male readers of Goosebumps.

Jean's Story About John, School, Masculinity, and Goosebumps

At a time when my eldest son, John, had not yet started reading independently for pleasure, I had checked out Goosebumps titles the first time because, despite the gruesome graphic covers, the About the Author page that I flipped to highlighted Stine's work as head writer for *Eu-reeka's Castle* (a children's TV show)—how bad could they be?

> R. L. Stine is the author of nearly two dozen best-selling thrillers and mysteries for young people. Recent titles for teenagers include *Hit and Run, The Girlfriend,* and *Baby-sitter II,* all published by Scholastic. He is also author of the *Fear Street* series. When he isn't writing scary books, he is head writer of the children's TV show, *Eureeka's Castle,* seen on Nickelodeon. Bob lives in New York City with his wife, Jane, and twelve-year-old son, Matt *(Welcome to dead house, #1).* [This description varies slightly throughout the series.]

Recognition of Stine as the head writer of *Eureeka's Castle* was critical to my decision to first purchase Goosebumps. Stine's association with *Eureeka* quelled my fears about the gruesome Goosebumps covers. *Eureeka,* broadcast on Nickelodeon, is a show that exudes kindness and developmental appropriateness. It is geared to preschoolers and early childhood, so parents of primary grade and upper elementary children whose households subscribe to cable TV are familiar with it.

I read Goosebumps aloud to John, primarily to have him spend more time with reading (he had nearly stopped reading alone at home) and to reduce his stress (he often stated, "You don't know how tough it is at school" and, "It's tough being a kid"). John, an eight-year-old second-grader when we began this read-aloud odyssey that persisted through-out his second grade year, was willing to listen. I had mistakenly read my own meaning of assumed developmental appropriateness into the ref-erence to Stine's involvement with *Eureeka's Castle*. A more careful read-ing of the blurb reveals: "When he isn't writing scary books, he is head writer of . . . *Eureeka's Castle*."

Parental Fear of the Book Covers

Some of the covers concerned me gravely. The cover of *You Can't Scare Me* (#15) depicts muddy, rising-from-the-dead swamp monsters, with the phrase, "They're coming for you . . ." to the left of a monster's hand. *The Beast Under the Sink's* (#30) cover reveals a devilish, cross-eyed, vague, black beast peaking from behind the plumbing, with the words to the right of the eyes, "It's warm? It's breathing? And it doesn't do dishes?" Okay for fourteen-year-old adolescents, maybe, but second-graders? Having personally and systematically avoided horror as a genre myself, both books and film, my imagination was not as graphic as the Goose-bumps covers. I was also concerned about content, including both the child characters' meanness to one another (which my son tired of hearing me point out) and the young characters' dire plights in which adults either do not or cannot help them—which may indeed be the source of their problems.

I found myself experiencing a variety of emotions as we read and my son collected the books. Some covers seemed not so gory, such as the wolf on *The Werewolf of Fever Swamp* (#14) and the giant child's legs and sneaker-ensconced feet walking through miniature playground equipment on the cover of *Monster Blood III* (#29). This latter cover reminded me of Disney's *Honey, I Blew Up the Kids*—comedy rather than horror. I feared that I was becoming conditioned to the gore—worn down as a working mother, carrying the heavy burden of work and overseeing my children's cultural experiences. I was reluctantly giving my child what he asked for while forgetting that I had first encouraged Goosebumps purchases. I was shocked to be reminded by my son that I had indeed bought for him the Goosebumps Official Collectors Caps Book through a school book club.

John's Gendered School Days, Nonliteracy Related

Schools (including John's) give teachers the right to strongly regulate students' activities, movement, posture, talking, possessions, access to water, and time and manner of eating (Thorne, 1994). Such collective regulation pressures kids to conform as they are all treated as members of a group. Circumstances of high gender salience (Jones and Mahony, 1989) include gender-based groups (girls together and boys together), gender divisions ("girls versus boys"; athletic versus nonathletic boys and the girls), gender identities ("hegemonic masculinity," "hegemonic femininity"), and gendered daily meanings (e.g., John recently stated, "I lose respect. I am not athletic . . ." and now he also has to wear glasses for nearsightedness). The common school reference to children as "boys and girls" serves to differentiate children age-wise from teachers and to divide children by gender. This is common at John's elementary school; he refers to boys by name and to girls by name or as "the girls." In preschool he referred to kids by name only, as did his preschool teachers.

Children often separate by gender on the playground (Thorne, 1994). According to John, boys and girls play mostly separately as the girls "get together to plan or something" and boys play kickball or football. Children are being socialized primarily for girls to play with girls, boys to play with boys. Gender is highly salient as boys control several times more space than girls. Kids are often excluded by others, and gender is one source of exclusion that centers around conceptions of hegemonic masculinities and femininities. For boys, nonhegemonic masculinities (not being athletic, not joining the kickball game, chasing girls on the playground) is related to exclusion. For John, the ritual of being chosen last for kickball as dominant boys pick teams wrecked his days for weeks during second grade. My request for closer playground supervision was denied for lack of resources and due to the belief that children need time and freedom from the adult intervention present in soccer leagues and Little League baseball. "Pick-overs," the practice whereby a dominant boy who had chosen players for one of the kickball teams picks a new team so that he and his friends can be at base again, was common for weeks during John's second-grade year until adults intervened. The dominant kickball players had been the soccer stars the previous summer, when equal playing time had been ignored by a coach who appeared to need to win.

Gender segregation on the playground and teacher reiteration of "boys and girls" make gender highly salient to the children. Also, there was a girls' kickball and a boys' kickball in the classroom, distributed prior to each recess. John's reference group by the end of second grade was one of boys. Gender salience on the playground overshadowed his days in second grade. Although children "do gender" in their play and classrooms, the gender construction and hegemonic masculinities (and femininities, neglected here) are shaped by school routines, sensitivities, and language at school. John's lack of physical skillfulness, his quietness, and his deep interest in art are not the traits of hegemonic masculinities. Meanwhile, his identity as a male child was and continues to be constructed in relation to the dynamics of the school as a social institution characterized by gender hierarchies. At home he lives with serious older parents and an assertive little brother who probably adds to his stress as well as providing a playmate.

John's reference group for friends and for conflicts with kids has included mostly boys. He spoke gently of individual girls occasionally during second grade. His only outspoken anger was in response to his teacher leading a game of girls-versus-boys kickball during which the teacher gave the girls extra chances to kick. Her stated purpose was to help the girls practice skills but "the girls" against "the boys" set up a boundary that strengthened the sense of difference. This was evident in the angry verbal objections from several boys, including my son, in class after the event. The teacher responded by canceling any class kickball games for the rest of the year, which was a loss, since the teacher rarely played with the children, a circumstance John would like to see changed. After my objection to the principal later in the year, the school revised a "boys against girls" school playground field day to "boys from one room and girls from another" together as a team. Gender is easily identifiable, but it is not innocent or harmless as a marker for activity.

Teacher attempts to advocate for those less skillful or aggressive cannot be sorted so easily along gender lines, and gender-sensitive boys may be most likely to see such actions as sexist (Jones and Mahony, 1989).

In second grade John would not complain to the teacher, and he absorbed with pain and without retaliation periodic hitting and punching from boys whom he felt "liked him" one day but not necessarily the next. The common notion that all boys play in teams is inaccurate when one looks at all the boys—not just the most athletic and tough.

While in third grade John admitted, flashing a wide, dimpled grin, "If Steve hits me, first I check to see if the teacher is looking, and if she isn't, I bop him back. If she is, I complain." The anxiety has lessened, and circumstances have changed. John's third-grade teacher appears to be an unhurried, empathetic listener to children who herself does not have children—so she doesn't have the triple load of working mothers. John has grown three inches in one year, become more physically skillful, and taken advice from his dad to hit back. He has become more sports-oriented, which has provided him with a focus for more interactions with his dad and other boys. He is highly sports team–identified, as indicated by the pennants on his bedroom wall, a baseball-card collection, and experiences attending baseball and football games with his dad. John has begun to demonstrate greater identification with elements of hegemonic masculinities. The complexities surrounding the construction of masculinities have led John to sports identification and physical aggression, which contribute to the foundation of patriarchy and help him to cope with male cultural norms (Jones and Mahony, 1989). John likes to play indoors as well as out but had ceased drawing as something to do—replacing it with much reading, Lego ships and Playmobile castle sets, and Super Nintendo Super Mario World and Basketball GrandSlam. The recent addition of art lessons has resulted in John choosing to draw during free time.

In summary, there are multiple masculinities available. John has moved toward hegemonic masculinities in his identification with sports and privileging of sports as a favorite interest. He continues to love art and to take private group lessons, but his talk is increasingly sports talk, which is directed toward his dad and friends.

John's Gendered Life and Goosebumps

Why did I continue to read Goosebumps and allow John to do so? Without all the anxiety described above, I would not have allowed Goosebumps. The decision to promote Goosebumps was conscious and immediate, questioned often but always within the busyness of working and parenting full-time and the hegemonic masculinities dominant at John's school and in the culture. I was attempting to support my son through a socially difficult school year as he negotiated a distant relationship with his teacher and on again–off again aggression and friendships with boys in second grade.

Goosebumps provided John with common ground with some of the more aggressive boys with whom he had to negotiate recesses and lunchtime—the least supervised times of the school day. He talked with them about collecting and informed them of which titles he owned. They competed to be first to purchase newer titles.

John's second-grade teacher, teaching and parenting full-time, was likely very busy. She provided gendered reading suggestions to children, encouraging John and other boys to read Matt Christopher books (which I consider to be run-of-the-mill sports books). The teacher, aspiring to support boys' reading, overlooked that Christopher used sports terminology unfamiliar to John or to his sports-illiterate mother.

John had been read to by me, his dad, his grandmother, and his in-home child care providers since about age one—often daily for fifteen- to sixty-minute slots. I had read him the entire Narnia Chronicles the previous summer. Kindergarten had been a happy time as his teacher expressed appreciation of his sensitivity to others and accepted his quiet shyness. First grade had been troubling: His teacher desired more verbal participation from John, resisted parental efforts to enroll him in more art classes (his heart's desire), and coped, as a parent of two small children, with a move to a new home in February of that school year. It was not a good year. Beginning second grade, John was not yet a fluent reader who would read by himself for pleasure. During fall 1995 he stated at home that he did not really like reading—just being read to. I replied, "That is not an acceptable attitude for this family." The compromise with my child was to read and buy whatever he might read, and he wanted Goosebumps. Teaching, parenting, being a kid, and coping with popular culture artifacts such as Goosebumps is not easy.

John as Reader and Collector

John does not have favorite titles. The books are numbered, apparently to fill a marketing purpose, since the narratives are freestanding, with the exceptions of the Monster Blood and Night of the Living Dummy miniseries, which do not exhibit the complexity of character development, plot, setting, and dialogue that typifies another series John had read, the Narnia Chronicles. Within Narnia, it takes serious thought to sequence the books—yet John had done so. The Narnia temporal sequence is different than the title-listings sequence on Narnia back covers. John believes the Narnia titles should be listed in chronological order, "Because then if you want to read them in order, you know what the order is." No such discussions are possible with Goosebumps, because settings and characters are not sufficiently developed or interrelated. Reflection on and critique of Goosebumps is hard for children, because it is primarily the marketing that undergirds connections among Goosebumps titles.

Some children's horror has more depth of character and setting and provides insight into what Goosebumps might have been. For example, John Bellair's *The Ghost in the Mirror* provides more of what I wish for my son: central characters (adolescent Rose Rita and sixty-four-year-old Mrs. Zimmerman) who have a caring, dependable relationship. The horror experiences are encapsulated in specific events of limited duration. They connect in complex ways with well-developed plots, settings, and characters—all of which provide a backdrop of safety and reality. Goosebumps, in contrast, lacks these points of reference since actions dominate with little character or setting development available to the reader. Like Goosebumps, Bellair's works alert readers to books for older readers. The cover copy of "The Ghost in the Mirror" states, "Will appeal to young Stephen King Fans." Goosebumps publicizes Fear Street titles, thus again not recognizing child readers as distinctive. This trend of marketing down to younger age selections and genres previously reserved for older persons contributes to a reconstruction and possible disappearance of recent historical, cultural, and economic constructions of childhood whereby childhood is discrete from adulthood (Aries, 1962; Elkind, 1984, 1988).

In Bellair's work and in Narnia, boys and girls play and work together, often being kind and generally thoughtful toward one another. The contrast with Goosebumps is startling. Goosebumps's young characters are sometimes kind to a friend, but more often they are helpless alone and, less often, helpless together. Children abandon one another in Goosebumps, and the parents and grandparents are unavailable to help children, whether at summer camp (*Welcome to Camp Nightmare*, #9) or while visiting grandparents who are themselves threatened (*The Scarecrow Walks at Midnight*, #20). In some books the children are placed in circumstances where as a result of their actions horrible things happen to their younger siblings. In *Cuckoo Clock of Doom* (#28) the older sibling moves the hands on the cuckoo clock, ultimately transporting the family back in time, with the result that a younger sister will never be born (the older child is gleeful at that circumstance). Another example of horror done to a younger sibling, less directly at the hand of the older, occurs in *The Haunted Mask,* where the mask that the older sister brings home is found and put on by her younger brother—it can never be removed and will transform his personality to that of an angry monster.

Parental Exercise of Censorship

I censored the ending to *The Haunted Mask*, extemporaneously changing it to end with the mask put away forever. I continue to have major difficulty with the age of the audience reading Goosebumps, particularly if parents and teachers are not reading aloud and discussing the books with the children. This apparently is not a concern for Stine, who, as detailed earlier "has to come up with ideas" because of the demand for the books (Verney, 1994). This statement obscures the wealth that he is accruing. The question is inadequately addressed by Stine's assertion that children have the right to read literature without socially redeeming qualities. The question is whether adult writers and parents, myself included, have obligations to children in response to their moral, cognitive, social, economic, and family situations.

Tony Reads Goosebumps

During 1995 we also interviewed Tony about his reading of Goosebumps. Tony, of Greek ancestry, then age thirteen and soon to enter the seventh grade, lives in an small city in the upper Midwest, only two houses from John. He attends junior high and has two parents with doctorates in the fine arts—one working as a music professor and the other as an Catholic elementary school principal. Tony appears comfortable with his keen interest in sports and is on the school football team. He is a slightly stocky child who smiles readily, is active in a Boy Scout troop led by his former fifth-grade teacher, and appears comfortable with his skill playing the piano. He has recently experienced his parent's divorce, and he lives at both homes.

Tony began reading Goosebumps "about third grade" when he borrowed a book from a "friend and it was a Goosebumps." He recalled, "Then I saw them at the store and started buying and reading them and I liked them and didn't have a good collection. John tipped me off of the good price at Target and at this point I'm only four or five off the whole collection." Just as adults share information about places to shop for good deals, so do children. Tony frames his reading of Goosebumps within the context of collecting and completing the entire collection rather than through recommendations for individual titles. Tony explained why he likes Goosebumps:

It is not so much that they are scary—more adventurous—the suspense is holding, it's enjoyable to read. One that I thought was scary but not really scary but enjoyable that was *Ghost Beach*. It is the scariest of what I've read . . . the setting about a ghost, kids find this cave and explore and it turns out to be this graveyard and there's this one guy who lives in a cave and he's the one said to be the ghost but he's alive and he's trying to trap some of the bad ghosts in the cave and in the end the old man gets trapped in the cave with three ghosts. He is [stuck there forever] because it's a sanctuary-type cave and that's the kind ghosts can't go through. . . . He had to sacrifice himself otherwise he couldn't get the ghosts there. The kids and the old man's dog went to stay with their aunt and uncle and it turns out they're [the aunt and uncle] dead too. . . . In early times the whole town was ghosts because of sickness. It just kind of strikes me as suspense. The kids didn't know he [the uncle] was a ghost. It took a wide turn.

Tony read the books again and again:

If I didn't read them over and over again, my mom and dad would say it's just a waste of money . . . something I believe is kind of true 'cause I can read them kind of quick. If something is boring it takes forever to read, but if it's really interesting you can go through it quick. I like that saying—like a hot knife through butter.

When asked about how many books he owned, he replied,

I would have to look. . . . I have most, not the one behind the *[Revenge of the] Lawn Gnomes*, and not two behind *Lawn Gnomes* and not *Night in Terror Tower*. I have too many to list what I do have. I like to buy because I'm not just a reader, I'm also a collector.

Tony commented on his age:

Even though I am an older kid going into seventh, and it's [Goosebumps] for fifth-grade readers, I still think it's enjoyable for more than one age group. . . . Somewhere on the book—I don't recall where—[it says] it's for fifth or sixth grade depending on how hard the book is, how big the words are and stuff.

Tony is aware younger kids are reading the books. When asked whether girls read these books, he replied: "A tough question—I'm not sure of any I've known or I've seen reading these books. I know a couple of my male friends do read these books. . . ."

Tony reads Goosebumps at home and in the car but indicated there wasn't too much time to read them at school. They are not part of the formal curriculum. He has turned in "a couple of Goosebumps book reports," and his reading teacher has noticed that he likes them: "She basically just reads them. I do a good summary—a page."

John Reads Goosebumps

John, reading independently and fluently since the end of second grade, reminded me that his first Goosebumps book came from a new-books display at the public library. He stated: "I continued and now that I'm into them it's like I can't stop. It might be the mysteries I like. I don't pay much attention to how the kids treat each other." John does not think Goosebumps books are scary, and when asked which was scariest, he noted, "I don't pay attention to that." John at nine years old was unable to identify the scariest one: "It's hard to tell because they are all different . . . like so many different ideas, you know?"

Having something to do, avoiding being bored, is important to John. "Yes, it [reading Goosebumps] keeps me busy when I didn't have anything to do." John knows he owns thirty-four Goosebumps and commented, "It's just as fun as reading them again." He could not say how he got interested in collecting: "I pretty much just know I collect them and read them over." He commented that the age the books are written for "varies. A little older than me yet I can understand it and it's my reading level. The kids [characters] are like twelve and sometimes ten." He is right. He also commented about girls reading Goosebumps and about lending them: "Yeah. Some people [girls] in our class, but they just read them—they don't collect them. I read them over again. Somebody borrowed my #16 and it is missing. I know I let somebody borrow it—I can't remember who."

He does not bring his Goosebumps to school, "because then people are 'Can I borrow this?' and I'm going to have all my books borrowed and then forget about it." John read Goosebumps "just about everywhere— in the car, in my room, on the couch, in the kitchen." He didn't mention school but noted that his teacher "hates them [Goosebumps] and she likes Matt Christopher [the author]. Matt Christopher is boring—the kids [characters] are way older and I don't understand them that much—a bunch of the words are sports words." In John's class, Goosebumps are allowed for oral book reports to parent-volunteers. John stated that the moms [parent-volunteers] comment, "So and so has read this too. Another one of these?" John, tired of questions, sighed and put his head down on the kitchen table. I asked John more questions another day. About collecting, John noted that the others collect the books: "Too many to name, girls and boys. [Why?] I don't know." John stated: "I started and I got attracted to the series although I don't like that you have to think 'Oh, you can't read this book—it looks too scary or it turns out bad. [You're being pretty nosey!]' John has not seen any horror movies or videos and, upon questioning, is not clear whether mysteries are scary horror: "Like if you would say mysteries—are mysteries scary?"

Reading Goosebumps is desirable, but John would not enter a haunted house: "I don't think I'm up to that. I'll watch it but I don't want to go in it."

John differentiates his life from that of Goosebumps characters: "I don't have that much adventure. Mostly just schoolkids that are in here—only kids in Goosebumps have this much adventure."

Conclusion

The horror genre with its monsters is traditionally a site for commentaries on social changes as exemplified by classics like Mary Shelley's *Frankenstein*. Today's children's horror novels also chronicle the psychic struggles involved in growing up at the end of the twentieth century, as children seek and also fear independence and separation from their parents. As F. Moretti (1992, 81) notes, the monster "makes bearable to the conscious mind those desires and fears which the latter has judged to be unacceptable and has thus been forced to repress." A series like Goosebumps imaginatively recodes the struggles around those desires and the social changes surrounding childhood today. Although Goosebumps constructs these transformations as primarily relational and psychic, they are economic and political as well.

Moretti (1992, 68) also suggests that the monster expresses anxiety of a monstrous future. Goosebumps describes a fictional world in which adults are not there for children. Children must solve their own problems and, in so doing, become powerful. In becoming more adultlike, these children do not acquire social power and recognition. They still are regarded as dependent by their parents and other adults. M. Cherland (1994) notes that children often chafe at the restrictions adults place on them and read fiction to fulfill in fantasy their desires to occupy more powerful discursive positions than those they perceive to be available to them in everyday life. In Moretti's study of popular children's fiction reading, readers experienced satisfaction with overcoming their fears in a manner similar to John's and Tony's enjoyment of the suspenseful aspects of Goosebumps and the characters' unusual adventures.

Series novels like Nancy Drew, teen-romance fiction, and *The Baby-Sitters Club* facilitate children's incorporation into existing capitalistic social and economic relations (Cherland, 1994; Christian-Smith, 1991, 1993). Goosebumps presents a striking example of the ways children's literature connects the socioeconomic with psychic structures. Through collecting books and purchasing Goosebumps spin-off products, children like John and Tony are being positioned as male "possessive individuals" so central to the continuation of capitalism. Goosebumps taps into boys' existing pastimes of collecting sports cars and the like. John's interviews indicate that the traditional social positions of mothers as consumers are being contradictorily reproduced through the Goosebumps phenomenon. Goosebumps represents the bind working mothers are in when promoting literacy with boys, which is often difficult given the social construction of fiction reading as a feminine activity (Cherland, 1994). Goosebumps may also work intertextually with other fiction and social texts in children's everyday lives (video games, name-brand clothing, and the like) to situate them within a children's culture increasingly organized and orchestrated by the corporate sector.

Goosebumps is primarily read by boys and presents a striking example of how popular children's fiction constructs subject positions around masculinity. The four readings provided in this chapter suggest how contentious and contradictory this is. In taking up gendered social subjectivities as an increasingly separate person, children are engaged in constant social negotiation as they struggle to develop and maintain a unified and coherent sense of self out of a diversity of possible, actual, and contradictory selves. John's interviews and his mother's concerns poignantly reveal the struggles around masculinities. John's quiet shyness and sensitivity toward others are in contradictory relation to the more aggressive, hegemonic masculinities he is under pressure to adopt if he is to get along in a world structured around strong gender divisions. Yet what will be the consequences for John, other boys, and society if boys lose touch with their sensitive and compassionate sides? John's art lessons may keep him linked to these important aspects of his masculinities, but will it be enough? Reading Goosebumps figures in these struggles. All of this is of no small consequence, for his mother is a feminist professor of education, a political progressive, and a supporter of the positive values of literacy.

Is Goosebumps a safe scare as R. L. Stine contends? As entertainment and as a window on childhood today, Goosebumps's tales from the dark side present dark visions of what it means to be a child at the end of this century.

References

Anderson, G. L. (1989). Critical ethnography in education: Origins, current status, and new directions. *Review of Educational Research* 59 (3): 249–270.

Aries, P. (1962). *Centuries of childhood: A social history of family life.* New York: Alfred Knopf.

Askew, S., and Ross, C. (1988). *Boys don't cry: Boys and sexism in education.* Milton Keynes, England: Open University Press.

Berlak, H., and Berlak, A. (1981). *Dilemmas of schooling: Teaching and social change.* New York: Methuen.

Cherland, M. (1994). *Private practices.* London: Falmer Press.

Christian-Smith, L. K. (1990). *Becoming a woman through romance.* New York: Routledge.

_____. (1991). The perils of Nancy Drew: Social identities in popular children's fiction. Presented at the Mid-Western Educational Research Association's Annual Meeting in Chicago, October 18.

_____. (1993). *Texts of desire: Essays on fiction, femininity, and schooling.* London: Falmer Press.

Connell, R. W. (1987). *Gender and power.* Oxford, England: Polity Press.

Cooper, D. (1993). Retailing gender: Adolescent book clubs in Australian schools. In L. K. Christian-Smith, ed. *Texts of desire: Essays on fiction, femininity, and schooling.* London: Falmer Press.

Derma-Sparks, L., and the A. B. C. Task Force. (1989). *Anti-bias curriculum: Tools for empowering young children.* Washington, D.C.: National Association for the Education of Young Children.

Director of Corporate Affiliations. (1993). *U.S. Private Companies.* Vol. 3. New Providence, NJ: National Register Publishing.

Eaglen, A. (1989). New blood for young readers. *School Library Journal* 35 (December): 49.

Elkind, D. (1984). *All grown up and no place to go: Teenagers in crisis.* Reading, MA: Addison-Wesley.

_____. (1988). *The hurried child: Growing up too fast too soon.* Reading, MA: Addison-Wesley.

Gray, P. (1993, August 2). Carnage: An open book. *Time* 142 (5), p. 54.

Jones, C., and Mahony, P., eds. (1989). *Learning our lines: Sex and social control in education.* London: Women's Press.

Lewis, C. S. (1950). *The lion, the witch, and the wardrobe: A story for children.* New York: Macmillan.

Luke, C. (1989). *Pedagogy, printing, and Protestantism: The discourse on childhood.* Albany: State University of New York Press.

_____. (1990). *Constructing the child viewer: A history of the American discourse on television and children, 1950–1980.* New York: Praeger.

_____. (1991). On reading the child: A feminist poststructuralist perspective. *Australian Journal of Reading* 14 (2): 109–116.

Moretti, F. (1992). The dialectic of fear. *New Left Review* 136: 67–85.

Nathan, P. (1995). The show biz angle. *Publishers Weekly* 242 (March 13): 18.

Provenzo, E. F. Jr. (1991). *Video kids: Making sense of Nintendo.* Cambridge, MA: Harvard University Press.

Rose, J. (1984). *The case of Peter Pan.* London: Macmillan.

Standard & Poors. (1995). *Register of corporations, directors, and executives.* Vol. 1. New York: McGraw-Hill.

Steedman, C., Unwin, C., and Walkerdine, V., eds. (1985). *Language, gender, and childhood*. London: Routledge and Kegan Paul.

Shelley, M. (1831, 1965). *Frankenstein*. Rpt. New York: New American Library.

Stevenson, R. L. (1886, 1967). *The strange case of Dr. Jekyll and Mr. Hyde*. Rpt. New York: Bantam Books.

Stoker, B. (1897, 1965). *Dracula*. Rpt. New York: Signet.

Thorne, B. (1994). *Gender play: Girls and boys in schools*. New Brunswick, NJ: Rutgers University Press.

Twitchell, J. B. (1985). *Dreadful pleasures: An anatomy of modern horror*. New York: Oxford University Press.

Verney, S. (1994). R. L. Stine. In K. S. Hile and E. A. Des Chenes, eds. *Authors and artists for young adults*. Detroit: Gale Research Inc.

Walkerdine, V. (1984). Developmental psychology and the child-centered pedagogy: The insertion of Piaget into early childhood education. In J. Henriques, W. Holloway, C. Urwin, C. Venn, and V. Walkerdine, eds. *Changing the subject: Psychology, social regulation, and subjectivity*. London: Methuen.

8

Reading Children's Magazines: Kinderculture and Popular Culture

Alan A. Block

> At the age of seven, I saw my first movie, Intermezzo . . . I fell in
> love with the background music. I couldn't fathom why it felt so
> good to hear a specific combination of notes in a certain order
> with a particular rhythm, but it gave me such pleasure just to
> keep humming that sweet melody over and over to myself. It was
> like having a secret companion. I couldn't wait to tell Mischa
> Goodman that I wanted to learn how to play Intermezzo. But he
> obviously didn't share my enthusiasm.
>   "Intermezzo?" he sneered. "That's not right for you."
>   His words reverberated in my heart. That's not right for you!
> This was not merely a turndown of my request. It was a
> universal declaration of war upon the individual.
>
> —Paul Krassner

IN THIS CHAPTER I DISCUSS POPULAR CULTURE and children and the magazines of popular culture that are directed specifically
at children and to which we adults subscribe—on behalf of our children—in extraordinary numbers. We buy these magazines for our children because we read magazines ourselves—and we assume our children will want to read them as well. Children's magazines represent the
culture of adults organized for children. Why adults read these magazines and how we read them will be part of this discussion, because children's magazines are marketed on the same basis as adult magazines—
that is, they promise information in entertaining and/or palatable
forms. *Highlights for Children*, for example, is subtitled *Fun with a Pur-*

pose, which to my mind negates the very essence of fun. In this era of the perfect child (a middle-class invention), we purchase for our children materials we hope will ease their way to success while we assuage our consciences that our children are being pressured to be grown-ups before they have first been children: For the most part these magazines are, you will recall, fun *with a purpose*! Nevertheless, our children read these materials of popular culture, and so we must look not only to the content of that culture but also to methods of reading it if we are to understand the potential effects these magazines have on our children. As adults we are "in the world" and, therefore, have access to these magazines without having to subscribe to them—but the same cannot be said of our children. What they read is often what we purchase for them; as adults we invite certain exemplars of popular culture into our homes to enrich (we hope) our children's lives.

These magazines are designed to be read, and so inevitably this essay must also be about the reading of popular culture. Walter Benjamin (1969, 257) writes, "There is no document of civilization which is not at the same time a document of barbarism. And just as such a document is not free of barbarism, barbarism taints also the manner in which it was transmitted from one owner to another. A historical materialist therefore dissociates himself from it as far as possible. He regards it as his task to brush history against the grain." So as a historical materialist, I would like, on the one hand, to read these children's magazines against the grain by situating my own reading of the magazines of popular culture against the grain. I would discover how these magazines occupied my time and my thinking, that I might understand their power and gather my own for the benefits of my children. On the other hand, I would like to read these magazines against the grain, that we might understand how they might be understood not only as documents of civilization but as documents of barbarism as well. In that way we might understand the silences that these magazines produce and give them voice. Not only are these magazines evidence of a corporate takeover of childhood—only *Stone Soup* is published by children—but they are given authority by the pedagogy of the school and the reading instruction that is offered there. It is nevertheless possible to offer an alternative pedagogy that will result in an informed pleasure, a type of reading pedagogy that facilitates reading against the grain so that these magazines might be enjoyed and used—fun with a purpose other than that organized by the publishers and editors.

I, for example, love to read *People* magazine. And *Us*. And many of the other popular magazines (*Time, Newsweek, U.S. News and World Report, Ladies Home Journal, Cosmopolitan, Self, Better Homes and Gardens, National Geographic, Popular Mechanics* [though I can't put together a hammer and a nail]) that purvey, define, report, and engage me in what we refer to as "popular culture." *We*, of course, refers to those of us who imagine themselves intelligent enough to actually know another culture than that of the popular variety.[1] I think that this condescension is often our problem, those who think of themselves as *us*; this conceit in some very real way has led not only to this important book but specifically to this chapter about the culture of children's magazines that are so intimately embedded in popular culture. This chapter (indeed, as do all of the chapters in this book, as do these magazines), to some extent addresses adults who subscribe to magazines for their children; thus this chapter inevitably concerns popular culture as it translates into kinderculture.[2] This chapter is about us and about what we want for our children and how as adults we have been persuaded by the culture of the magazines to subscribe for our children. This chapter is about how our children may too often be purchased for the price of a subscription.

We (an alternative pronoun for *us* but more clearly an *I*) are (*am*) always more moral about our (*my*) children than about ourselves (*myself*); *I* have enough experience to read this material, but *my* children may be so easily persuaded; this stuff is for *their* children but not for *mine*.

We insist that only particular materials enter our house for our children, hence the vituperative arguments against television and sometimes severe restrictions on its viewing. (I have never yet heard nor heard tell of a parent restricting his child to only one hour of reading a day—even if that reading is of a preapproved [censored] selection, but perhaps that topic is best left for some other time.) However, we do decide to invite certain subscriptions into our house, and hence the focus of this chapter. To discuss children's magazines as kinderculture is really a discussion of the adult culture of children's magazines. For if we are talking about children's magazines and the culture therein, we are talking about popular culture. Whether we consider popular culture what we do with what is out there (as does John Fiske), or whether we agree that popular culture is what is manufactured to be uncritically consumed by the greatest numbers, popular children's magazines must be considered popular culture.

There is a plethora of magazines out there for our children, more, probably, than I am aware of—some of which may even derive from some overtly fascist sensibilities, though I have yet to come across one of them—and certain of these magazines enter certain houses, or are available at certain locations, for clearly ideological reasons. We want our children to have available these specific magazines. These magazines are specifically designed for children. (I use that phrase, of course, cautiously. I do not mean all children generically, I mean all children who fit the definition of children held by the particular journals and parents who purchase these magazines for their children. That indeed is another story and is pursued in historical accounts of childhood.)[3] But children's magazines are undoubtedly steeped in popular culture and are intended to offend absolutely no one and to appeal to the greatest population[4] and are given entrance wherever children—or a particular class of children—may be in attendance. The majority of children depicted in these magazines seems to be in the middle class, and the environments in which they play—and remember that they do mostly play: fun with a purpose—are almost always clean, safe, and child-friendly. There are no drive-by shootings in, say, *Highlights*. There are no dangerous toxic chemicals, and AIDS does not exist. Jonathan Silin (1995, 40) writes that "too much of the contemporary curriculum brings a deathly silence to the being of childhood and not enough of it speaks to the things that really matter in children's lives or in the lives of those who care for them." I think the same can be said for the curriculum to be discovered in children's magazines. Not enough is said about injustice, about the Holocaust, about the genocide that wiped out the Native American population, or of the war in Bosnia-Hercegovina. *Zlata's Diary* has not yet been excerpted in *Highlights*. Anne Frank is an historical figure and no longer a living image. The world portrayed in children's magazines is intended to offend no one; it sells magazines but it is not our world.

Adults buy these subscriptions—not children. And it is adults who determine not only what will enter the home but also what will be published for children's consumption. As parents, we are careful, but the corporate executives are clever. I mean to say that they are in it for the money. Their aim is to appeal to their sense of the social child and, in addition, to construct their image of that child in order to make a profit. But adults make the subscriptions, and so it is what adults think of magazines and of children that determines the availability of the magazines into the home.

My five-year-old daughter, Emma, is a subscriber to *Highlights*, circulation 2.8 million, and *Your Big Backyard*, circulation 450,000. We read *Cricket*, circulation 130,000, and *Ladybug*, circulation 120,000. At various locales she will come across *Jack and Jill* (327, 000) or *Sesame Street Magazine* (1.2 million) or *Humpty Dumpty* (350,000). There are others that I do not so readily find—*Cobblestone: The History Magazine for Young People* (47,000); or *Stone Soup: The Magazine by Children* (10,000). And I have been thinking about what happens when Emma reads these journals. I have been thinking about the magazines of popular culture for kids—about kinderculture.

Toto, I have a feeling we're not in Kansas anymore!
—**Dorothy, in *The Wizard of Oz***

Children's popular (and not-so-popular) magazines can be broadly classified, as can adult popular (and not-so-popular) magazines, as those that address issues of general interest—stories, games, activities, jokes, letters, advice columns, and informative articles about people and events (e.g., *Highlights, Sesame Street, Cricket*); and special-subject magazines (e.g., *Your Big Backyard*, published by the National Wildlife Federation and intended to teach children about the natural world around them); *Calliope*, a magazine that explores one issue of world history per issue; *Humpty Dumpty*, which focuses on issues of health and safety for young children, though I doubt if there is an article that may offer suggestions about avoiding AIDS, drive-by shootings, or even cigarettes; *Boy's Life*, which addresses issues of scouting and boy's life but probably doesn't address issues of military injustice or squad conformity, sexism, or date rape.[5] There is even *Barbie: The Magazine for Girls*, a quarterly featuring beauty tips, Barbie news and stories, and articles on topics of concern to young girls—hobbies, baby-sitting tips, and sibling rivalry, though no word about the dangers of silicone implants or anorexia or bulimia.[6]

These journals are purveyors of popular culture, that is, they present a selected and unreflective world of surfaces and everyday experiences in such a way that a pedagogy of existence can be displayed. The substance of the magazine itself—the world it presents—is never held up for critique, nor does it look at the values it espouses as anything but universal. The world of the magazine is the world. Goofus is always Goofus in *Highlights*, and his behavior is always inappropriate; in contrast, Gallant always acts correctly. The world presented is almost always monocultural, which is to say that although multiculturalism informs all of the children's magazines (e.g., *Skipping Stones: A Multicultural Children's Quarterly* whose circulation is 2,500 and whose editorial content is designed to "encourage cooperation, creativity, and celebration of cultural and linguistic diversity"), I have never seen actual cases of prejudice appear (as it does appear so centrally in, say, *To Kill a Mockingbird*)—except with regard to odd clothing. All races are represented in Halloween illustrations, though the presence of class and the dangers of tainted treats are not in evidence. In these journals every culture's values are the same, that is, monocultural and seamless, though sometimes the practices between cultures differ. And the cultures are usually presented as complete and not as influenced by and influencing history. Cultures whose values do not coincide with our own Western white culture—such as, say, non–print literate cultures—are rarely if ever presented, nor are, say, differing definitions of literacy within our cultures. Social problems are usually ascribed to individuals; systemic interrogation or critique are also a rarity. You see, children's magazines are not too much different than adult magazines. And since this is an essay on kinderculture—which is not much different than adult popular culture—I can truly only address my adult response to the kinderculture in the popular children's magazines.

> *I listened because it was the price I paid for his attention.*
> —E. L. Doctorow, *The Book of Daniel*

In E. L. Doctorow's novel *The Book of Daniel*, from which I have quoted above, the narrator, Daniel Isaacson, interrogates an aspect of the relationship he has had with his father, a man executed by the U.S. government for conspiring to commit treason by giving atomic secrets to the Soviets. Daniel's narration in the novel is an attempt to construct his life by making connections between all the occasions and people that he can remember in his experience. He is learning to read, to make connections. In this scene he is evaluating the consequences of his father's lessons regarding the ideological content of the productions of popular culture—the magazines and other aspects of popular culture that abound in the home. The effects of such training, as Daniel recalls, was to make of his son a psychic alien, one who has been estranged from the world by the discovery of its devious duplicitousness and insidious superficiality. Daniel has become incapable of being at home in the world in large part because of his father's lessons, and this alienation denies Daniel the knowledge of the origin and realization of his own desire. He can discover pleasure nowhere. And so I want to offer to you a substantial quotation from the book to set the stage for what I would like to think about with regard to the kinderculture of children's magazines. In this passage, Daniel constructs his relationship to his father:

> He wrestled society for my soul. He worked on me to counteract the bad influences of my culture. That was our relationship—his teaching me how to be a psychic alien. That was part of my training. He had to exorcise the influences, the bad spirits. Did I ever wonder why my radio programs had commercials? He'd find me reading the back of the cereal box at breakfast, and break them down and show what it appealed to, how it was intended to make me believe something that wasn't—that eating the cereal would make me an athlete. There were foods one didn't eat, like bananas, because they were the fruit of some notorious exploitation. . . . He gave me pamphlets with titles like *Who Owns America* or *Rulers of the American Press*. When I could barely read. He told me things I could never find in my American History. . . . Putting it all together. *Everything was accounted for: even my comic books which he studied with me, teaching me to recognize and isolate the insidious stereotypes of yellow villains, Semitic villains, Russian villains. . . .* (45–46, emphasis added)

What I want to point out is the relationship between Daniel and his father (Paul), the social interaction that is reading. On the one hand, though Paul decries the substance of popular culture, exposes its ideological and hegemonic bases, it pervades his household in the substance of daily life—the breakfast cereals, the radios (which Paul fixes in his repair shop), the foods that give sustenance to his family, and the print media that his son enthusiastically and enjoyably reads. You see (and I believe), as Paul understands *because he* reads the materials themselves (as I read the magazines of popular culture), that there is no place to escape popular culture. One can't critique a culture until it has been seen. TV may be a vast wasteland (I do not believe that it is or ever has been; traditional school-based reading instruction, Madeleine Grumet [1988] notes, has prepared us for television and not the other way around), but one has first to view it to know what a vast wasteland might look like. So in reading the materials of popular culture—the comic books and magazines Daniel consumes—Daniel's father, Paul, insists on exploring the operations of that popular culture, its subterfuges, its deceptions, its mechanics.

I understand Paul's instruction as a form of reading education. Paul is teaching Daniel to read. That is, Paul is revealing to Daniel the world in the word and the word in the world—and how to find the world in the word and the word in the world. He is teaching him to read against the grain; I think finally it is an activity of which I can only approve, given my own understanding of popular culture and of reading. However, there is something insidious in Paul's attentions to his son's growth, something that has always troubled me in this novel and in my life. Finally Paul discovers only purpose in reading and not pleasure. Unlike *Highlights*, there is no fun in reading here, *only* purpose; but also very much like *Highlights*, there is no fun *without* purpose.

And the result of Paul's work is to create out of his son a psychic alien, one who is estranged from the world in which he lives. Perhaps more disturbing, Daniel is estranged from himself as well, and that must be a painful position, because from this position one experiences isolation and alienation as powerful and as real as that which the left (with which I align myself) argues results from the reification and commodification that is the work of popular culture. Discovering—being made to discover—the ideological basis of the popular world situates Daniel in a world space by himself, dubious of every act and at home nowhere. All of the materials in his daily world are tainted; one must exist outside of the world in order to be free from its oppression, but this could mean only death.

Happiness and desire are unfulfillable in the world. However, since one's desires can be realized only by the daily world, desires are ideologically suspect. From this position no place is safe or comfortable. Paul, in making all the connections himself for his son, Daniel, gives him no opportunity to learn for himself the operations of popular culture—in which Daniel so eagerly partakes—that he might discover his desire in popular culture. Rather, Paul poisons the very breakfast cereal that Daniel eats. Paul denies Daniel's place in the word and, as a result, in the world as well. I would not have that unhappiness for my daughters—who would? You see, Paul occupies the word as dangerously as the popular culture he decries: Daniel is a psychic alien because his own pleasures have been denied in the word—from which pleasures he might have discovered his own desires and how they are manipulated by popular culture. Daniel's alienation is not only from his culture but from himself. He can take pleasure nowhere because his pleasure has been denied. What remains is pain.

> *Meet the new boss. Same as the old boss.*
>
> —Pete Townsend in "Won't Get Fooled Again," *Who's Next* (1971)

> Admitting that the kinderculture of children's magazines is popular culture, what am I to do with it? I certainly cannot do away with it: One popular culture always replaces another. And besides, what my daughter does not gather from the magazines I exclude she will harvest from the library books she brings home to read. I suffer the dilemma of Paul Isaacson, but I would like to conceptualize it in an alternative manner: How do I teach Emma to read so that she might discover popular cultures even as she enjoys them (as I do when I read *People* or *National Enquirer* or *Newsweek*)? They make me angry at times, but I enjoy them nonetheless. How do I play Toto to my daughter's Dorothy so that the Wizard can be exposed as merely a man but who will still get her back to her home in Kansas?

> I would not have my daughter be a psychic alien, but I know enough about cultural studies and Marxism to understand that not to teach her these things would create a psychic alien of a different sort. One who will never look like Barbie and live regretting it. One who will search for Prince Charming and find only toads. One who thinks that all the news that's fit to print is anything less than a corporate decision.

I learned to read formally in school. I learned the meaning of words. "Look, Dick. See Jane. See Jane run." Ad nauseam. All I remember from reading instruction is the familiar sight-word methodology. I learned that words have meaning and that reading comprehension resulted from the accumulation of meaningful words slammed together, as in the familiar model of atomic fission detonations that permeated life during the 1950s. Meaning was produced by the explosion, and emotion, like radiation, followed as the aftereffect. I never conceived of an alternative perspective on reading; I spent my primary and secondary school years mining for gold in the received texts of the selective tradition. I read these texts as I read the magazines of my popular culture: for lessons and information.

I recall *Hot Rod* by John Felsen because it was about youth gone astray: It was explicitly meant to caution youth against racing—the kind that might be associated with James Dean and Marlon Brando and that was reinforced in the popular culture of rock 'n' roll: "Last Kiss" by J. Frank Wilson and the Cavaliers, "Dean Man's Curve" by Jan and Dean, and "Tell Laura I Love Her" by Ray Peterson. I read *Tale of Two Cities* and waited for the blood of the French Revolution to come alive for me but only remember Madame Defarge sitting and knitting. Wouldn't she have made a fitting picture on the cover of *People* or *Newsweek*? I consumed Ernest Hemingway because he seemed to represent in fiction what I saw in the textbooks and magazines of popular culture: a world governed by machismo, by war, by male action and female submission and silence. I learned to read the material of popular cultures in school in formal reading instruction and in formal texts.

But I learned to read informally out of school and also in the realms of popular culture. I was lucky to have lived in the particular confluence of time when this popular culture turned on itself and yet was readily available through the radios that Paul Isaacson fixed and through the hi-fi recordings that became ubiquitous on the shelves and bookcases of America. My parents had one: I used it for purposes they could not imagine. I learned from those voices that texts did not necessarily contain wisdom: Dylan spittingly sang, "You've read all of F. Scott Fitzgerald's books. . . . /But you know something's happening, but you don't know what it is, do you, Mr. Jones?" The Rolling Stones railed contemptuously about a "man [who] comes on the radio telling me more and more about some useless information, supposed to try my imagination." The Beatles spoke satirically about the person who produced the texts of popular culture because "I want a job so I want to be a 'back writer, paperback writer."

I learned from these and many, many more how to read popular culture even as I engaged joyfully in it. For there was no getting around the fact that rock 'n' roll was popular: It probably sold many more copies than the periodicals of popular culture that I found in my environment. I was discovering my desire in it—pleasure—even as it taught me how to be cautious of that desire. I was taught doubt; I learned to doubt. I learned to produce knowledge. The language was often cryptic, some-

times opaque—it had to be; we were talking about forbidden things—
but I learned how to read because those meanings I produced were not
the same as those of my parents. They never understood.[7] And those
meanings worked. Even when they put them on the cover of the popular
journals these people never seemed to take seriously the form that was
taking them so seriously. I learned irony.

I would expect that the magazines of popular culture, both the adult
and children's varieties, offer a perspective that derives from the culture
in which they are solidly steeped, a culture from which they emanate
and to which they owe allegiance, reverence, and even tribute. Now the
elite always decries the stuff of popular culture; Plato meant to keep
music and poetry out of the *Republic* because their meanings could not
be controlled. Allan Bloom and William Bennett would control the materials of the curriculum. The religious right would censor the libraries.
There is no end to the decrying of popular culture. Yet I would suspect
that these magazines of popular culture for children are no better or
worse than those that permeate the adult world. Kinderculture mirrors
the selective tradition of adult culture; its purposes are the production of
citizens who maintain the present power relation, which focuses much
of the power in a small band of others.

I think it is necessary that we adults teach children to read their magazines of popular culture. We must allow our children to discover themselves in the word and the world in the word. We must ask of them more
questions than we answer; we must have available ways of knowing that
provide alternative perspectives to the responses to our questions.
Emma wants the Barbie she sees advertised on television, but she knows
that the commercial is meant to entice her to buy. We must allow our
children to discover their desire in the materials of popular culture even
as they learn to critique that desire and—we would hope but cannot demand—that they learn to reexamine it. We should teach our children—
using the magazines of popular culture, of course—so that they may
read; we would not have them be psychic aliens but become effective
critics of the cultures in which they live. I will not deny my children the
pleasures of playing *Intermezzo*. I will not deny my children. But I will
help them learn.

Tonight I sit with Emma and we look through *Highlights*. We read
about a boy who fearfully envisions the opposing soccer goalie as a
many-legged tarantula. During the course of the story he learns how hu-
manly fallible the goalie actually is when, in approaching the goal during the final seconds of play, he accidentally burps, causing the goalie to
laugh, lose his concentration, and let in the winning goal. The two shake
hands as friends. Emma and I tell a few jokes. We read another story, this
one about Native Americans. What else does Emma know about Native

Americans? I ask. A few things. Does she notice that the Native Americans are always making peace with the European, white strangers? I quote and explain Buffy Saint Marie's song "Where Have the Buffalo Gone." We talk of Thanksgiving. And then it is time for sleep. Emma says we should sing a song, and she gets to choose which one. I agree. We sing:

> Oh you can't scare me I'm sticking to the Union,
> I'm sticking to the Union, I'm sticking to the Union,
> Oh you can't scare me I'm sticking to the Union
> Sticking to the Union, 'til the day I die.

Good night, Emma. Pleasant dreams.

Notes

1. The journals I read are popular among a small cultural group and this, by all definition, qualifies them as journals of popular culture. But we prefer to be us.

2. It interests me to consider that the adult horror at the popularity of *Barney* may be situated in the disdain Barney evidences for adults. Unlike characters in *Sesame Street*, Barney pays no attention to adults during his show.

3. See Phillipe Aries's *Centuries of Childhood*, or David Nasaw's *Schooled to Order*, or my own "It's Alright Ma (I'm Only Bleeding): Education as the Practice of Social Violence Against the Child" (*Taboo*, 1995).

4. Let us not be naïve: These magazines are intended to make someone money.

5. I read the other day that a Muslim was denied leadership in the Scouts because of religion. So much for multicultural issues. I do not think this issue will be addressed in *Boy's Life*.

6. For adults there is the *Soap Opera Digest*, among others.

7. I recall when my parents, upon listening to Bob Dylan sing "Stuck Inside of Mobile with the Memphis Blues Again," derisively commented that he sounded like he was in pain. What they never knew was that we were.

References

Benjamin, W. (1969). In H. Arendt, ed., *Illuminations*. Trans. H. Zohn. New York: Schocken Books.
Doctorow, E. L. (1971). *The Book of Daniel*. New York: Bantam Books.
Grumet, M. R. (1988). *Bitter Milk*. Amherst: University of Massachusetts Press.
Silin, J. (1995). *Sex, Death, and the Education of Children: Our Passion for Ignorance in the Age of AIDS*. New York: Teachers College Press.

9

Professional Wrestling and Youth Culture: Teasing, Taunting, and the Containment of Civility

Aaron David Gresson III

ARIANE, MY DAUGHTER, was two years old when she saw her first professional wrestling match on TV. We were traveling away from home and had spent the night in a motel. Trying to find a suitable children's show for her while her mother and I readied for the next leg of our journey, we came upon Saturday-morning wrestling. Wanting to see the latest cast of characters, I left the show on, and Ariane became immediately mesmerized by the match of the moment: A huge black male, Papa Shango, was working voodoo on his handsome, courageous, but clearly overwhelmed white opponent. Dressed in native costume, complete with his staff and human skull, this fearsome creature called forth fire and smoke (stage effects), making his opponent spit forth some greenish liquid reminiscent of Linda Blair in *The Exorcist*. The arena audience screamed and jeered, my daughter's eyes bulged in their sockets, and I only just managed to free myself to change the channel and break the spell that held both her and me.

I cannot say with certainty what my daughter saw or understood by this encounter with professional wrestling. I do know that when I reached for her, after changing the television channel, she initially recoiled from me. Was I momentarily Papa Shango? Had she seen me when she watched him inflicting great though faked pain upon his hapless opponent? It would be fruitless to speculate long on these questions. They are obviously unanswerable. Still, although we cannot know what Ariane saw and felt, there are some related questions worth asking that might allow conjecture. What place does professional wrestling have in the lives of the young? Is the effect of these constructed dramas largely benign, or is there some unhealthy dimension to this sport?

In this chapter I consider these questions by exploring some of the psychological and cultural dimensions of professional wrestling in the construction of consciousness in youth. I first briefly describe the structure and function of professional wrestling. Here, as a prelude to examining the ways in which wrestling engages youth's self-understanding, I will consider the peculiar constructions it has taken within recent American history. Next I reflect on psychosocial implications of wrestling's organizing themes for youth. I conclude with a reading of the possibly unintentional role wrestling plays in reactionary cultural politics.

Professional Wrestling: Its Structure and Function

Somewhere around the age of fourteen I discovered the world of wrestling. This was a remarkable event, as I reflect on it some thirty-five years later. After all, back in 1960 wrestling had not yet become the multimillion-dollar multimedia drama it is today. When I attended those Thursday-night matches at the Norfolk, Virginia, arena, I was often *the* black audience. Back then—as now—professional wrestling was working-class and white entertainment. Few racial minorities were even used as wrestlers: BoBo Brazil and Chief Big Heart were the notable tokens. Virtually no racial minorities were present at the live arena fights. (Even in the 1970s, one critic of the sport could declare: "To their credit blacks don't participate much inside or outside the ring" [K. Mano, 1974, p. 705]). For the most part, wrestlers portraying white ethnics made up the local arena cards as promoters sought to provide identifiable heroes for the hometown crowds.

Still, there is a logic to why I, despite the relative nonparticipation of African Americans in the wrestling ritual, was turned on by this entertainment: Professional wrestling engages something primal in humans. This primal quality—passion—is triggered by the twin cultural themes encoded in the professional drama of wrestling: There is goodness in the world; but evil seems to be ubiquitous. Perhaps this is a first clue to the significance of professional wrestling in the United States and to how its structure and function have evolved to the present forms.

Modern Professional Wrestling: The Struggle of Good and Evil

Most wrestlers are cast as either good or evil. Within their carnival world, the wrestlers call the good guy a "face" and the bad guy a "heel." The referee is the judge; he stands for justice. But justice can be conveniently blind, and the referee often sides with the "evil" wrestlers. This "unholy alliance" is, in fact, what stacks the odds in favor of evil. By managing, routinely, to miss blatant "illegal acts"—actions perfectly evident to the audience—the referee induces the audience to identify with the "face." Roland Barthes (1972, 21, 22) has argued:

> But what wrestling is above all meant to portray is a purely moral concept: that of justice. Justice is the embodiment of a possible transgression. It is therefore easy to understand why out of five wrestling matches, only about one is fair. One must realize, let it be repeated, that "fairness" here is a role or a genre, as in the theater: the rules do not at all constitute a real constraint; they are the conventional appearances of fairness. So that in actual fact a fair fight is nothing but an exaggeratedly polite one. One must understand, of course, here, that all these polite actions are brought to the notice of the public by the most conventional gestures of fairness: shaking hands, raising the arms, ostensibly avoiding a fruitless hold which would detract from the perfection of the contest.

The drama described by Barthes is a modern invention. Prior to the mid-nineteenth century wrestling was largely a participant sport. It was almost solely controlled and attended by those participating in it (Ball 1990, 52). Only after 1900 did the audience become directly involved in the sport, only then were the themes of good and evil organizing themes for the passions and performances of audience and wrestlers alike.

When wrestlers themselves were largely the audience, personal development was an important motivation for participation: "The building of skill, physical agility, and general health, the learning of sportsmanship, the excitement of competition and the development of self-defense techniques . . . were all stressed" (Ball 1990, 52). Today professional wrestling has virtually no emphasis on personal development. It is orchestrated for an audience whose main interest seems to be the spectacle of brutality and violence. What took place with this shift from amateur to professional wrestler was a shift from personal development to communal celebration of certain basic yet largely destructive proclivities. This is perhaps best seen in the teasing and taunting that the drama calls forth in the audience. To achieve this level of audience involvement, wrestling promoters turned to stereotyping the wrestlers themselves. For example, professional wrestling traditionally engaged the audiences by staging battles between local favorites and a variety of "aliens" or "others."

One of the favorite stops for promoters at this time was the ethnic communities of large cities, where wrestlers would play in school auditoriums or community centers. A favorite trick was to manufacture ethnic heroes billed as Italian in Italian neighborhoods or German in German neighborhoods. It was not unusual for stars to change ethnicities and names overnight to cater to a specific ethnic crowd (Ball 1990, 51).

This form of ethnic stereotyping was intended to overcome the boredom associated with amateur wrestling. Whatever the rationale, this playing to the audience no doubt had an impact on the values and attitudes of the audience. But what precisely did professional wrestling bring forth through the use of ethnic stereotypes? Was it truly nothing more than the juxtaposing of good and evil, the emotional lashing-out at injustice, as suggested earlier by Roland Barthes?

Unfortunately, Barthes's analysis is insightful and useful, especially for understanding the European matches of the pre-1960 period; it does not seem sufficient for understanding the deeper passions—violence and rage—characterizing the modern American wrestling world. Professional wrestling has gone from a relatively boring participant ritual to an action-packed form of theater. Although its progress as a sport may be questioned, it is clear that wrestling has adapted to the ritual needs of audiences and successfully provided spectacular shows in return for spectacular profits. And the drama it has become is contagious, especially among the poor and oppressed. A case in point is Mexico. It was recently reported that in Mexico professional wrestlers are considered to be warriors, superheroes, celebrities, and saints (*Atlanta Journal and Atlanta Constitution*, November 26, 1992). Such representations belie the more brutal, destructive side of this entertainment.

That professional wrestlers might be viewed as saintly is uncanny, if we recall Barthes's observation that wrestling is symbolically a morality play. But such representations belie the more brutal, destructive side of this entertainment. Wrestling is violence; it is brutal and savage. Yet some argue that the faked aspects of the fights themselves neutralize the sport's brutality. Challenging those who view professional wrestling as a harmless form of lower-class entertainment are those who see the psychological and social problems accompanying it. For instance, William C. Martin (1972, 86) wrote in *Atlantic Monthly*, "Professional wrestling offers fans an almost unparalleled opportunity to indulge aggressive and violent impulses. . . . They want hitting and kicking and stomping and bleeding. Especially bleeding." Further, it has been cogently argued by Michael Ball (1990, 61) that

[although] the actual inflicting of pain and the punishing of opponents are more histrionics than fact, that does not diminish the glorification of such tactics. In such a scenario, wrestling becomes a lamination . . . of brutality. Its theatrics are not meant to diminish the viciousness and ferocity of wrestling but to enhance it while saving the wrestlers themselves from real injury. Wrestling, while containing little or no actual brutality, becomes the embodiment of brutality.

Thus, a ritual drama pitting good against evil, or local ethnic heroes against some other less favored ethnic group member, is not the essence of professional wrestling: Animal savagery is the drug that has entranced so many to this sport. It remains true that justice, good, and evil are organizing themes for the ritual drama called wrestling. But the passions called forth are not a better understanding of justice, good, and evil in the world—or even one's own small part of the world. On the contrary, the taunting and teasing only serve to intensify and deepen the rage and anger within one. The taste for blood, so to speak, has been increased by a steady diet of manufactured madness, where minute after minute men maul and maim each other. That the damage is fictional has been seen, by some, as exonerating; however, it has been correctly observed that the very fakeness of the violence betrays the sickness of the message. Beyond this, televised fights add yet something more to the celebration of ethnic chauvinism and the thirst for bleeding. It has brought the manipulation of oppressive stereotypes into the purview of youth like my daughter (whose only guilt was a father whose curiosity exposed her to the scary Papa Shango).

Postmodern Wrestling and Oppressive Stereotypes

The growth of television and professional wrestling has been seen as symbiotic, and the expansion of the stereotyping tendencies of this entertainment is very much implicated in this mutuality. Through the course of time wrestling went from a participant sport to audience entertainment. The audience also changed, or rather enlarged, to include an anonymous television audience. These two changes—from sport to entertainment and anonymous, diversified television audience—are critical factors in the arrival of wrestling as a media-driven ritual that exploits negative stereotypes.

Wrestling promoters would likely deny any intentional negative stereotyping; they would most probably argue that their characters are reflections of audience desire or just harmless fun, humor (Gresson 1995). Even more, they would certainly deny a connection between the televised wrestling and an intensified exploitation of negative stereotypes. Yet, writing in the *Saturday Evening Post* nearly three decades ago, Myron Cope (1966, 90) saw the collusive bond: "The advent of television in 1947 multiplied fans at least a thousandfold, and created such outrageous caricatures as wrestlers in long blond hair, Indian headdress, and fur capes. This mixture of showmanship and violence packed arenas as tightly in New York City as in Wichita Falls, Texas."

Interestingly, wrestling promoters have deemphasized the violence, arguing instead that television enlarges the demography of the audience to include the middle class and other traditionally absent groups. This position has not been substantiated by the little available research (Ball 1990). What is evident, however, is the persistence at arena matches of those behaviors associated with the working lower class. But let's assume that a more diverse audience has become attracted to televised matches. What precisely is being presented?

Professional wrestling began to prosper through television while America was entering the radical 1960s. A dominant feature of this period has been the various liberation movements: black power, women's power, kid's power, gray power, gay power, and white power. Because wrestling promoters have reproduced daily events and dramas in their wrestling matches, they have reproduced the very stereotypes that were challenged in the 1960s and 1970s liberation movements. Thus, ethnic neighborhood scenarios were replaced with larger societal themes.

There are two major issues embedded in the contemporary multimedia manufacturing of "wrestlemania." First, there is the fact that promoters have settled on using the stuff of daily life to construct their dramas. Included here are classist, sexist, and racist themes that reproduce specific characters such as the Junk Yard Dog (a black male), Miss Elizabeth (a pretty but dominated white female), Macho Man (a narcissistic, sexist white male), Country Cousins (two unkempt "hillbillies"), and the Ultimate Warrior (a muscular blond/white Indian brave). Michael Ball's (1990, 94) characterization of Junk Yard Dog is suggestive of the stereotyping issue: "JYD, as he is known, wears a spiked collar with a heavy chain attached. The crowd throws him dog biscuits which he eagerly retrieves and eats. JYD is characterized as a poor black who grew up in the projects and survived through street tactics, including violence and theft." It is perhaps clear why blacks are not heavily represented in the wrestling drama as either wrestler or audience: The basic characterization of black wrestlers is unabashedly racist. Few blacks are likely able to disassociate themselves sufficiently from the regular negative stereotyping of blacks to enjoy the live matches. But the increased use of negative social stereotypes to stimulate the audience is not the only modification televised wrestling has witnessed.

By using television and the special effects of high technology, the old traditional stereotypes both reach a wider potential audience and impact in a more intimate way. Additionally:

> On television, the audience acts as a combination backdrop and cueing device for home viewers. The audience is lighted as deeply as possible, and the lighting drops abruptly where the audience ends. This emphasizes the large audience-filled auditorium events . . . and gives the impression that

the audience continues into the darkness in case of smaller . . . events. The cheers and boos of the studio audience act in the same way as canned laughter in situation comedies, cueing a similar response from home viewers (Ball 1990, 75).

Perhaps one of the more critical outcomes of this use of the television audience is the domestication of the brutality: Anyone watching televised matches cannot help seeing—and being influenced by—the large percentage of females and small children in the audience. For some time now female attendance at professional wrestling matches has been a paradox: Professional wrestling is unabashedly sexist, so why do women attend? Various answers have been offered, but none of these are conclusive. What is usually agreed is that professional wrestling is a "family affair." The presence of women and children as regulars at the wrestling matches affects the structure of the arena; it is not a males-only site. We might say that the "rhetorical condition" (Asante and Atwater 1986) or persuasive message of the setting itself dissuades accusations of sexism, racism, or brutality. The brutality and violence enacted on the wrestling mat reaches a televised audience buffered by a live audience of men, women, and children. This fact, moreover, clues us to the complex character of the audience and highlights the profound fact that children are learning to receive and own wrestling's stereotypes and the audience's shared savagery under the watchful eye and collusion of their parents.

The Psychology of Wrestling

Let me now suggest how wrestling impinges on the psyche of the developing child. First, wrestling rehearses "horseplay." As such, it is a ritual expression of something very familiar to most children: Children wrestle and tussle "naturally." Without the presence of adults or other "judges" to regulate this play and aggression among children, there are two or three basic scenarios that have psychological implications. First, through the bodily contact that wrestling allows, children become psychosexually aroused, in the Freudian sense, that is, they may feel strong connective arousal ("libido"), strong disconnected feeling ("aggression"), or a combination of both ("ambivalence"). Most of us have at one time or the other during childhood known these feelings. If we were stronger, we pushed on with the attack; if we were weaker, we pulled away, often getting angry at the other's overwhelming power.

In short, wrestling, even more so than boxing, carries powerful emotive potential. I believe that it is this highly eroticized potential that is critical to the child's attraction to wrestling. The developing child is at the height of her emotional vulnerability and exposed to two simultaneous fictive constructions: One is the possibility of these strong, powerful men to brutalize each other without serious harm to anyone; the other is the "naturalness" of conflict and conflict resolution through violence. Because the child may come to wrestling by way of play, she or he may already have an experiential basis for these two constructions of professional wrestling. Attendance at live matches or watching televised fights becomes a context for expanding the child's understanding of this "natural" child's play or conflict. New layers of meaning are offered, and a validated context—"they do it on TV"—as well.

Professional wrestling, then, becomes a participant in the education of children regarding the use of their bodies on another. But children occupy different positions in society; the need to understand and use their bodies differs accordingly. Two boys may wrestle each other without much criticism, but a boy and girl, or two boys of different classes or races, may be less favorably received if they are found locked in bodily combat. Thus, race and gender influence our understandings of wrestling.

But what is most important is that wrestling is primarily working, lower-class, white entertainment. There is evidence that some middle-class children do watch televised wrestling matches; there is even a minority audience at live arena matches. Yet by and large the wrestling drama is intended for and supported by lower-class whites. And discussion of kinderculture must address this specific condition.

Wrestling Social Consciousness and Class

Professional wrestling has taken on a peculiar or uncanny function for the lower class: In the years before 1950, the chief frustration of white ethnics was "the social order," and "good" and "evil" were the organizing principles. To exploit these conditions, it was sufficient to portray different ethnic groups as the good and bad guys. Today, "government" is the chief frustration, and "affirmative action" and "white as victim" are the organizing principles. Accordingly, the wrestling drama has routinely reconstructed its rituals to rehearse a recovery from the evils associated with stereotypes reminiscent of the radical liberation period. Characters such as the Million Dollar Man, Slick, Virgil, Junk Yard Dog, Coco Beware, Macho Man, Sergeant Slaughter, Sheri, Miss Elizabeth, and the Nasty Boys are constructed to achieve this end.

Professional wrestling's fuel is the outrage generated among the audience: Truly, like the stand-up comic, the professional wrestler "lives for the taunt or tease." This is so because the constructed action, "professional wrestling," is contrived for an audience that is aware, at some level, that this cannot be real (for the most part). Yet the audience experiences the action as real. This capacity to experience the "unreal" as "real" is precisely what makes the wrestlers' gestures "genuine" and the constructed stereotype "true."

The traditional appeal of wrestling to the lower-status person has been interpreted by social researchers and critics as a function of the "defective mentality" attributed to them. For example, Gregory P. Stone and Ramon A. Oldenburg (1967, 526) argue, "Lower-status persons seldom question the concrete world about them. Consequently, they are more susceptible to staging than persons on higher status levels."

Perhaps "concrete operations" are more evident among lower-class persons than middle-class persons. I think that the evidence on this point is mixed and best explained in terms of specific contexts or issues. There are many issues about which middle-class persons seem as conservative—that is, gullible, rigid, and inflexible—as those identified as lower-class. The predominance of lower-class persons as wrestling fans is related less to their concreteness than to their need for certain "safety valves." Professional wrestling allows a particular group, privileged by skin color but damned because of class, to vent its frustrations. A variety of working-class whites share this need.

Have you ever seen the "little old ladies" at wrestling matches? In years prior to the 1980s, they were a familiar part at arenas. It was common for the television cameras—again, in a normalizing gesture—to focus in on one of these "small, frail creatures" flaring out at the wrestler with her purse. This sight, despite its relative infrequency, invites us to see professional wrestling as intergenerational in its appeal. And there is a level of truth to this rhetorical turn. Wrestling audiences include a wide range of age groups—from little tots to senior citizens. Their presence together is suggestive of the familial aspect of the sport—a quality shared in common with many other sports. And yet this quality differs from those other family-oriented sports because it invites a certain kind of participation: emotional outburst. In recent history this shared quality across the life span found expression in such post–"Black Power" concepts as "Kid Power" and "Gray Power," allusions to the empowerment needs of children and the elderly.

But what precisely are these empowerment needs? I believe that they are essentially the need for nonalienation, nondetachment from the heart of the community, the heart of—and here is the clear disjuncture—the "heart of the social order." Of course, there is no heart within social orders; this is the essential message of the early sociologists, men such as Ferdinand Toinnes and Robert Redfield, who wrote cogently about the shift from the agrarian communities to the urban societies, a shift away from more intimate and "primitive" visions and missions to more rational and legalistic forms of understanding and living. Of course, it was precisely at the zenith of the industrial revolution and urbanization that the old became obsolete and the youth became exploitable capital.

I believe that wrestling, always an intimate form of connection and communication, became even more pivotal for expressing certain frustrations around self and other—and the nature and quality of the relational bond and contract in force. It is here that wrestling becomes especially pertinent to unfulfilled desire bordering on angst and in search of catharsis—these terms being particular to the rise of modernism.

It is against this contextual backdrop that the problem of child consciousness must be understood. I return briefly to my opening story: Ariane's entrancement by the televised drama and her recoiling from my touch immediately upon watching a black man seemingly hurting a white man. I shied away from constructing her understanding of the wrestling event or her reaction to me. But let me now use that event to construct my own understanding of the invitation such a spectacle offered her young mind: She saw a black man dressed differently than any of the white males in the ring; she saw him do "magic."

All this is seen by the young child, whether at the arena or on television. The difference afforded by viewing site is thus less significant than might be otherwise expected. This is so because the oppressive codes of society around race, sexuality, gender, and so forth are paralleled in the larger society. The consciousness of the young child, or even the adolescent, is greatly influenced by the given. The given social codes of oppression are among the organizing codes of the society that the child uses to make sense of her or his place in society and her or his relationship to others, especially different others. For example, the concept "white boys can't jump" is a social construction that belies experience; white males can jump, but this fact is compromised by a pervasive social message that jumping is an animal quality possessed largely by black males as evidenced in the person of a Michael Jordan.

This illustration is one indicator of what we mean by consciousness. By consciousness we mean the awareness of oneself as self, the ability to look at oneself as object, to assess one's place and processes. During the years of six to twenty, the age range most associated with attending and watching wrestling matches on television, the child is especially aware of his/her body and increasing competition with others. Wrestling is full of social codes that impinge on the operation of consciousness in the young. This is particularly true of the working-class male youth because of his special investment in the rituals and dramas of wrestling. In an important sense, professional wrestling helps teach the working, lower-class family how to feel and express its feelings. If it is true that this group is nonreflective with respect to the ritual drama called professional wrestling, perhaps this is so merely because consciousness would be even more dangerous and deadly. Remember, wrestling for some is like religion—and religion has been long understood to have addictive qualities, to be, in the words of Karl Marx, "an opiate of the people." Yet despite this capacity to contain the bodily explosions of the working-class white family, professional wrestling represents the occasion to transgress the codes of "civility" as much as it encourages the rehearsing of society's oppressive codes toward women and various minorities.

The Containment of Civility

Civility, the soothing and constructive channeling of irrational, erratic, and sometimes destructive passions into socially mediated and sanctioned behaviors, is never a complete achievement. Sigmund Freud is credited with saying that humans are only partially socializable. By this he meant that we forever retain spaces or places within our being that may say "No!" to the reigning social order. Thus, for example, society may dictate that shoes be worn by its citizens, but some will find occasions for going barefoot, even turning it into a countercultural gesture, as during the so-called "Hippie" era.

Civility, for the socially oppressed, the least fortunate, becomes a yoke precisely because society's strictures seem to do double duty with respect to them: They already occupy a "one-down" position due to the machinations of the "cognitive elite"; yet they are told by a "blind" social order to "behave," to "play by the rules." And for the most part the masses exercise their agency within the boundaries set for them. But then there are times when they, like the hero of the movie *Network,* open the window wide and shout: "We're not going to take it anymore!"

This, I believe, is largely the emotional environment that professional wrestling came to occupy in the years before television. Audience participation was an opportunity for emoting. And though some saw clearly its role as perpetuating violence (Arms et al. 1979), whatever violence occurred was restricted to the world of the lower class. Indeed, what was perhaps seen but not voiced was the convergence of mid-twentieth-century professional wrestling with the two forms that existed in the late 1800s, when both football and wrestling were under siege as brutal sport:

> The professional style was used in urban areas and was bureaucratically restricted by rules and regulations. A referee was always present to enforce the rules and often the matches lasted for many hours. By contrast, the

rural style of wrestling resembled a barroom brawl. Circuses, county fairs, and individual promoters would often feature the "World's Champion," willing to wrestle any challengers. Because of the unsophisticated nature and lack of knowledge of rules of many challengers in small towns, rules were few and enforcement was lax. Wrestlers were often unequal in ability, so the matches were relatively short, bloody, and action-packed (Ball 1990, 41).

Over time and through several transitional phases of the sport, these two styles converged. And because professional wrestling is essentially orchestrated, the "real violence" is minimal. But the emotions stimulated continue to be much like those of the rural wrestling of the past; it is these emotions that were largely an excess of affect or feeling associated with the frustrations necessary to group life. For group life demanded, under the economy of civility, the suppression and sublimation of affect that might lead to conflict and destruction. And that segment of American society permitted to address this suppression of affect is largely the working, lower-class white. Other lower-class groups—African American, Native American, and so on—share the class frustrations but were not permitted the exercise of this "safety valve." Ironically, this access to a restricted—"for whites only"—mode of acting out, while itself repressive, serves as a kind of status symbol, evidence that even the poor white is superior to "those other wretched souls."

There is also evidence that some of these people actually internalized feelings toward various wrestler archetypes, sometimes attacking them in the arena as well as on the streets (Ball 1990). By and large, however, wrestling and its impact on the imaginations and behaviors of the citizenry seemed to be a rather provincial matter. I have had reports from several teachers (students in my class on minority education) concerning the growing popularity of wrestling among working-class white males at school. They note that these youth like to try out the various wrestling holds on each other.

The arrival of television and, later, the pluralistic, radical 1960s effected a dramatic repackaging and remarketing of this primal play of suppressed passion. Yet the important quality remained this capacity to "live in the spectacle." As citizens, the audience relives the constructions of "fairness," "evil," and "good" through the visceral, the physiocerebral. This is important: Wrestling takes place in the audience's mind and is cathartic precisely because the audience is engaged in the ritual. This ability to enter the arena, to taunt and be taunted, to scream and yell, unabashedly, at the spectacle of injustice, vanity, and shameless and shameful hype, is critical for the "civilized" management of the necessity of "civility." After all, the central hypocrisy of civility is that truth and justice are essential and complete even as we live its barbarism and destructiveness.

The Middle Class as Voyeur

The middle-class spectator also derives enhancement from the wrestling match. Whereas the more sophisticated viewer may disavow belief in the "realness" of the action, he may still vicariously join in the pleasures obtained from the spectacle. Thus the expression, "Look at what they're doing!" Glee, at the very least, is contained in this utterance by the slightly detached, deeply amused, and entertained "elite viewer." This "social distance"—through giving tacit recognition to professional wrestling in much the fashion as I describe about my own interest in the sport—is part of the oppressiveness of the middle class. To be sure, many middle-class persons refuse to watch, to give "life" and license to the sport. But isn't this too a role in the structural arrangement? I am here reminded of a favorite comeback of KKK apologists when facing off with so-called white liberals: "You're just like me, you're racist too; you let me do the dirty work, say what we really feel." Perhaps this gaze from afar—in the privacy of our television rooms—is the most subtle and deadly oppressiveness of professional wrestling. What precisely do we mean when we say "look at them"? Are we not fusing both wrestler and audience, constructing them as an "other" without subjectivity? Are they truly mere "peasants," "mindless automatons," willing to believe anything, watch anything, do anything? And if they are, what does that say about us, for doesn't the lower working class exist, in part, because of those of us who consider ourselves middle class? And aren't their frustrations and their drugs also partly constructions of those of us who gaze upon them?

And what of our children's vulnerability to professional wrestling? Has not our quest for and formulation of civility created this vulnerability? For professional wrestling partially thrives because it serves as a corrective to the "denial of play" where play is read as an unprescribed, indeterminate possibility, an explosion of energy. The rise of civility is an assault on play; this assault, moreover, is signaled in genteel situations—when two youngsters lock in combat—with the exhortation "Stop it!" The exhortation to "Stop it!" is, after all, inspired by a need for order, stability, containment. These are precisely the threatened objects of professional wrestling as unharnessed energy. To be sure, wrestling does entail discipline, order, and application of will and body to a set task and timeline. But the spectacle itself, beyond the control of the professional, invites chaos.

Conclusion

Professional wrestling allows one segment of American society, notably the lower-class white ethnic, to derive primary entertainment and enhancement from the variously constructed rituals. In much the same way as stock-car racing,[1] fishing and hunting, and country music are available to all Americans but earmarked for the working-class white, so is professional wrestling. And through this entertainment all are invited to internalize certain oppressive stereotypes, but it is for the working-class white male to assimilate all of the petty biases associated with the stereotypes and to construct his consciousness of self as a physically violent, aggressive self. This fact, moreover, clues us to the character of the audience and the profound significance that children are learning to receive and own these and related stereotypes under the watchful eye and collusion of their parents.

In order for one to understand the consciousness of the child in relation to wrestling, I believe one must understand wrestling as possessing control and containment qualities not unlike basketball does for African American youth. We must see its evolution from a participant-dominated sport to rural and urban poor entertainment in much the same way as stock-car racing, rodeos, and country music have become "proprietary" for this class.

Professional wrestling is a massive enterprise. With more than three major promotional organizations, thousands of wrestlers, prime-time and weekend matches, and a strong presence in the toy industry, this once small-time sport has grown to multinational stature.

Capitalism's economic elites control the drama and its operation. Fuel for the drama comes from the critical events marking everyday life. Primal passions are elicited by the dramas as they have come to be played out. These passions are unlikely to be stimulated by a more boring form of wrestling—as the history of the sport indicates (Ball 1990). Still, there is evidence that even the promoters are unwilling to push certain buttons; for example, racial conflict is not dramatized for the most part.

Because wrestling has become largely a family affair, it is not readily feasible for parents to critique the drama. To ask this is to miss the current status of the sport. The family that wrestles together stays together. Self-reflection is thus suicidal to family unity, solidarity, togetherness.

Parents are most essential to containing the play, especially for the very young child who is less able to distinguish play from real physical violence. Of course, the more significant danger is the possibility of misreading the kinds of things that the wrestlers can really do without severe damage to themselves—this is, after all, what is really concealed. Helping children to see what really is involved in terms of physical preparations for these stunts is one possibility. Another is introducing the child to amateur wrestling. This form of wrestling retains much of the fast-paced excitement of the professional match but employs clear, real rules and procedures.

Ultimately, I believe, professional wrestling's containment function will be recognized and its brutality—once recognized as such—will be identified by its name and societal purpose. Until then children and adults alike will continue to rely upon it as an occasion and context for primal screaming. Likewise, there will continue to be "spillage," where young people, notably but not exclusively the lower-class white male, act out their frustrations and aggressions in public-school gyms, on playgrounds, and similar sites. In such a condition, the call to civility will remain a mockery, a sham.

Notes

1. It is noteworthy that recently professional wresting and automobile racing became linked formally: World Championship Wrestling became sponsor of a racing team. This gesture, though mostly economic in motive, reveals a consciousness of the shared audience.

References

Arms, Robert L., Gordon W. Russell, and Mark L. Sandilands. 1979. "Effects on the Hostility of Spectators of Viewing Aggressive Sports." *Social Psychology Quarterly* 42 (September): 275–279.

Asante, Molefi, and Deborah Atwater. 1986. "The Rhetorical Condition as Symbolic Structure in Discourse." *Communication Quarterly* 34 (Spring): 170–177.

Ball, Michael R. 1990. *Professional Wrestling as Ritual Drama in American Popular Culture*. Lewiston, New York: Edwin Mellen Press.

Barthes, Roland. 1972. *Mythologies*. New York: Hill and Wang.

Brean, Herbert. 1957. "Wrestling Script Gone Awry." *Life* 43 (December 2): 165–166.

Cope, Myron. 1966. "The Rich, Full Life of a Bad Guy." *Saturday Evening Post* 239 (February 12): 88–89.

Deegan, Mary Jo. 1989. *American Ritual Dramas: Social Rules and Cultural Meanings*. Contributions in Sociology, No. 76. New York: Greenwood Press.

Gresson, Aaron David. 1995. *The Recovery of Race in America*. Minneapolis: University of Minnesota Press.

Mano, K. 1974. "Heavyweight Fraud." *National Review* 26 (June 21): 705–706.

Martin, William C. 1972. "Friday Night in the Coliseum." *Atlantic Monthly* 229 (March): 83–87.

Stone, Gregory P., and Ramon A. Oldenburg. 1967. "Wrestling." In *Motivations in Play, Games, and Sports*, ed. Ralph Slovenko and James A. Knight. Springfield, Ill.: Charles C. Thomas.

10 Dealing from the Bottom of the Deck: The Business of Trading Cards, Past to Present

Murry R. Nelson and Shirley R. Steinberg

SECTION ONE: FROM THE PAST
Murry R. Nelson

By the age of nine I was hooked, a user, clearly addicted and a threat to those around me. I stole to support my habit and would barter away my possessions to get my fix. My need was cards—initially baseball cards but also football, Zorro, TV Westerns, Rails and Sails, Funny Valentine, Flags of the World, Celebrities, Davy Crockett, American Presidents, and any other card that fed my collecting instinct.

Gum cards, most notably baseball cards, were once largely the province of preadolescent boys, predominantly ages eight to twelve. Today, despite the extended adolescent habits of many adults (mostly male) the "hobby" is still mostly populated by male preteens, but their motivations and practices have become altered by a highly saturated and more scrutinized economic market.

Card collecting appears to be one aspect of a practice that most youngsters begin as toddlers when they might have saved pebbles, gum wrappers, or shells. As they mature and become both more literate and discriminating, the items collected become more "sophisticated"— stamps, coins, cards, dolls, gems and rocks, or books by an author or of a genre. Kids naturally categorize and acquire that which is of interest to them and available. For more than 100 years, cards have been produced to take advantage of that fascination and to sell a product. Cards have been marketed as vehicles for product purchase as well as being the end product itself. Today, millions of cards are produced each year, with millions of dollars spent on such products. The appeal is still to children, and more females than ever are part of the overall marketing strategy.

Cards, particularly sports cards, are a part of many children's lives and today have gone high-tech in both production (holographics) and marketing (computer generated television advertising). The products seem innocuous enough; in fact, many are interesting and educational. But along with the development of interest comes the development of key marketing strategies and consumer habits that carry over directly into adolescent and adult consumer patterns and worldviews.

Early Cards and Their Appeal

Between 1865 and 1900, "the major form of American advertising was a small colorful card known today as a 'Trade Card'" (Handelman 1983). These cards were a high-quality chromolithograph printed on thin cardboard. They advertised a specific product, a local business establishment, or both, and no attempt was necessarily made to link the subject pictured on the card to that which was advertised. The cards were distributed by jobbers and salesman to general stores and left on counters as giveaways for customers. The cards were so attractive and popular that people began to collect them and mount them in scrapbooks. By the year 1880, collecting trade cards was one of the nation's leading hobbies (Handelman 1983, 1).

In a nation only just beginning to take advantage of newly found leisure time, card collecting appealed mostly to adults, though the interest of children was clear. Baseball was a popular and convenient topic of trade cards—as were specific team cards such as those of the "Atlantics" of Brooklyn in 1868 or the "Red Stockings" of Cincinnati in 1869. The modern baseball card can be traced directly back to the results of a fierce cigarette war in the late 1880s. Competing companies began to pack coupons and, later, lithographed cards featuring subjects ranging from world flags to leading actresses. The jump to baseball players as the subjects of these cardboard strips was natural and quick (Olbermann 1979, 1).

These cards still appealed to adults, though collecting cigarette cards quickly captured the youth market and led manufacturers to consider linking card subjects appealing to kids with products with the same appeal. Tobacco cards had an enormous variety of subjects—birds, flags, colleges, presidents, explorers, jockeys, fish, boxers, mammals, as well as baseball players. Baseball cards must have had more cachet with kids, because by the late 1900s, when candy companies began issuing cards as premiums, baseball players (and some boxers) were the subject. These candy companies included the American Caramel Company, Standard Caramel Company, Philadelphia Caramels, Blomes Chocolates, C. A. Briggs Company, Mello Mints, and Williams Caramel Company, among others. As with tobacco, the card was the hook to land the kid (or adult) customer. Little media advertising was used to promote these products. The enticement was the packaging, and word of mouth was used to enhance interest. Except for a few exceptions in the early 1900s, the reverse sides were blank or contained advertising data. The overwhelming majority of cards had on their faces, then, pictures with no real message transmitted other than by the choice of the card topics or the individual subjects selected within those topics. Exceptions were some early tobacco baseball cards, the Cracker Jack baseball cards of 1914–1915, and a few other assorted sets.

Messages of the Prewar Era

The 1930s put an end to the absence of verbal messages. Starting in the early 1930s, baseball cards began to be sold as the premiums for the gum (usually bubble gum) of various companies. These included DeLong, Goudy, National Chicle, Gum, Inc. (which evolved into the Bowman Gum Company), and Leaf. Baseball cards were the dominant cards offered by these companies, but were not the only ones. Others included comic strips, North American Indians, pilots (referred to as "sky birds"), and cowboys.

Beginning in 1936, Gum, Inc., issued various series of cards with strong political and social messages that sought to inculcate as well as educate. In 1936, the G-Men series of cards was issued. This set focused on the actions of government agencies in hunting down and apprehending criminals like John Dillinger, Ma Barker, "Machine Gun" Kelly, and Bonnie Parker.

During this period in the United States, there was a concern among the general populace that crime was, if not rampant, then highly publicized and romanticized by the media. During the 1920s, Prohibition had created a whole new division of criminal acts and behaviors. The battles among gangs over territory for the distribution of liquor and beer were played out on the streets of many urban areas. In the 1930s, the desperation of the Great Depression made crime an option that many people might not have previously considered. Thus, some criminals were viewed by an economically deprived public as heroes in a sense.

The G-Men series, subtitled Heroes of the Law, sought to counter these antisocial ideas among young boys. Each card noted that "G-Men Trap Wily Fugitives Across the United States." The messages were clear: Crime is wrong, the agents of the government are heroic, and people who commit crimes will be apprehended and punished.

It is impossible to assess the effect that these cards might have had, but surely the manufacturers were convinced of the effectiveness of the cards in generating product sales and support for law enforcement. With the lessons of G-Men learned, Gum, Inc., sought to generate support for the prevention of another cataclysmic world war by issuing a set of cards in 1938 called Horrors of War. This series included pictures of mass slaughters, starvation, wild dogs chewing on corpses, bombed cities, and other horrifying devastations. The message on each card was that citizens must act in order to prevent the horrors of war. The set also had cards of antiheroes: Stalin, Hitler, and Mussolini.

By 1939, when the war started in Europe, the manufacturers of Gum, Inc., issued a series that was ostensibly noncommittal, but when examined it proves to be clearly interventionist. Isolationists like Republican Senator William Borah of Utah were stymieing President Franklin D. Roosevelt's efforts to aid the American allies. Roosevelt attempted to tread the fine line between assistance and intervention. This new series of cards, called The World in Arms, sought to build support for American intervention among younger Americans. Few schools addressed the topic, though *after* the United States entered the war many schools altered their curriculum to include subjects like "Wartime Geography" and "Aviation Training in the Classroom" (Nelson 1986).

The World in Arms series consisted of 120 cards: forty airplanes; thirty ships; ten iron cavalry; ten fired artillery; ten fortifications; and twenty miscellaneous world arms. Clearly the attempt was being made to build up fear of future conflict in the hope of interceding in the war in Europe. After a description of the front of the card, each card back asked in large bold type, "Can America Maintain Peace with THE WORLD IN ARMS?"

Most cards were merely factual descriptors of the war machinery pictured, but some of the cards were far more than that, containing fictitious depictions of horrifying circumstances. Take, for instance, "British Portable Steel Air Raid Shelter" (miscellaneous card number five). The obverse of the card depicts a conflagration brought about by low-flying bombers. People rush to shelters about the size of large phone booths as a city smolders in the background and bombs blast nearby buildings. The reverse of the card notes that the British shelters have been tested, though never used (and weren't) and that "these bells were designed for 'key personnel'—military police and other public officials who would have to keep their posts during an air raid." The card cautions that "a scene such as shown in the picture might well happen if children or adults were caught in the path of disaster."

Not to be outdone in the war card game, Goudy Gum issued its first war series in 1940—First Column Defenders. Each card had a red, white, and blue border with an insignia of red- and white-alternating stripes and a blue field centered at the top of the card. Emblematic of the American flag, the words "First Column Defenders" appeared in the blue field in place of white stars.

The card's reverse notes, "This card is one of a NEW SERIES! Start your collection now." Again, this was a thinly veiled attempt to build support for entry into the war. The card "Soldiers of the Sea" presents the glory of the U.S. Marine Corps, noting that the Marine Corps can "well be proud of the service it performs and the glorious record it has made." The card concludes, "The Marines provide protection for American lives and property abroad," the carte blanche used to justify American invasions in the Dominican Republic, Mexico, and Cuba and, since World War II, in Vietnam, Grenada, and Panama.

By 1941, the United States had turned to a strong defensive mode as the anticipation of American entry into World War II became keener. Gum, Inc., sought to sell their products by capitalizing on this feeling and issued its National Defense series. Each card carried the statement, "Save to get all these picture cards showing Uncle Sam's soldiers, sailors, marines, airmen, and civilians in training for NATIONAL DEFENSE." The familiar use of "Uncle Sam" rather than America was clearly designed to evoke a sense of the large American family pulling together for all of us. The need for readiness was apparent, and even kids could now play some part—even if it were only to speak up for the war effort at home.

Card number one of the National Defense series sets the tone. Labeled "Uncle Sam—Soldier" (all were "Uncle Sam" with some ending), this card is sublabeled "You're in the Army Now." The text seeks to prepare prospective recruits for the routine of the army. "Uncle Sam's Army gets up early. At a quarter to six the bugle blows." This, it is explained, is reveille, followed by roll call and then breakfast in the "mess hall." "The American soldiers are said to be the best fed in the world." Then comes the call to "fall in for drill." The rationale for this is offered along with the comment, "Military training, with its drill and exercise, keeps a man healthy. The real purpose for all military training is to win battles for Uncle Sam." No subtlety here. The messages are clear. Army training is great—good food, good exercise, and good discipline. And this culminates in the battles that are fought and won for our great family. What? There *aren't* any battles? Well, then, let's get into some. It's good for all Americans and America!

As noted above, card commentary, though often banal, was hardly ever subtle. In 1939, for example, the Play Ball—America series from Gum, Inc., had a card of Burgess Whitehead, former Cardinals second baseman then with the New York Giants. Whitehead had missed all of the 1938 season voluntarily because, as the card notes, he had had "a nervous breakdown." This was a revelation that would not have been made in the later "happy talk" years of baseball's golden age of the 1950s, but in 1939 straight talk was the order of the day.

Messages of many baseball cards in the 1930s focused on playing tips. With no youth leagues, and coaching still generally limited to older youth, some card sets took on the task themselves. The Diamond Stars set from National Chicle Co., produced from 1934 to 1936, was one such set. Many had pitching, fielding, or hitting tips, but among the tips were statements of value to conformity. One card focuses on fielding and notes that "only poor or inexperienced fielders kneel down to stop grounders." Though it's a minor point, many excellent major leaguers do, in fact, drop to their knees at times when a ball is hit swiftly on the ground toward them. Grace and beauty (form) becomes a slave to function (stopping the ball). The best players often develop their own individual style, but that message would have belied the mandates of many coaches.

During 1933 Goudy Gum issued a set of 240 baseball cards. One problem: Goudy issued only 239 cards, deliberately omitting number 106 (Nap Lajoie) to keep kids buying to complete their incomplete sets. The ploy worked until 1934, when consumer pressure forced Goudy to print the Lajoie card—but the company provided it only to those who wrote to ask for it. The card is now valued at more than $20,000.

Postwar Card Collecting

During World War II there were no card sets issued because of a paper shortage. Following the war it took awhile for the card companies to adjust to the new conditions. The first major set of antebellum cards to be issued were from Bowman Gum, the successors to Gum, Inc. In 1948, Bowman issued a forty-eight-card set of black-and-white cards. For three years, Bowman made the only postwar cards (the Topps Company entered the card market in 1951).

Jackie Robinson broke baseball's color barrier when he joined the Brooklyn Dodgers in 1947, but it wasn't until 1949 that he and legendary Negro Leagues pitcher Satchel Paige got their own cards. Roy Campanella, Don Newcombe, Sam Jethroe, Hark Thompson, and Larry Doby—all black—were ignored until 1950. Robinson's 1949 Bowman card notes that he was the first "Negro" to enter professional ball; Bowman apparently viewed the Negro Leagues as unprofessional.

Bowman's cards looked similar from 1950 through 1952, when it switched to modern technology and Kodachrome photographs. Included on the reverse were player statistics, apparently in response to what had been included on 1952 Topps cards. In 1955, Bowman reflected modern cultural progress and values by "enclosing" the color photographs within a wood-grain, plastic-looking frame that represented the chassis of a color television set. Just to make sure kids understood this wonderment, every card noted "color TV" on the front panel in a place where television controls would be.

The reverse of these cards also offered a variety of commentary: Some discussed the player depicted; some offered baseball tips; and others had the player describing his "biggest thrill in baseball." This latter group included a most unusual message on the card of Edie Waitku. He noted, "In 1950 I was shot by a deranged girl." Like Whitehead's revelation mentioned earlier, this was highly unusual, and from that year on no such candor exists on baseball cards.

When Topps entered the card market in 1951 with four small sets, no one would have predicted that it would drive Bowman out of the market. In fact, the opposite seemed more likely: Topps had trouble signing players to contracts, though some happily signed exclusive card contracts with either card company (Weidman 1954).

In 1952, Topps issued the largest set of cards to date (407). This set included most of the black players on major-league rosters. The card backs for 1952 and 1953 spoke only about baseball accomplishments, though Topps also noted that the "negro" players had only recently entered professional ball (i.e., formerly all-white leagues).[1] This note was prevalent in 1954, but, judging by the numbers of black athletes who were depicted, Topps was seemingly more accepting of the racial integration that was occurring in baseball than was Bowman. In 1954, twenty-two of Topps's 250 cards depicted African American or Latin American players. Bowman's set of 224 cards depicted eight blacks, though contractual agreements might have had some impact.

Topps had two- or three-panel cartoon depictions of some event in each player's life shown on the back of the card. Many of the "incidents" portrayed player successes as functions of perseverance, often in the face of adversity. These were messages for youngsters: try hard, a man's reach should exceed his grasp, and the like. Some messages were frightening, however, in their ingenuousness. David Hoskins's "story" chronicles "when Dave was with Dallas on June 9, '52, he got 2 letters threatening his life if he pitched that day." In the next box it says, "But Dave wouldn't be frightened. He hurled the game and won! And that year he chalked up 22 wins." No reason is given for why his life might have been threatened. Hoskins was black, and the South was still living under "separate but equal" (the *Brown v. Board of Education* decision would not be issued by the U.S. Supreme Court for another two years). Being one of the only blacks in the Texas League in 1952 was not a comfortable position for Hoskins to be in. Topps deserves some credit for acknowledging the courage of Hoskins, but by failing to contextualize the incident the depiction becomes almost noneducational.

Topps, being Brooklyn-based, was both supportive of the local team (which was the first to have black players) and the integrative practices of major league baseball. By 1956, Topps was depicting twenty-nine black players among its 340 cards. Fifteen of sixteen teams had added black players to their rosters; almost all of these players were pictured on cards. The attention paid to them by card companies, however, was not always as careful as it could have been.

The 1956 Topps baseball card set had on its card obverses a bust of each player with a background action shot. The card of Hank Aaron, entering his third full season in major league baseball that year, displayed an example of less than appropriate attention on the part of Topps. Aaron's background shot shows him beginning his slide toward home plate as the umpire rips off his mask to make the call. It's a nice action selection, except the shot wasn't of Aaron. For whatever reason, Topps either didn't take or couldn't select a good action shot of Aaron for the card, so it arrived at a unique solution: It substituted a shot of Willie Mays and airbrushed the front of his shirt to remove the team name and crudely reinked his cap to make it appear to be a Braves cap.

How can one tell it's not Aaron? Easy. Looking at the card makes it obvious to anyone who followed baseball in that era. Mays's facial features, including his puffed-out cheeks, are obvious, as are his slightly bowed legs and pigeon-toed gait. In an era of greater television coverage, particularly in color, no company would have attempted such an obvious sham. The message being sent was, "All blacks look alike. It's so hard to tell them apart that we can depict one young star as another and no one will know the difference."

The racist naïveté involved in this line of thinking is unbelievable considering that the center of card production and purchase was New York City—where Willie Mays played for the Giants! Did Topps think their young customers so oblivious that they might not notice? Or did Topps simply not care? (To redo the card would cost time and money by delaying the entire set of cards, and a whole sheet of eighty-eight would have had to have been destroyed.) I suspect that economic factors made the difference in this decision, but the racial arrogance shines through. Would Topps have printed a card of Duke Snider with Mickey Mantle portraying Snider? I think not.

The next year, a similar incident reoccurred—revealing the low esteem Topps held for its young consumers and its baseball stars. Aaron's photo was printed with the negative reversed, so Aaron is depicted on his card batting left-handed; the logo and one of the numerals on his uniform also are clearly reversed. Again the question: Would a white superstar have received such shabby treatment? Treating a young black hero in this manner reflected poorly on Topps's quality control, of course, but it also reinforced an attitude that blacks were of less consequence, even as professionals.

One might ask how Bowman was depicting black players at this time. The answer is that it wasn't. Early in 1956, Topps had purchased its competitors—creating a monopoly that existed for the next twenty-five years. To be a baseball card collector was to be a *Topps* card collector. Topps created dozens of card issues to keep the nickels and dimes of youngsters flowing into Topps coffers year-round.

In 1955, Topps had a football set that depicted All-America players since the early 1900s, because Topps couldn't get pro football players out from under Bowman contracts. Beginning in 1956, Topps began producing pro football card sets since Bowman was no longer a competitor. Topps also did sporadic issues of pro basketball and pro hockey cards. Of more interest, however, were the various nonsport sets produced by Topps to fill the void between baseball seasons. Topps's selection of these sets offers some insight into their views—and the view of corporate America in general—toward youngsters and their interests. Topps selected topics of educational and cultural interest as well as topics of almost no redeeming "social value"—but which could be produced cheaply and quickly.

One quick source of card ideas was the cache of previous card issues—the "old chestnut" approach. In the early 1950s, Bowman had issued a series of American presidents—one per card. The set was obviously quite small since there were fewer than thirty-five presidents. Nevertheless, Topps copied the idea and in the late 1950s issued a set of forty cards that included one of the White House, the Capitol, and other scenes.

The cards included text on the reverse that was mostly factual. What is interesting is the particular data selected for inclusion on these cards and the messages these facts might send to young collectors. George Washington's card, for example, says nothing of his role or accomplishments as the nation's first president. Instead, his great strength as a young man is emphasized as a model for youngsters to aspire to: "Public surveyor at 16; major in Virginia militia at 21. Went on a 500-mile errand for Governor Dinwiddie. Found way by North Star. Slept in frozen clothes on pine boughs." Sounds a bit like the preparation of an Eagle Scout. There is no mention of his wife or his politics. Almost all of the other cards followed this model. A larger-than-life youth is mentioned, followed by political offices and election to the presidency. Though so much more could have been made of this opportunity, the cards were at least mildly educational.

Another set, drawn from early tobacco card issues, was the 1957 Flags of the World series, an attempt at understanding others—or so it seemed. Each card's obverse depicted a large flag with two background scenes illustrative of that flag's nation. The reverse had information drawn directly from an almanac: capitol, area, population, type of government, monetary unit, language, main products, and air miles from New York City. This latter point reflected the "New York centricity" many Americans decried—but it wasn't surprising given that the series was issued by a New York–based company. Why not measure air miles from our nation's capital? Why not measure to the nearest American shore?

The choosing of the "official" language (and there was only one for each country) also reflects interesting cultural views. For Switzerland the language is German, which ignores the Italian and French speakers that had long made Switzerland officially trilingual. There is a similar insensitivity as to Nationalist China and the People's Republic of China. Only one Chinese dialect is printed for each country—providing a hegemonic rather than heterogeneous view of the population and culture of these diverse peoples.

More culturally interesting, however, are many of the scenes depicted on the front of the cards. Asian countries were ill served, since their cultures were often reduced to the American view. The card of the Philippines shows two scenes: a barefoot man climbing a rubber tree and General Douglas MacArthur (with two GIs) and explosions in the background. Is this a fair depiction of Filipino culture? South Korea also has a war scene with a GI, fighter planes overhead, and smoke and fire in the background. The other scene is a woman in front of a thatched hut. Both Nationalist China and the People's Republic of China had cards with armed troops on the front. Clearly the cultures of these countries were depicted from an American point of view—the countries' import presented in relation to the United States.

Non-Asian countries also received unusual depictions. Norway had one scene—Vikings on a longboat, circa 1100. Surely a cultural depiction of a country in the middle of the twentieth century can do better than this in imparting some understanding of the nation. Iceland fared only slightly better. In addition to a depiction of another Viking ship, there was a depiction of Icelanders fishing on a small, open boat. Switzerland shows the Alps, bobsledding, and a skier. Is there no more to culture and commerce in Switzerland—one of the richest countries in the world and one undamaged by World War II?

It is clear that the Flags of the World set was well-intentioned but culturally distorted by ethnocentrism. Card backs were, as noted, merely data (and some data were inaccurate); card fronts were drawn from dated and largely ignorant views of the countries—most likely from illustrations in reference works. Most of the text at that time and into the 1970s was written by Sy Berger, the sales manager and head of the Topps sports department. He also approved most card photos (Boyd and Harris 1973), but the Flags decisions were made by staffpeople in the Topps art department, most of whom were apparently unconcerned with a legitimate portrayal of any country. Why not a revolutionary war soldier and a log cabin to portray the United States rather than the Capitol and the Statue of Liberty?

In the 1950s and early 1960s, Topps constantly sought to fill the void between September and March with cards that would appeal to children, because Topps was, in Sy Berger's words, "basically in the children's entertainment business" (Boyd and Harris, 1973, 24). Keeping that in mind, Topps produced many cards with "entertaining" appeal. Transportation was presented in Rails and Sails, a series on antique railroads and classic sailing ships. Fighter planes were depicted in the Wings series from 1953. This was clearly a product of Korean War fears—the back of each card had a quiz that had as its subject matter the overhead silhouette of various fighter planes. The alertness to such planes (enemy or friendly) fit the era of air-raid drills.

What Topps did more of, however, was reflect cultural pop "idols" that were famous from films, records, or television. In 1975, Topps presented Hit Stars, a series of ninety-nine movie, TV, and recording stars with publicity photos on the fronts and text largely drawn from studio public-relations information on the backs. The recording artists represented were black and white, rock 'n' rollers, rhythm and blues artists, and balladeers like Frankie Laine.

The movie stars were usually noted as starring in a particular upcoming film. Here was a great medium for Topps sales—the photos and text data were provided without charge by studios and/or agents since the cards were "free publicity" for them, and kids got color photos of their favorite stars, many of whom they had either not seen or seen only in black-and-white photos or television. Media-corporation marriages with card companies have continued for over forty years and have been instrumental in creating tie-ins with later movie-related products like dolls, equipment, and clothing. The James Dean card describes an early life of loneliness and sadness. This is particularly interesting in light of his death at 1955 in a one-car crash after making only three films.

The card of Elvis Presley was the forerunner to an Elvis Presley set and, in the mid-1960s, a Beatles set. Similarly, other individual cards inspired sets, including Batman, Partridge Family, Charlie's Angels, Welcome Back, Kotter, and Happy Days issues. The entertainment tie-in was a clear economic winner for Topps. Capitalizing on TV's Western craze of 1958, Topps came out with a seventy-one-card set highlighting different shows. The bigger shows (*Gunsmoke, Have Gun Will Travel, Wagon Train*) got long story sequences over six to fifteen cards. Less popular shows like *Boots and Saddles* and *Union Pacific*—which were independently distributed and not network productions—had two or three card stories each.[2]

The most extensive tie-in with Topps, however, was with Walt Disney. The phenomenon of the mid-1950s was the Disney-produced TV series *Davy Crockett*. Every kid, it seemed, owned a coonskin cap, a Davy Crockett T-shirt, a fake Bowie knife, and a fringed leather jacket. Reinforcing all of this were the two series of Davy Crockett cards, which included film scenes on the front and scene descriptions on the reverse. Since Topps essentially acted as a Disney mouthpiece, there is little to critique other than the Disney perspective on the world as viewed through the Crockett films and television episodes. So, too, with the Zorro series of eighty-eight cards issued in 1958. Based entirely on the Disney TV series, the scenes, like in the Davy Crockett set, were taken directly from the shows; the text was also drawn from the show—and likely first written by Disney publicists.

Summarizing the postwar vision of children and of card collecting offers a view of a number of significant issues of the period—race and gender relations, the fear of future war, the ethnocentrism of Americans, and a recognition of children's value as consumers of low (pop) culture. Regarding race, Bowman avoided most black ballplayers except for the superstars. Admittedly, there were few blacks in the major leagues from 1948 to 1955, but Topps represented them more equitably on their card issues. The Negro Leagues were disparaged as semipro, a cruel and untrue characterization furthered by both card companies.

The difficulties of being the lone black on a team, in a league, or even in a town were ignored. Were Topps or Bowman even aware of the traumas faced by early black major leaguers? Unlikely, but it would not have been difficult to discern. For their part, most black players were eager to make the bigger bucks in the major leagues and to keep discrimination—which they were often embarrassed by—to a minimum. These white and black attitudes were typical of the 1950s—an era of superficial happiness with anger or resentment often smoldering beneath the surface. Kids were being protected from these feelings by upbeat baseball cards. Topps had many African Americans in their Hit Stars series, but all were recording artists. Discrimination against black actors and actresses in film and television was reflected by their absence from that section of the card set.

In the Crockett and Zorro sets, as in the Disney video versions, the Indians were portrayed as savage enemies (early Crockett) or simpletons (Zorro). In Crockett, the Mexicans were depicted as bloodthirsty killers, despite the fact that Texans were the ones who invaded Mexico, then sought independence. The *Zorro* TV series presents a different angle (since it takes place in Spanish California). All of the key heroic players are Anglo, however, with one of the few Hispanic actors left to play the obese comic foil—Sergeant Garcia.

If cards reflected cultural import, women also had little influence. Though sports cards in the early 1900s through the 1930s and even the 1925 Berk Ross set (truly an anomalous set with two females) depicted women, the largest postwar card issues ignored the existence of women with one exception—Celebrities/Hit Stars. Women were not portrayed as athletes, which reflected attitudes of the majority of the male population and a significant minority of the female population in the period before the passage and implementation of Title IX of the Civil Rights Act of 1968. Into the 1980s, women were still barely shown on card issues unless they were shown bare or nearly so. Playboy Centerfold cards and cards by other, less-respected models became adult card sets. Did kids care? I would guess that some certainly did. Women have generally been ignored by trading card manufacturers.

The period of war and war fears was manifested in the Flag set and the Wings set, as well as in the violence of TV Westerns and Davy Crockett. Despite the end of World War II, fighting in China, Korea, and Indochina and the takeover of Eastern Europe by the Soviets made for an uneasy peace. This Cold War tension was apparent in postwar Topps cards, just as the prewar cards had sought to first stress isolationism then intervention. These card "worldviews" were reflections of ideological positions that spoke directly to children. The ethnocentric view of the world was also indicative of an America both convinced of its rightness and unwilling to consider little that other countries or cultures had to offer.

The recognition of kids as consumers of pop culture was a plan of the Topps company. As Sy Berger notes in talking about the various nonsports issues, "We've been years ahead of our time on every one of them. You have to anticipate way ahead on these things. You have to work out a particular trend before it breaks" (Boyd and Harris, 1973, 27). Obviously, companies are in business to make a profit, and once Topps identified its market clientele it was very aggressive in marketing its products and eliminating much of its competition.

After purchasing Bowman in 1956, Topps signed exclusive contracts with all baseball players. These contracts remained in effect until 1980, when a federal court ruled that other companies *could* produce and sell baseball cards—but not with gum. The slab of gum in Topps cards had never been the main source of pursuit by youngsters. Thus, Topps carefully analyzed its market and produced other goods to appeal to seven-to twelve-year-olds—mostly boys. Rather than create a market, Topps found it more profitable to expand or piggyback on an existing children's market as popularized by television, film, and music. Topps became a reflector of children's interests in popular culture.

With its ascendancy to a monopolistic position in card production, Topps grew pedestrian in its issues. Baseball commentary was reduced to make room for more data because, as Sy Berger notes, "The kids are in love with statistics. So of course we have to give them what they want" (Boyd and Harris, 1973, 25). Thus, Topps baseball cards became less a reflector of cultural activities than previously—with a few notable exceptions. In 1972, borders were nearly "psychedelic" in their colors, print face, and logos. In 1975, in a similar vein, the borders were at least two colors with the team name in a third. This was, however, as bold as it got. A lack of competition often leads to a stale product.

As for nonsports issues, they shrunk in number and creativity as Topps dedicated its presses to more and more sports issues. In 1956, Topps began producing professional football issues, which have continued, in one form or another, ever since. Professional hockey cards began to be released in 1954 but were not annually produced until 1957–1958. In 1956, Topps presented its first basketball cards, which were regionally sold and were obviously not very popular since no other set was issued until 1969–1970. Topps dropped the basketball cards in the late 1970s and did not return to them until the 1990s.

Occasionally, a Topps nonsports issue is produced and successfully marketed. The 1985 Garbage Pail Kids series (satirizing Cabbage Patch dolls) was one such set. For the most part, however, Topps cards means sports cards. Since 1981, Topps has battled with Fleer, Donruss, Upper Deck, and other companies for market share in a split market. Though adult collector/speculator/dealers have created a new market niche, cards continue to be purchased primarily by preadolescents. Thus, the nonsport, cultural-reflection market has become part of the niche of smaller companies, particularly collection-oriented presses that have seen few images that cannot be converted into card sets.

In addition, card collectors can now be the subjects of cards (such as Little League baseball players or Pop Warner League football stars) as companies market cards of them. One can even write one's own copy. We continue to collect, and the companies continue to sell.

SECTION TWO: TO THE PRESENT
Shirley R. Steinberg

One of my greatest collecting coups of all times occurred in 1996 when Murry Nelson was able to purchase a vintage baseball card for me. I do like baseball, do not collect cards, and have watched *General Hospital* since I was in fourth grade. Consequently, it was logical for me to want a card of John Beradino (aka Dr. Stephen Hardy), a former infielder for the St. Louis Browns. As I now examine this card for the umpteenth time, a validating process is taking place. Maybe it is legitimation, historical verification that my favorite TV star also played baseball. Berardino lived next door to my stepfather; they were raised together and went to the farm leagues together. Dad had to return home to help his eight brothers and sisters; Johnny went on to play in the major leagues. Somehow, I have a history within this baseball card.

I had a Roger Maris rookie card, a Frank Howard card, and a Sandy Koufax card. I really didn't see the import of collecting cards—I only knew that boys liked that I knew who certain baseball players were. I knew Sandy was Jewish, and I wish I still had the cards.

Werner Muensterberger calls collecting "an unruly passion" (Muensterberger 1994). He connects human behavior and conduct with the spectacle, the "unquenchable thirst" of collecting. Muensterberger examines habits of collectors and the distance to which they would travel in order to collect. I don't think I am a collector, at least I am not serious about one collection, but as I peruse my habitat I realize I do *collect* stuff. Walter Benjamin collected books; he observed, "One has only to watch a collector handle the objects in his glass case. As he holds them in his hands, he seems to be seeing through them into their distant past as though inspired" (Benjamin 1931). Now this seems a bit overstated; the reverence implied makes me nervous. However, after living with my four children and watching two of them obsess with collecting cards, comics, posters, and models, I have felt the romance, although second-hand, with collecting.

Our two boys . . . is collecting a boy thing? Why is it that 95 percent of comic-book store clients are male? Why do boys play card-role games more than girls? Why is it so impossible to throw these things away, even after the interest is gone? Our girls have passions, but there is something mystical (a bit obnoxious), enigmatic, about our sons and what they collect. Their collections are thematic, comics leading to cards about comics, cards from comics and TV shows to models, costumes, and clothing—*Star Wars* begot our sons' T-shirt wardrobes, defines their drinking mugs, and decorates their rooms. *Beavis and Butt-Head* and *The Simpsons* cards and comics splatter over their floors, *X-Men* come in third, and if they had the money, they would be buying $5 worth of cards every week.

Somehow violence, blood, guts, fantasy, and science fiction define their collections. Originally, Chaim started collecting baseball cards. He has a huge collection; however, aside from his trading them in fourth grade, I never saw him do anything with them. The acquisition was everything. What does one *do* with cards? Trade them? Then what? That moment of opening up the packet and discovering who was residing in the foil—that was the high. The cards disappeared into books and boxes; Chaim still gets bored with baseball games—they are too long. What does Murry *do* with his books of cards? Show them to people? And then?

Chaim's brother, Ian, got him started on comics, all kinds of comics. We traipsed all over the country going to vintage comic stores and making coveted purchases. Getting a #1 issue was always great. I encouraged Ian's collecting; as a former *Superman* fan, I remembered my mother not understanding why I spent my entire allowance on comics, and I was determined to not repeat this pattern. I read comics, devoured them, but I wasn't a *collector.* However, I never encouraged the girls, Meghann and Bronwyn, to collect comics or cards. Was it just a boy thing? This obsession with acquisition? Or did I just encourage the boys to acquire representations of adventure, fantasy, and sports?

There are Barbie cards, *Barbie* comics; as Murry mentioned, there were Garbage Pail Kids, the obvious answer to the Cabbage Patch Kids cards. But "girl" cards somehow seem unexciting; they are unexciting. There are American Girl cards: "There are 300 American Girl Trading Cards. Trade with your friends and collect them all! For a free catalogue about the American Girl Collection, call . . ." Redefining American history, these cards are faded with Renoiresque pictures of the days gone by. Each girl has a story, and in a short summary on the back of the card she somehow "saves the day" for humanity. Coincidentally, Barbie cards and comics have a similar theme—"saving the day." What is the power that these blonde bimbo dolls and bourgeois quasihistorical dolls have that the entire world comes to a stop and they can remedy all ills, solve all problems, and create new paradigms?

Do children really enjoy opening these cards, reading the story, and filing them away? What do they eventually *do* with them? In order to get all 300 cards, one would have to buy thirty packs at $2.25 each. Assuming that all of the cards were different, a parent would only be out $67.50 for the collection. However, I have yet to see cards not be duplicated; that's the trick—the kids get hooked for the acquisition and then have to complete the set.

So we've established that cards are collected by kids and by adults. Boys do collect cards more than girls, as a rule, and "girl" cards are tame, pretty, and educational. Muensterberger traces collecting to an anal behavior. Benjamin claims that "ownership is the most intimate relationship one can have to objects, not that they come alive in him; it is he who lives in them" (Benjamin 1931). Scary thought. At least getting bubble gum or cigarettes gave the purchaser incentive; now the incentive is the purchase.

In this chapter I look at the content of the cards that our children collect. I will leave Muensterberger to his conclusions about the obsession of collecting. At this point I have an image in my head of the young woman in Tennessee Williams's *Glass Menagerie*, collecting her little glass animals; her world, her definition of self was involved in these animals. If collecting tells us something about ourselves, does the content of what we collect further deconstruct us? I hope not.

The innocence of childhood card collecting speaks to the joy of acquisition, trading, displaying, and possibly game-playing. Muensterberger calls it a "promise of pleasure." Examining what the cards say in the late twentieth century sends chilling messages down the spine. I don't think they are just cards.

Blood and Guts

I spent $7 for a set of Death Cult Jonestown Massacre Memorial Cards (Worden and Honath 1988). Over 4,000 of these sets were reproduced, including several stickers and cards telling the story of the suicide/murders. Several cards: "Cyanide Convulsions," "Brains Blown Out," "Jones Shot." The cards were on the shelf next to the X-Men cards and the Sesame Street cards. The selling point for the cards was the historical/educational significance of the event. The text however, reveals a strong preoccupation with death, fear, coercion, and blood.

RIP Good Ghoul Art cards are in the shape of a coffin. "Each card is a haunting document of a chilling event . . . actual encounters with true ghosts, human monsters, fiends, weird mysteries . . . you'll want to read these in a well-lit place!" (Kitchen Sink Press 1994). Relating stories about the "Texas Terror" or "Human Fireballs," the cards graphically describe "real-life" occurrences. These were on the shelf by the Coca Cola cards. Why would anyone want to collect product cards? These cards contain pictures of old Coke advertising campaigns, nostalgic for those days gone by. I will address advertising cards later—things were simpler then; there weren't serial killer trading cards.

Butchers, Shooters, Tax Evaders, and Junkies

The True Crime Series was created in the early 1990s to "teach" about authentic crimes. Series Two is specifically about serial killers and mass murderers. Collectors learn about people like Peter Sutcliffe, the "Yorkshire Ripper"; the back of the card describes Sutcliffe's killings of prostitutes and his use of a hammer. Dates are given, as is the result of the trial and conviction of this killer. Readers are treated to a detailed narrative about the methods of the serial killers, their personal habits, and their backgrounds—a real historical peek into the personal life and nature of some of the cruelest men in history.

The absence of women or nonwhite men is disturbing in this series. There is one card that portrays a female, Anna Sage (aka the Lady in Red). Anna was an associate of John Dillinger; she was also a madame, running brothels in northwestern Indiana. Anna never killed anyone; however, she appears in the True Crime Series One: G-Men and Gangsters. The other cards in the series focus on "great" crime lords, memorable days in crime, the St. Valentine's Day massacre, and mass street executions. Anna is strangely connected to this violence by her friendship with Dillinger and the fact that she ran a whorehouse. One questions her degree of "infamy" and her placement in this violent series.

Attention to nonwhites is given in a card called "Slum Gangs—The Roots of Organized Crime." The card's discussion of the influx of European immigrants, "primarily Irish, Italian, and Eastern European," implies that the lack of gainful employment for these immigrants helped create urban criminals; "the stage was set for the entrance of organized crime." It appears obvious that without immigration the United States may have totally avoided the plague of criminal organizations. Right.

Nathaniel White is portrayed on card number 196. A black man from Albany, he is accused of killing six women. However, he is "being held pending trial." He merits his own card, alongside Juan Corona, Ted Bundy, and Richard Speck; they were all convicted; Nathaniel wasn't; he is still waiting. Evidently there is a shortage of convicted black mass murderers, so Nathaniel got his own card. If he is not convicted, one wonders if his card will be rescinded.

One of the newest series is called Crime and Punishment. In these packs, collectors read about notorious trials held in the United States. A short synopsis gives the prosecution's angle and then that of the defense. Many graphic descriptions of the crimes are included.

The Drug Wars Trading Cards set gives us "the straight dope on America's dirtiest deals." Thirty-six cards strong, it costs $8.95 to get the "inside" and "true" story on drugs. Card number one fittingly describes President Bush's campaign against drugs; quoting the president, the card informs the collector that narcotics are "the gravest threat facing our nation." The card instructs the reader that since Nixon, every president has been deeply committed to fighting drugs. After going through the cards, I found that eight cards out of thirty-six discussed drugs, narcotics, and criminal activity in an informative way. Twenty-five cards discuss drug crimes and citizens from countries other than the United States, indicting all countries in South and Central America and South-east Asia, India, the Middle East, France, and Cuba. My favorite card, number 6, discusses "Jewish gangsters like Meyer Lansky and Arnold 'The Brain' Rothstein [who] controlled the heroin trade." On each of the twenty-five cards, ethnicity of each criminal is discussed and highlighted. This set counters the serial killers; evidently, we conclude, white men murder women and children en masse; men of color, non-WASPs, distribute drugs and narcotics. Trading cards become a lesson in categorization, the essentialization of historical "facts." In all fairness to Drug Wars, I do believe the initial creation of the cards was to prevent and educate about drug abuse. I am still at a loss to know what one does with these cards after reading them. Put them in an album? They are hardly flash cards for fourth graders.

War Games and Education

Fine—so all trading cards are not violent. We can teach our children through these cards. For $10.95, Columbia Games, Inc., gives us Dixie: 1st Bull Run Edition. "Each Dixie deck contains 60 cards . . . the series depicts every regimen, battery, and general at 1st Bull Run. Bull Run was the first major battle of the war and the uniforms seen on this battlefield were especially varied and colorful." So our children can play a card game with dice with the Dixie cards and view colorful and varied uniforms. Somehow, the depth and significance of the Civil War seem diminished by this narrative. Half of the cards are backed with a picture of a Union soldier proudly holding the Stars and Bars above his head as he smashes it over the body of an enemy, bayonets pointing to the sky. The other half pictures the same soldier, only as a Confederate warrior trouncing a Union soldier. Or maybe the man holding the Dixie flag is a rebel with a Union hat and the man holding the fifty-starred flag(?) is a Union soldier with Johnny Yuma's hat on. Either way, the historical significance seems clouded with the bloody, violent scenes of war. I am uncomfortable with a card game having Yankees and Rebels killing one another, reworking and rewriting the Civil War at each hand. I also don't think we had fifty states during that particular conflict.

Searching through the memory lane of card shelves, I was able to collect some Desert Storm Victory Series cards. These cards were printed in 1991 by Topps, the sports card company, with the emblem "Coalition for Peace" written patriotically under a tank with a gun pointing to the left. The cards are bordered in blue stars, and the descriptions on the cards range from the types of fighter jets and ships used to the habitats of the soldiers. I was disappointed to not get a Saddam Hussein card in my three packs. The repetition of descriptive words like "largest," "best," "greatest," "fastest," and "world's first" preface every implement of war described.

Civics and political science govern many of the new trading cards. Illuminati: New World Order by Steve Jackson Games is a set of cards based on a game of political intrigue. Delineated on the box is a set of *rules* that control the game:

- Conservative opposes Liberal.
- Straight opposes Weird.
- Corporate opposes Government.
- Peaceful opposes Violent.
- Fanatic opposes Fanatic.
- Criminal has no opposite.

"The world is stranger than you think . . . everything that you read in the tabloids is true. The telephone company is controlled by the Moonies. The Congressional Wives have taken over the Pentagon. The Druids are casting spells to destroy the IRS." What's more, "Hitler is still alive . . . or at least his brain is, in a jar . . . mad scientists are building Orbital Mind Control Lasers . . . aimed at you! You've always known it. Secret conspiracies are everywhere. They're out to get you—unless you get them first" (Jackson 1995). The game is intended for ages eight to adult.

If the creator of this card set had the intent to frighten the players into action, I question the Moonies and Congressional Wives being given such terrifying power. The word *Illuminati* usually refers to a secret conspiracy of Jews that wishes to take over the world. It is interesting that Jackson has selected this name (used for more than a century by right-wing fundamentalists and anti-Semites) to title his card game. As in all card packs, the consumer buys a startup pack then must constantly replenish the supply by purchasing additional packs. Naturally, the packs will include duplicates; one can trade them, but one still needs to keep buying in order to complete the incompletable set. I believe this section was to highlight educational trading cards; for nonviolent cards we need to search further.

Nonviolent, Pleasant (Nice) Trading Cards

I don't want to give a unilateral view of the trading cards our children are collecting. There are indeed many nice, nonviolent cards. I was impressed by the preponderance of cards that advertised products, showed beautiful women, displayed acts of love, described TV-show characters and rock stars, and replicated comic books. In most card and comic stores, sets of trading cards are categorized by sports, fantasy/science fiction, and other. Many times, the nonviolent, pleasant, and nice trading cards are found sitting close to the war, crime, and blood cards.

Aesthetically Pleasing Cards

It would be unfair to not mention the artwork in trading cards. Many cards, both violent and peaceful, display excellent pen and ink work, intricate art, and usually less-than-articulate prose. The art can be whimsical, graphic, or realistic. The Women of the World Collection proclaims that "Trading Cards Just Got Better!" Surrounded by the flags of different countries, these cards display the beauty of the young females from different countries. Once again educational, these cards discuss the country in which a woman was born, where the capital of that country is, and what the prime export is. For example:

> *Michele: Colombia*
> Height 5'3" Weight 105 lbs.
> Measurements 36–22–34
> Birthdate: September 19th
> *Michele was born in Bogota, the capital of Colombia. Coffee is Colombia's most valuable export* (Gatefold Cards 1994).

Michele wears a transparent corset and is sitting on her knees leaning forward. Some cards serve to promote public relations and tourism for countries, as in the case of Amy Weber, from Italy: "Amy represents Italy which has enriched the world with the arts, sciences, and law." Amy's picture shows a tall brunette bending over a bale of hay in jeans, holding a horse blanket with a lace bra on. These cards were available next to the Married with Children and All My Children card sets. There was no age appropriateness printed on the package.

Many card sets available at comic and card stores can be found behind the register or on higher shelves. Gentlemen's Clubhouse Diamonds Series cards include twelve adult trading cards and one gold-foil card. Although the words "ADULTS ONLY" are printed at the bottom of the package, I observed males of different ages purchasing the packages. Obviously twelve-year-olds can be considered adults; who is to determine the age? However, most twelve-year-olds don't have credit cards, and on the reverse of each card is a 1-800 phone number for collectors to phone their favorite card model.

California Dreaming Cards bare both the tops and bottoms of the models; little text is involved, merely listings of height, weight, and measurements. A small photo of the woman is in a box on one side, and a full body shot adorns the back. Exotic names like Monique, Lana, and

Shawnee are in abundance. There are no age restrictions on the package. My particular favorite is a card with the torso of a naked woman, from below the breast to above the knees, with one hand pulling a pair of panties off, below the pelvis. Very graphic, no-name, severed woman.

Ladies, Leather, and Lace is created for collectors but is labeled "ADULT ORIENTED" at the bottom of the package. Each package is a collection of different women depicted in lively positions through an airbrush medium. Olivia is the artist, and she paints live models and also "patches together body parts from magazines, postcards, catalogues and other reference materials to form one image" (De Berardinis 1994). There are no age descriptors on this package.

Looking nostalgically back to the good old calendar days, Pin-Up Girls is a collection of "8 Premium Collectible Trading Cards," which historically trace the calendar *girls* from pre- and postwar days. Each card discusses the qualities that the *girls* needed in order to be used for the calendar. "Varga Girls decked out in corsets and garters were rare birds indeed. Such trappings were for the demimondaine, not the girl-next-door or Hollywood star qualities of *Esquire's* leading lady." Cards of "June Brides" in their nightly garb adorn some of the cards, as do nightie poses and one particularly unusual card of a bride in a veil with a teddy and high heels on.

There are no age restrictions for purchasing any trading cards; indeed, I found distinctly pornographic cards nestled comfortably among hockey and *The Simpsons* cards. I am able, however, with these particular cards, to understand that young people, presumably most young men, would indeed, be able to *use* the cards more regularly than perhaps the True Crime cards. There are only so many times one would like to look at "Machine Gun Kelly," but viewing "Blake," "Mikki," "Misha," and "Bijou" and their 1-800 phone numbers could facilitate hours of pleasurable viewing.

I looked for flora and fauna cards, assuming that they, too, would add to my aesthetically pleasing portion. However, short of a few kindergarten-type cards for children, I found few educational cards of artistic worth to collect in this genre.

Hype Cards

I am not sure if I am titling this section correctly; I wish to examine cards that contain either advertisements or promotional material from media. Somehow, after going through many packets, I still feel that the main objective is to *sell* cards and *promote* certain products. This brings back my laborious question: What *does* one *do* with these cards after opening the package (realizing that there is no longer any bubble gum), reading the back, and looking at the art?

Products

Possibly one could categorize product cards as educational. For instance, Coors Collectors Cards each explain in detail how malt, beer, and distilling is accomplished. Additionally, at the bottom of each card in tiny type (next to the copyright symbol), a socially responsible note is reserved for each reader: "Coors Products are for adults—21 means 21."

Other manufacturers have trading cards: Pepsi, Campbell's Soup, and Hershey's Chocolate are all packages ranging from $2 to $3 for eight or ten trading cards. The cards historically trace the advertising history of each company, reminding older consumers of the original advertising campaigns and educating young consumers of how "it used to be."

TV cards seem to rise to popularity quickly and descend just as promptly. Depending on the impact of particular shows, some cards have maintained their collectability. Others come and go. On the same shelf I found *Saved by the Bell, Baywatch, GI Joe, Ren and Stimpy, Mighty Morphin Power Rangers,* and *All My Children* cards. The *Baywatch* cards could double in the "aesthetically pleasing" section of this paper—lots of skin, physical statistics, and the like.

And where to put the Hooters cards? Are these aesthetic or just promotional? Each card shows a different waitress, lists her measurements, and identifies which Hooters restaurant she can be found at. Politically sensitive, these cards may truly end up to be collector's items. Will they continue if Hooters hires male waiters? The mind wanders.

The Unique

To conclude this chapter, I wanted to look at cards that were making a political or ethical difference—maybe cards that suggested social justice or compassion. I found none. I did find, however, one set of cards worth mention: AIDS AWARENESS TRADING CARDS: AIDS FIGHT IT, AIDS STOP IT AIDS—A Free Condom in Every Pack. Thirteen cards educate the reader about the disease. Twelve cards depict white men; one card shows a heterosexual white couple. The condom was red.

Conclusion

Why the obsession for collecting? As a child, I thought collecting was finding old things and continuing to accumulate them. I now find that collecting is new, and with an appropriate amount of money I can instantly *collect* an entire set of something. We have moved far from Murry Nelson's concept of cherishing, collecting, and sharing our trading cards from generation to generation. Our postmodern move to hyperreality has demanded that collecting become instant, that no time be involved in the accumulation. As quickly as sending an e-mail or a fax, one can become a collector. The commodification of collecting allows our kinderculture to instantaneously identify with collectors who have spent their lives accumulating and categorizing objects.

Children quickly enter into this desire to collect. Collectibles pervade every medium and genre of kinderculture. From collectible Barbies, circa 1996, to collectible nostalgic postcards, circa 1996, we are surrounded by a demand to buy, save, and keep incidental objects that only create meaning by the text included in the $2.25 package.

Well-known collectors have delighted the world with their lifelong pursuits. Peter Bull and his teddy bears, the Capuchin monks and their skulls, Robert Opie's mugs, Andy Warhol's art deco, and the skulls collected by the village chief of Dubu Diama of Urama, Papua, New Guinea (Muensterberger 1994). For decades, these collectors have meticulously pursued and kept objects of their desire. Now our children are able to instantly create a collection with less time, money, or dedication.

What is next? Sex, drugs, and rock 'n' roll are prolific in the trading card business. Sports cards are still popular, and with every new TV show or movie, cards are created. Companies sell cards to advertise their products; birth control can be marketed through trading cards. Where is there to go—to sarcastically suggest abortion trading cards, junkie trading cards, deadbeat dad cards? That seems too close to the truth. Can I stretch my imagination further? Bodily fluid cards? (Can you recall the scene in *Slackers* of the entrepreneur selling Madonna's pap smear?) What about serial killer victim cards—the half-eaten corpses of Dahmer's victims? (There are, of course, already Jeffrey Dahmer cards.) The manifestation of hyperreality is that outrageousness is commodified to the point that nothing is outrageous. Somehow my Johnny Beradino seems more significant.

Notes

1. The 1954 card of Bob Trice refers to the powerful Homestead Grays as a "semi-pro team." Considering the number of future Hall of Fame players on the team, it is an interesting reference.

2. During the 1958–1959 season seven of the top ten TV shows were Westerns—*Gunsmoke, Wagon Train, Have Gun Will Travel, The Rifleman, Maverick, Tales of Wells Fargo,* and *Wyatt Earp.*

References, Section One

Boyd, B., and F. Harris. (1973, 1991). *The Great American Baseball Card Flipping, Trading, and Bubble Gum Book*. New York: Ticknor and Fields.

Handelman, W. (1983). "Trade Cards." In L. Lipset, *Encyclopedia of Baseball Cards, Volume 1: 19th-Century Cards*. Centereach, NY: Lew Lipset.

Olbermann, K. (1979). "Trading Cards." In B. Sugar, ed. *The Sports Collectors Bible*. 3rd ed. Indianapolis: Bobbs-Merrill.

Nelson, M. (1986). "Some Possible Effects of World War II on the Social Studies Curriculum." *Theory and Research in Social Education* 15(4): 245–256.

Weidman, J. (1954). ". . . Anybody got a Solly Hemus?" *Sports Illustrated* (August 16): 38.

References, Section Two

Benjamin, W. 1931. *Illuminations*. London: Fontana, 1952.

De Berardinis, O. 1994. *Ladies, Leather, and Lace*. Saddle Brook, NJ: Comic Images.

Gatefold Cards. 1994. *Women of the World*. Beverly Hills, CA: Gatefold Cards.

Jackson, S. 1995. *Illuminati New World Order: Unlimited Edition Starter Set*. Austin, TX: Steve Jackson Games.

Kitchen Sink Press. 1994. *R.I.P. Good Ghoul Art*. Eric Nesheim and Kitchen Sink Press.

Muensterberger, W. 1994. *Collecting: An Unruly Passion, Psychological Perspectives*. Princeton, NJ: Princeton University Press.

Worden, D., and W. Honath. 1988. *Death Cult: Jonestown Massacre Memorial Cards*. Somerville, MA: Arnage Press.

The Bitch Who Has Everything

Shirley R. Steinberg

THIS IS THE BOOK of the Generations of Barbie.

1 In the day that Ruth created her, in the likeness of Ruth's daughter and a German whore, she made Barbie.

2 Female first she created her, and blessed her and called her name Barbie after her first-born.

3 And Barbie lived three years and Ruth created Ken, male and female she created them both.

4 And Barbie begat Skipper and friends, by the year of our lord nineteen hundred and sixty four, they were three.

5 And Barbie lived thirty and seven years until this record. Within those years, ten friends were created for Skipper. Midge was created to be Barbie's best friend.

6 And in the year nineteen hundred and sixty eight, Christie was created. Christie was unlike any other creation; her skin was black.

7 And these are the years and days of Barbie, the days of Barbie and the Rockers; the days of Barbie and her pets, including puppy Sachi and horse Rosebud; and the years of Barbie's family, cousins Francie and Jazzie; siblings Tutti, Todd, and Stacie.

8 And through Stacie, friends were born, Whitney and Janet.

9 And through Ken, multiple male friends were born, and like Ken, none of them ever married, and verily their manhood was always in question.

10 However, Barbie was most plentiful with friends, by the year nineteen hundred and ninety four, having twenty and six new girlfriends. Among them Cara who was also black, Teresa who was made Hispanic, and Kira who was Asian.

11 Hence, Barbie was known through the land as diverse and multicultural.

12 And these were the days of Barbie, and it came to pass, when Barbie
and her friends began to multiply on the face of the earth, little girls began
to buy more, as verily, one doll was never enough.

Okay, maybe I am taking an artist's license in rewriting scriptures. It only
seemed appropriate, as Mattel has been rewriting history and children's
play for years.

Playing Barbies in the fifth grade consisted of lugging plastic cases
laden with "outfits" to the playground and constructing scenarios
around Barbie and "getting" Ken. I knew at this early age that Barbie
(seeing as how she was female) must have an "outfit" for every occasion
and that wearing the same thing within some unspoken frame of time
was just not done.

When I was twelve or thirteen I began meticulously recording what I
wore each day on a calendar. I made sure that at least a month would go
by before I wore something twice. While I was a high school teacher my
students called attention to my idiosyncrasy by applauding the first day
that I duplicated an "outfit" in the classroom. Did Barbie construct this
behavior, or do I just love clothes?

Where does the text of Barbie begin? Thirty-seven years ago, Mattel invested in the production of a slim, blonde doll who (that?) wore a variety
of coordinated "outfits." While on vacation in Europe Mattel's cofounder,
Ruth Handler, discovered Lily. Lily was a prominent star of comics—a
sexy blonde with lose morals who adorned the dashboards of men's
autos throughout Germany and Switzerland. Her origin is not well documented, although her lineage has been traced to a Lily comic strip. Handler decided to bring the model of Lily with her back to the United States
and create a doll that could wear multiple "outfits"—she would name
her Barbie, after her daughter, Barbara. The promotional "hook" that
Handler cited as most essential was the possibility that girls could own
only one doll yet the doll could have multiple "outfits."

Physiologically, Barbie had perfect breasts (although no nipples), a
tiny waist, and long, slender legs. Much has been written within a feminist framework about Barbie, discussing the unrealistic body shape and
the like. I won't "go there." Barbie was made slim so that layers of designer fabric would flow nicely and realistically on her body. She was,
first and foremost, a model—fabric by Dior, designs by Mackie; nothing
was beyond reach for her. I am not offended by her figure; I do wonder,
however, about her poorly constructed private parts.

Speaking of private parts, four years later Barbie was given a
boyfriend, Ken—he had no genitals. Ken's crotch was (and is) as flat and
smooth as is Barbie's—I remember specifically my disappointment in
disrobing my first Ken (nothing to see). Possibly that physical defect is in

line with the personality that Ken has displayed throughout the years (though Earring Ken seemed to have a certain flare). Ken and Barbie have gotten as far as their wedding but never past it. The couple has never had a wedding night, and Barbie is always seen pushing the strollers of cousins, younger siblings, or friends but not of her own. Indeed, the only machismo sexuality found is radiated through Ken's friends of color, Derek and Steven—yet still crotchless.

Within months of her creation Barbie was a sensation. Mattel had transformed toys, especially dolls, and Barbie became "us." Little girls were frenzied to own a Barbie, each one coming in her own long, thin box and wearing a black- and white-striped swimsuit. Barbie had earrings and a blonde ponytail. She was a teen model. Girls moved from cradling baby dolls to demanding the latest in haute couture à la Mattel. Barbie was sexy, although most of her owners were not even aware of the genre of sexiness—they just loved their Barbies.

From Research to Obsession

I take my work seriously. Indeed, I think I am a superb researcher. I love the challenge of finding strange and wonderful factoids of trivia in little known academic nooks and crannies. However, this chapter has caused havoc in my life. Four years ago I became fascinated with the effect that Barbie had on little girls. I started to pick up Barbies, Barbie furniture, *Barbie* comics, *Barbie* books, Barbie jewelry, and Barbie toys wherever I went. I was able to even find the Benetton Barbie in Istanbul's airport (under the sign featuring the Marlboro man).

In order to do thorough textual analyses of Barbie and Barbie accoutrements, I needed to purchase my artifacts. I sit now, with great embarrassment, in an office with no less than forty Barbies, ten Kens, several Skippers (including a beauty princess and a cheerleading Skipper) and a plethora of "ethnic" and "special-edition" Barbies. I have three Barbie watches, a $300 Barbie jacket from F.A.O. Schwartz, a Barbie McDonald's playset, a Christmas playset, and a bakery set. I have two Barbie board games, one computer game ("Barbie Goes Shopping"), and a floppy-disc game ("Barbie Design Studio"). My life is out of control. I am only thankful that this research came long after my children were finished with playing with toys—consequently I am the only one in the home who lays claim to this Mattel treasure trove. However, when children come to visit, they plow through my Barbies within an hour and then inquire, "Do you have anything else?" Obviously, I don't have enough. My thoughts roam to my colleagues: Did Peter and Janet buy a host of Power Rangers? Does Doug sleep under a veritable canopy of *Beavis and Butt-*

Head posters? I know Murry owns more trading cards than anyone. Does Joe really idolize Macauley Culkin? I know he craves McDonald's Arch Deluxes constantly. Or is this all just rock 'n' roll?

My ownership of Barbies and related paraphernalia qualifies me as an expert. I am a consumer and a scholar—no better combination. Historically, I come by the expertise naturally; I have had a Barbie since she was invented. However, as I trace my own Barbie autobiography I am able to single out only my fetish for "outfits" as a permanent influence à la Barbie. I hope that I remain untouched from other taint . . . unless one looks at my research.

What Barbie Doesn't Have

It is far easier to discuss what Barbie doesn't have than what she does have. The list is much smaller. Barbie doesn't have a locomotive, a battleship (although she is a sailor), a rocket (although she is an astronaut), or an Uzi (although she is a soldier). Thematically, Mattel still has not invented Homeless Barbie, Abortion Barbie, Alcoholic Barbie, or S&M Bondage Barbie. As far as special editions, Barbie still has not come out as a criminal—she has, however, come out in special editions of fairy tales (never a witch), "true" history, careers, and different ethnicities—different from white, that is. There is no Northern Beauty Barbie, but the Southern Beauty Barbie features "today's Southern belle with charm and style!"

Barbie doesn't have holes in her clothes (unless placed there by Bob Mackie), and she never walks because she has a plane, a boat, a Corvette, a bicycle, a horse, roller blades, and Ken. Barbie doesn't have a favorite color other than hot pink; she has only one logo and no last name. Actually, I once heard her last name is Roberts—so where are her people from? Barbie does not have holiday sets for Hanukkah or Ramadan, but she does have them for Easter and Christmas. K Mart does not have a K Mart Barbie, but there are Wal-Mart, Saks Fifth Avenue, Bloomingdale's, Avon, and Nichole Miller Barbies (you know, the designer whose ties cost $60).

It is also easier to look at what Barbie isn't. Barbie is never sad, never unavailable, and never fails to "save the day" within every story written about her. Barbie is timeless; she existed in the days of the Mayflower, she was in Oz as Dorothy, and she has run for president in the last several American elections. She has never been a cook but has been a chef; never been a construction worker but has been a fashion designer; she has been a soloist, a rock star, and the mythological tooth fairy. Barbie is exclusively thematic; Ken, Christie, and the rest are occasionally given only professions.

The Bitch Has Everything

She does. From the pink condo to the swimming pool to the RV to the recording stage to more friends than anyone. Everyone loves Barbie and Barbie loves everyone. Barbie proves to us that if we try hard enough we can own anything and everything. Barbie always succeeds. She becomes whatever she sets her mind to—she influences generations of children and adults and is a perpetual reminder to all that is good, wholesome, and pink in our lives. Barbie is a true American. She stands for the family values that our country holds dear. She is strictly heterosexual, self-providing, philanthropic, and moral. She is also ready to bring "other" people into her life, no matter what color or ethnicity.

Barbie is able to move in and out of social circles with ease. Her plate is always filled with helping charity organizations and doing "good." The Love to Read Barbie comes with two children (one black and one white) and a book; for every LTR Barbie sold Mattel donates $1 to the Reading is Fundamental organization. As consumers we are able to support reading by purchasing this doll. That makes all the difference.

Intercourse Barbie

As much as Barbie is a virgin in sexual relationships, she is a whore in the corporate world. Barbie has "been in bed" with more of the Fortune 500 than anyone. She has worked in and owned her own Pizza Hut and McDonald's, she is a special Wal-Mart edition, she is also the star of TV's *Baywatch*, she is a constant guest within Happy Meals, and Disney's Epcot Center features a "Magical World of Barbie" show complete with dancers, singers, and fireworks. Avon has just released a special-edition Barbie, and Hallmark has Barbie Christmas ornaments—a new one issued each year. I already mentioned the Benetton Barbie, my unlikely find in a broken down Turkish airport. Barbie wanders in and out of corporate headquarters with ease. Companies know that tapping her resources is a quick ride to increased profits. No one really wants the tiny hamburger in the child's meal; they all are looking for the Barbie—which one is she? The Kenyan? The Ballerina? The Wedding Barbie? As a professional, Barbie is able to chose from her cellular phone, her video camera, and numerous pink briefcases for "just the right thing" for breaking that glass ceiling.

As a professional, Barbie has set records for changing vocations. In the early days she was featured as a nurse, a baby-sitter, and a secretary. Within months of political correctness, she became a doctor, a pilot, and a businessperson. Naturally, many of her careers still smack of nurturing—how can one avoid it with a constantly pink motif? One of my favorite fashion sets is the Caring Careers Fashion Gift Set. These "play pieces for Barbie at work" include a firefighter suit with pink trim, a teacher set, and a veterinarian's smock. Dr. Barbie is a pediatrician with a little black child and a little white child—all adorned in pink and blue. Astronaut Barbie came out in the 1980s and has reappeared in the late 1990s. As a part of the Career Collection, this Barbie first came out as a space pioneer. The newest version highlights Space Week and NASA and "encourages children of all ages to discover the past and future of the exploration in space." All of the boxes featuring careers have the slogan "We Girls Can Do Anything!" ribboned across the front. Police Officer Barbie is a "friend to all in the community! In her glittery evening dress, Police Officer Barbie shines with pride at the Police Awards Ball. Everyone applauds as she receives the Best Police Officer Award for her courageous acts in the community." PO Barbie comes with a badge and a short formal gown for the ball.

No group of careers could be complete without acknowledging our armed forces. There are more military Barbies than any other profession. As sergeants and majors, these booted girls march to the beat of proud, patriotic America. Choosing a favorite would be hard; I guess mine is the Desert Storm Barbie. "Wearing authentic desert battle dress uniforms of camouflage material—Sergeant Barbie is a medic, and she's ready for duty! Staff Sergeant Ken is ready too!" Their berets bear the distinctive 101st Airborne insignia with the motto: "Rendezvous with Destiny. Both are proud, patriotic Americans serving their country wherever they are needed."

To round out the professions, in 1992 we found the Barbie for President Gift Set. This was a Toys 'R' Us limited edition. "Barbie hits the campaign trail in spectacular style! Dressed in her winning red and gold suit she's the picture perfect candidate to get out the vote. Then, at her inaugural ball, the festive crowd cheers as Barbie enters in a sensational sparkling gown sprinkled with silver stars!" We girls can do anything. Is it any wonder that the latest Barbie is the $75 Statue of Liberty Barbie? Holding the torch of freedom, this golden-haired doll stands perched upon a plastic island, adorned with a shimmery crown, beckoning all who will listen to join her in liberty and justice for all.

Herstory

Barbie's other identities lie in ethnic and historical roots. Not satisfied with the existential Barbie, Mattel allowed Barbie to revisit, ergo, rewrite the past through a series of historical dolls. Each doll belongs to a collector's set, usually priced $5 to $100 more than a "regular" Barbie.

A collector's doll should be kept in her box, accumulating worth as the ages tick by.

One can only take a little boat down It's a Small World in Disneyland or go to Disney World to understand how ethnicity is defined by a corporation. Sailing down that channel, listening to hundreds of little dolls sing—constantly—we are able to see different peoples grouped together on their continents. Northern countries show a preponderance of buildings and clothing—countries from south of the equator seem to exhibit dolls with scant clothing selling vegetables, taking a siesta, or climbing trees. No buildings are evident in Africa, and only huts appear in the South American countries. Taking It's a Small World seriously as a metaphor for The World, we are able to understand the consciousness that constructed Mattel's line of ethnic Barbies.

Imagine we are sailing through our own small world and meeting these diverse Barbies; we hear their words describing their heritage. Each Barbie is distinct in native dress and manner. The Jamaican Barbie comes with large hoop earrings and a red bandanna. Many exclaim how much like Aunt Jemima or a slave she looks. Jamaican Barbie claims that her people speak patois, "a kind of Jamaica talk" filled with English and African words. She also insists Jamaicans are a very "happy" people and are "filled with boonoonoonoos, much happiness." Culturally, this Barbie teaches us that her country is filled with higglers (women merchants) who sell their food in open markets. Along with pictures of Bob Marley, sugarcane, and palm trees, the Jamaican Barbie is pleasantly packed in hot pink.

In keeping with the island theme, we move to the Polynesian Barbie. The box never mentions which island she is from—somewhere within the thirteen groups of tropical islands. We are told that people live closely together and are kind to one another. Polynesians like luaus and like to eat.

Another Barbie "of color" is the Indian Barbie. Unlike those of her island cousins, her box shows a picture of one building: Taj Mahal. We are reminded that India is a very old country and that most people eat only vegetables and rice "with their fingers." It is not mentioned whether or not Indians are happy or kind. None of these Barbies discuss their skin color or hair texture; there is no mention of physical attributes. Naturally, they are all standing on tiptoe.

As we visit northern Europe, we do not meet any amalgamated Barbies. For instance, there are no British Isles Barbies or Scandinavian Barbies. Each has her own country. The German Barbie looks splendid in her milkmaid's outfit and her long, blonde braids. We are welcomed to a country that is known for its "breathtaking beauty and hard-working people." Evidently the south-of-the-equator Barbies do not work—at least hard. Mentioned on the box are the modern cities, the museums, the art galleries, and the industries. The Norwegian Barbie tells us of her mythological tradition and describes her people as "tall, sturdy, fair-skinned, blonde, and blue-eyed." Food is not mentioned nearly as much on north-of-the-equator Barbie boxes as on the south-of-the-equator counterparts; evidently the farther north one moves the less they talk about or think about food.

There is no actual American Barbie—I mean a regular American. However, there is a Native American Barbie in the Dolls of the World Collection. NA Barbie is part of a "proud Indian heritage, rich in culture and tradition." She tells that long ago her people belonged to a tribe. Her dress is that of a Plains Indian, yet she describes homes like Eastern Indians. She reminds us three times of how proud she is of her people.

What's going on here? Mattel has defined ethnicity as other than white. Blonde, regular Barbie is the standard from which the "other" comes. As it emulates the dominant culture, the norm is Barbie; without a title, all other Barbies are qualified by their language, foods, and "native" dances. Attempting to be multicultural, parents buy these dolls for their children to teach them about "other" people. No "regular" Barbie ever talks about her regular diet, the personality of "her" people, and what her customs are. Only the designated "ethnic" dolls have those qualifications, much like the sign in the local K Mart that designates the location of ethnic hair products. Barbie has otherized dolls into dominant and marginal cultures. Barbie's whiteness privileges her to not be questioned; she is the standard by which all others are measured.

The New Social Studies

A couple of years after the introduction of the ethnic line of Barbie, Mattel introduced the American Stories Collection that featured a Civil War Nurse Barbie, a Pilgrim Barbie, a Pioneer Barbie, and an American Indian Barbie (there she is again). Each doll comes with a storybook that places Barbie in the middle of historical action. Each book ends with Barbie "saving the day" and changing history for the better.

As you have probably guessed, Pilgrim Barbie meets Squanto, and he teaches her how to plant corn: "He wasn't savage at all." She grows a successful crop of corn and decides to share it with her neighbors—hence the first Thanksgiving, and Barbie was there. Conveniently neglected are the Pilgrims' grave-robbings, confiscation of Indian lands, and oh, yes, the sticky matter of genocide.

Since Betsy Ross had already made the flag in 1776, Colonial Barbie decides to make a quilt to celebrate the thirteen colonies. The quilt was embroidered "Happy Birthday America," and Barbie and her female helpers were congratulated for the quilt and treated "with great respect." Western Barbie cleverly brings dried apples on the long journey during the westward expansion; when her friends get hungry, the apples are produced to make a delicious apple pie. American Indian Barbie takes care of a papoose, parentage unknown, and tells stories to the little Indian villagers. I will stop here, fearing an overload of saccharine.

Each book is signed on the back with a personal note from the author. History becomes firm in the eyes of the reader as it is legitimized by the author. Here are a few excerpts:

> During my research for Western Promise, I learned a lot about pioneers. The more I read, the more I admired these courageous, self-reliant people.

*   *   *

> Even though it's fun to read books, I still love to hear someone tell a good story! In the early days of the American Indians, there were no books or schools like there are today.

*   *   *

> In writing this story for you, I have learned so much! What I noticed most about the story of the Pilgrims and Thanksgiving is how the Native Americans became their friends and helped these strangers in a new land.

*   *   *

> I hope you enjoyed imagining Barbie as a colonial girl. Perhaps you will think of her on the next 4th of July and what it must have been like during the early days when America was first "born."

Consumers are told that history is being taught in a friendly way, via Mattel. Children now place Barbie within historical contexts in order to understand what really happened.

Fairy tales and fiction are not immune from Mattel's rewriting. The new Children's Collection Series features heroines from different stories. "Childhood favorites 'come to life' with Barbie. Play out the story of *Rapunzel*." Barbie as Scarlett O'Hara promises to be one of the most successful dolls of the decade. Promoted in a thirty-minute infomercial by Cathy Lee Gifford (TV's Barbie), the doll is sold as essential for anyone who was affected by the novel or movie *Gone with the Wind*: "See Barbie as your favorite character, Scarlett," Cathy Lee advises us. She recalls that Barbie was her favorite doll as a little girl and that there is nothing more special than having her best friend become Scarlett. One gets somewhat uncomfortable trying to find where reality begins and ends. Barbie acting as a character? Misogynist Henry Higgins Ken mentors Eliza Doolittle Barbie in a $150 *My Fair Lady* Limited Edition. *Star Trek* Barbie and Ken command a cardboard bridge for a mere $80 more. Barbie and Ken can be anyone.

Barbie as Literary Text

Mattel recognizes the importance of reading and education within its merchandising, creating hundreds of types of reading materials that feature Barbie. Not satisfied with the toy market, Mattel has branched out themes in magazines, books, newspapers, and film.

The Adventures with Barbie book series features a set of paperback books in which "Barbie stars in her own series of fabulous adventures that tie inspiring messages in with action, suspense and fun with friends—and set an example of independence, responsibility and kindness for young girls everywhere." *BARBIE*, the magazine for girls, is a subscription magazine that gives fashion tips, promotes new Barbie themes, teaches fun crafts, and gives beauty advice. The comic market promotes *Barbie Fashion* and *Barbie*; both comics are monthly and tell "stylish stories" and give "trend-setting tips." So as not to ignore toddlers, Little Golden Books have several Barbie titles, among them, *Very Busy Barbie* (Barbie as a model who gives up her career), *A Picnic Surprise* (Barbie finding an old lady's puppy, instead of having fun), and *Barbie, the Big Splash* (Barbie's photo shoot is spoiled, but she is able to take disappointment). We constantly are bombarded by the altruistic blonde (in the books, she is usually monocolored) giving up something sensational for the good of all humankind. Little girls are taught at an early age that it is more important to give up one's goal than to disappoint anyone else. Disney did it well with *The Little Mermaid* and *Beauty and the Beast*. It is a female's place to sacrifice for the good of others. What about Pocahontas? Esmeralda? You get the point.

Not to be outdone by three-foot-tall competitors, adults have their own Barbie literature: *Barbie Collector's Magazine* and several weekly and monthly newspapers, the most circulated paper being *Miller's Market Report: News, Advice, and Collecting Tips for Barbie Doll Investors.* This tabloid features Barbie events; in an April issue there were nineteen "don't-miss" gatherings advertised, including The Great Barbie Show of Southern California, Barbie Comes to Bloomingdale's, 7th Annual Barbie Grants-A-Wish, and many regional conventions. Barbie clubs adorn the United States from sea to sequined sea. There is an annual Barbie world convention and classes on Barbie, and a couple of years ago there was a Barbie Summit in New York. To emulate a global consciousness, Mattel organized this summit for women and girls alike to caucus about their needs and desires from Mattel for the twenty-first century. Always the educator, Barbie proves to us that reading and schooling cannot be left behind. Math becomes essential in order to add up the values of vintage dolls and collector items. Barbie, for many, is a full-time profession. Barbie is also the only nonhuman figure in Madame Toussand's famed wax museum in Hollywood. Naturally, she has her own Barbie Boutique on Fifth Avenue adjoining F.A.O. Schwartz, a store that provides scads of books, magazines, videos, and objects devoted to Barbie. The market flourishes.

What Could Possibly Be Next?

Are Barbies good for children? Should our girls play with them? How many Barbies should a child own? Do the dolls teach us what true beauty is? Can a child have self-esteem and not look like Barbie? Should we bend to peer pressure and allow our children to abide in pink-trimmed junior condos, dreaming of faraway places and exotic men? Does Barbie assist in constructing childhood consciousness?

Of course she does—just like any other feature of kinderculture. And just like any other feature of kinderculture, the affect of the Barbie curriculum is idiosyncratic: For some it facilitates conformity; for others it inspires resistance. Multiple readings aside, Barbie does operate within the boundaries of particular cultural logics. She does celebrate whiteness—blonde whiteness in particular—as a standard for feminine beauty; she does reify anorexic figures coupled with large breasts as objects of male desire. She does support unbridled consumerism as a reason for being. She never questions American virtue and supports the erasure of the colonial genocide of America's past. Make no mistake, she is a Christian, not a Jew, mainstream and not countercultural. No poor girl, Barbie, as she repeatedly proves her upper-middle-class credentials. Again, the curriculum may not take—no affect is guaranteed—but we must be aware of the terrain on which Barbie operates.

We feel great anticipation about the next line of Barbies. Having featured professions, movie stars, stories, sports, and fashion, could it be possible that Barbie could run out of themes? Ever maintaining authenticity, Mattel is able to continue rewriting history and life.

Following the popular *Baywatch* Barbie, we may find an *X-Files* Barbie complete with unknown blobby substance and missing/replaceable metal limbs. After Barbie has been Scarlett, will she be offered the part of

Lady Chatterly? Following Rapunzel, could we see a hairless Barbie? In keeping with real-life professions, wouldn't we be wise to wait for a Factory Worker Barbie, a Prostitute Barbie, a Drug Pusher Barbie—can a Pimp Ken be far behind? What about more politically active Barbies? Protest Barbie, chained to her Dream House? Bisexual Barbie, complete with both Ken and Midge?

The mind wearies with the possibility. One knows for certain, however, Barbie is with us, verily.

13 She who is known as Barbie will walk the earth through the millennium, being praised by both women and men and ushering in a new day for all humankind.

12 Multiculturalism and the American Dream

Jeanne Brady

MULTICULTURALISM IS A TREND in the toy industry in the 1990s, and today's dolls, with their caricatured ethnicity, are in full splendor, lined up in the aisles of toy stores everywhere. Even Barbie, still in her trashy pageantry, can be purchased in African American or Native American garb. In addition to fostering diversity, today's dolls can foster a form of literacy as well. As we know, Barbie has long been offered in a talking, albeit garrulous, version. It is important to note that dolls and books encode the cultural values of their creators. Barbie's cultural capital, however, cannot compete with the American Girl Collection.

The American Girl Collection is no exception to this multicultural trend. It too embraces diversity and literacy. American Girl dolls come not only with authentic fashions of the times but with historically accurate clothes and accessories, which can be purchased along with a series of companion books that are intended to help children understand what a girl's life was like during a particular historical period.

Pleasant Rowland, creator of the American Girl Collection and president of Pleasant Company, has pushed her empire beyond playrooms and bedrooms of little girls and into classrooms, offering lending libraries and an American Girl curriculum to accompany the dolls and books. Many educators are constantly looking for children's literature that provides positive images and interesting characters for boys and girls in the hope that these books will deepen and expand a critical understanding of cultural and gender diversity in our classrooms. Rowland has attempted to fill this void for young girls by commercially marketing dolls and books about Felicity, Kirsten, Addy, Samantha, and Molly in an attempt to bring history alive and to show how growing up in America has both changed and stayed the same during the past 200 years.

The current intersection of education and popular culture and its relationship to a gendered politics of representation is clearly expressed in the marketing of the American Girl Collection. Gender makes a difference when it comes to dolls. This is seen not only in the marketing of dolls but in their very conceptualization and construction.

I would like to provide a brief introduction to the history of Pleasant Company. I will analyze the production, distribution, and circulation of social identities and a particular narrative of popular memory and American dreams inherent in the products it manufactures. Next, I will analyze how these books play a part in the construction of classroom knowledge within a narrow view of history. Finally, I will analyze how educators might rethink the American Girl Collection within a position of a feminist pedagogy of multiculturalism. My purpose here is to make a claim for developing a pedagogy of difference that takes both popular culture and gender as serious academic concerns. This allows an analysis for studying gendered American dreams.

Pleasant Company was founded in 1985 and is dedicated to providing girls, ages seven and up, with a quality alternative to mass-marketed books and toys. Pleasant Rowland's decision to create this company came from her belief that "there were no toys of quality based on positive values for young girls." The American Girl Book Collection was initially created around three nine-year-old characters, each depicted during different periods in American history. Over the next eight years two additional characters were added.

Within nine years of its conception Pleasant Company's sales rose to more than $74 million. In 1991 and 1992 Pleasant Company was identified on *INC.* magazine's list of 500 fastest growing private companies in the nation. As of today, more than 10 million copies of American Girl books have been sold.

These products cannot be purchased in stores but only through a glossy, oversized catalog, which is revised many times during the year. It packages the American Girl Collection to target white and upper-middle-class adults. The marketing success of these products in part comes from the politics of representation inherent in the images and text that are provided in the catalog. As a part of the commercial packaging, the images and text display messages of nostalgia, innocence, and safe and romantic notions of childhood that mobilize particular lived experiences and desires. Furthermore, the elegant packaging of the catalog creates a stylized world of aesthetics and consumption while keeping books and dolls alive for a profitable business.

The dolls are created to coincide with the texts and, in Rowland's view, are manufactured to "be dearly loved and well played with and then passed down to other generations of girls tomorrow." Yet when examining the prices of the dolls and their accessories, one can only conclude that they are manufactured for a very elite group. The price of one doll and a paperback book is $88. To purchase additional accessories for the doll, one could pay as much as $1,000. The lucky girl who has the complete collection of all five dolls and their accessories would have invested more than $5,000. All of this is part of a strikingly sophisticated marketing effort that includes authentic styles of clothing with matching outfits for a girl and her doll. Samantha's nightgown costs $18. The same nightgown in children's sizes cost $42. And if you purchase them together, the savings is $6. This, of course, denies many young girls the possibility of owning their own dolls, accessories, and clothing—yet with millions of books sold the American Girl narrative is not unknown to children, parents, and teachers alike, certainly creating the desire among economic groups for the doll and her accessories. A recent Scholastic Books order form, which children bring home from school, offers an American Girl Pack, five books in all, for $14.95 (individual books are $3.95 each).

Another concern centers on the intersection of popular culture in the form of the American Girl dolls and books and the influence these books have on the formation of gender roles and the construction of identities. The Felicity doll accessories offer a wooden tea caddie with a dark-blue china teacup and saucer advertised as everything for a proper tea ceremony ($22). To help girls dress like Kirsten, the catalog offers her springtime dress (sizes 6X to 16) and apron with scalloped hem and puffy, short sleeves, petticoat, pantalettes, and prairie boots for $221. Peppermint pinafore dresses, sailor suits, afternoon tea dresses, school suits, rose garden gowns, summertime gowns with rose-trimmed hats, and birthday sundresses are offered to girls to make their feminine wardrobe complete and allow them to dress up in the nostalgic, wholesome times of the dainty little character. Not to offend those who lack money but not cultural capital, pattern portfolios can be purchased for the experienced sewer. In addition, American Girl Pastimes offers cookbooks, craft books, theater kits, and paper dolls to participate in little-girl adventures from the past. On the "Special Little Extras" page in the catalog a skincare kit is suggested ($6) for your American Girl Doll to keep her vinyl body healthy with cleansing power and terry towel and facecloth.

Production of History

Educators often look for books that contain positive images and creative characters for boys and girls. Unfortunately, however, male characters continue to hold the lead in children's literature, both in picture books and in juvenile fiction.[1] One of the stated goals of the American Girl Book Collection is to provide young readers with books that feature smart, resourceful girls and that show how their lives are worthy of study. This, of course, is an important step in educators' and in the public's acknowledgment of the need for gender equality and democratic classroom relations, and, at first glance, these books appear to provide us with an opening. However, the American Girl series merely uses the past as a convenient vehicle to portray five girls' lives in trends and styles reminiscent of class, racial, and gender stereotypes and inequities that characterize the present. In this instance the stories fail to connect their readers with a critically interrogated past by providing dominant forms of representation and making claims on history and their targeted audience that serve to delete and reduce oppositional historical narratives and knowledge. In this instance, I am not challenging the historical authenticity of the texts but rather am attempting to engage both the grounds on which such authenticity is developed and the relationship between knowledge and authority—to critique how it is established and to explore what relationship it has to dominant regimes of representation. Through this type of analysis I hope to illuminate how scenarios that view the world within simple dichotomies, such as good or evil and right or wrong, reveal a commercial pedagogy that does little to question and challenge a history that a critical feminist multiculturalism calls into question.

Upon critical examination it is clear that the overall collection, with the possible exception of the Addy series, actually produces a narrative of national identity that is one-dimensional. This is seen in the alarmingly artificial formula that shapes the series. Each girl has a tale about a school story, a Christmas story, a springtime story, a summer story, and a winter story. The stories are for the most part uncomplicated and bland, with quick solutions and easy answers. What these books and dolls demonstrate is that life in the past, whether it be in 1774, 1854, 1864, 1904, or 1944, was simple, unified, fixed, wholesome, and complete. Even with moments of adventure, the texts are devoid of critical substance. Issues of struggle, conflict, imperialism, and repression are conveniently missing from this view of history.

Joshua Brown notes in his critique of children's historical fiction that in some cases "books offer a false totality, words and pictures reinforcing one another to create a closed, complete universe devoid of true detail, contradictions, questions or unsettling ideas."[2] Unlike most children's historical fiction, the American Girl series provides a brief postscript in each book that offers a "Peek Into the Past," furnishing documentary photographs and images of that particular time in history that unfortunately only complement the historical presentation of the narrow view of history contained in the texts.

Furthermore, ethnicity in these books is limited, and class positions are translucent and have no weight on the characters' ideologies—their values, behaviors, or ideas. On the contrary, everyone conforms to a modern, middle-class morality that conflates the past and present so as to narrate a dominant version of national identity. An example of this is Molly. Although the texts are placed within the period of World War II and take up issues of patriotism and the war effort that bolster hardship and adversity, Molly and her friends live in a world of bleach-white racial conformity. There is no serious discussion within the texts or the post-script that addresses other frames of history during this time, such as the evacuation of Japanese American children and adults into concentration camps in this country or profiteering.

The most recent doll series, Addy Walker (1864), made its debut in the fall of 1993 and is a possible exception. The promotional campaign that was launched months before the actual doll and books were available was enormous; posters, pins, Addy testimonials, and news releases preceded the products. An Addy Advisory Board that included an impressive list of scholars, historians, and filmmakers was constructed to legitimate her creation. Addy is portrayed as an African American girl living during the Civil War era. Connie Porter, a celebrated author in her own right, wrote the first three formula texts, which are well written and are beautifully illustrated by Melodye Rosales. (The illustrator later resigned over a conflict of artistic license with the corporate hierarchy, who deemed her illustrations too graphic and depressing for children—slaves should have smiling faces.)

These texts provide an important opportunity for the introduction to a multicultural understanding of history. In the introductory story, Addy and her mother escape slavery and are separated from the rest of their family. Yet in the succeeding tales Addy lives in Philadelphia and experiences a school story (the reader, of course, can purchase Addy's school dress for $70 and the petticoat to wear underneath for an additional $20), a Christmas story (Addy's dad arrives as a free man on Christmas Day to make the holiday complete), and so on. With the exception of the first text, *Meet Addy*,[3] this specific collection, when analyzed within the entire philosophy of Pleasant Company, reeks of a liberal notion of multiculturalism developed around a view of pluralism based on the concept of "common culture." Do these texts provide the opportunity to name the experience of oppression and then identify structures of domination that function to cause the oppression? Do these books erase America's shameful character? Or, instead, do these books legitimate diversity as a marketing strategy in the same way Crayola has in manufacturing a new line of "multicultural" crayons, which offers an array of browns and tans and signals difference as nothing more than fashion and consumerism? Soon an Hispanic American Girl Doll will make its way into the catalog, and I can only guess that her story will be the same.

Education and Popular Culture

School is an important site where the construction of a narrow range of identities not only takes place but can be challenged pedagogically. These texts and dolls, as well as other artifacts of popular culture, offer educators an opportunity to challenge the narrow range of identities they project. It is around the relationship between popular culture and education that an approach can be theorized that will enable people (teachers, parents, boys, girls, administrators) to intervene in the formation of their own subjectivities and to enable and exercise power in the interest of transforming forms of domination and conditions of oppression into emancipatory practices and democratic possibilities.

Educators must become more attentive to the various pedagogical sites (both in and out of schools) in which the politics of remembering and forgetting produce different narratives of a national past, present, and future. When history and politics are disguised in the image of nostalgia, innocence, and simplicity there is more at stake than the danger of simple deception. History in this sense becomes rewritten as a unified chronological record of events and exonerated of its contradictory, complex, and seamy sides. As critical educators we should provide students with the opportunity to read and understand history in all its complexity and narrative form so as to provide the opportunity for students to problematize the past and become active agents so as to challenge the present and create a more democratic future while recognizing the various constraints different social groups face in their struggle for self-determination and social justice. In effect, I want to argue that questions of identity and public life are central to any notion of schooling, and I will attempt to develop this point by focusing on elementary schools as important public spheres.

I believe that elementary schools are important sites where educators can intervene in developing curricula and classroom relations that attempt to eliminate sexist, racist, classist, and other oppressive social practices. This is a more complex approach to teaching and pedagogy, requiring teachers to redefine this relationship in terms of a mutually appreciated space for living in the world of difference. This does not mean adding new material to the existing curriculum by offering students bits of knowledge but rather a revisioning of a curriculum that fosters the relationship between schooling and democracy.

I want to be more specific here by looking at the important intersection of popular culture and a pedagogy of difference. The American Girl

Collection is an exemplary cultural text that can be taken up pedagogically because it offers the potential for a critical reading of how the politics of "nostalgia" works to conceal the ideological principles used to legitimate an innocent view of history and a dominant conception of family values.[4] Under the guise of play, entertainment, and fun a one-dimensional history provides a foundation for viewing historical events that appeal to a nostalgic past written as an unchanging narrative rather than providing texts that construct meanings amid diverse social struggles and modes of contestation. By erasing the political and ethical considerations that make history a site of struggle, the American Girl Collection produces a version of history/popular culture through a lens that rewrites history as sites of injustice without the potential for human agency. The issue for educators is not merely to recognize the importance of cultural texts such as the American Girl Collection in shaping social identities but to address how representations are constructed and taken up through social memories that are taught, learned, mediated, and appropriated within particular formations of power both in and out of schools.

Historical fiction texts can provide alternative interpretations and presentations of the past that will enhance and expand the sugary view of history that the American Girl series offers. I am not asking for historical fiction to expose children to the atrocities of the past but rather to transform an uncomplicated reading of history into a tangible experience that can offer the opportunity for students and teachers to engage the past and challenge the present.

The American Girl series is a good place to begin. Let's use these books as a jumping-off point to expand upon the cultural diversity of the past and the multicultural realms of the present and future. There are many texts that can be used to enhance and extend our understanding of the complexities of history. For example, *A Break with Charity*[5] takes place in 1706; its main character is a young girl who recalls the fears and accusations of witchcraft that tore apart her community in 1692. *Time Enough for Drums*[6] is the story of a sixteen-year-old African American girl who struggles on the home front during the Revolutionary War. *Who Is Carrie?*[7] is also set during the Revolutionary War; it is a book about a young African American girl living in New York City and grappling to understand her identity in the world. *A Gathering of Days: A New England Girl's Journal, 1830–1832*,[8] is a fictional diary kept by a young girl growing up in a small town in New Hampshire. *Lyddie*[9] is a story of a young girl determined to gain her independence by becoming a factory worker in a textile mill in Lowell, Massachusetts. *Number the Stars*[10] tells the story of two young girls living in war-torn Denmark and their courage and determination to fight against the Holocaust. *Rose Blanche*,[11] another story set during World War II (this time in Germany) teaches us about a young girl's strength and commitment to social justice. These are just a few of the many texts available.

We need to be aware that even though there is more multiethnic and multicultural literature being published, the quality of the literature for different ethnic groups, white included, may be questionable. Some of these texts are permeated with notions of patriarchy, colonialism, sexism, and racism. Therefore, we need to take up these books critically. What this means is that much of what is constituted as accepted knowledge must be analyzed for the exclusions, repressions, and privileges that often go unacknowledged in the language of educators in the classroom. This does not mean that we deny children the actual pleasures of play and enjoyment; rather, by historicizing culture and problematizing knowledge, we provide them with the opportunity to understand diversity and cultural difference represented in the past and present.

Finally, we have a responsibility to increase our knowledge of the distant and recent past in an attempt to generate insights into the conditions and multiple identities and ideologies that existed. We need to see beyond a single representation of fact and provide learning opportunities for students to engage in multiple references that compose different cultural experiences, codes, and languages.

Notes

1. See Kathryn Meyer Reimer, "Multiethnic Literature: Holding Fast to Dreams," *Language Arts* 69 (January 1992): 14–21.

2. Joshua Brown, "Into the Minds of Babes: Children's Books and the Past," in Susan Porter Benson, Stephen Brier, and Roy Rosenweig, eds., *Presenting the Past* (Philadelphia: Temple University Press, 1986).

3. Connie Porter, *Meet Addy* (Middleton, WI: Pleasant Company, 1993).

4. Henry Giroux, "Beyond the Politics of Innocence: Memory and Pedagogy in the 'Wonderful World of Disney,'" *Socialist Review*, in press.

5. Ann Rinaldi, *A Break with Charity* (San Diego: Harcourt, Brace, Jovanovitch, 1992).

6. Ann Rinaldi, *Time Enough for Drums* (New York: Holiday House, 1986).

7. James Lincoln Collier and Christopher Collier, *Who Is Carrie?* (New York: Delacorte Press, 1984).

8. Joan Blos, *A Gathering of Days: A New England Girl's Journal, 1830–1832* (1979).

9. Katherine Patterson, *Lyddie* (New York: Lodestar Books, 1991).

10. Lois Lowry, *Number the Stars* (New York: Houghton Mifflin, 1989).

11. Roberto Innocenti and Christophe Gally, *Rose Blanche* (Mankato, MN: Creative Education, 1985).

13 Anything You Want: Women and Children in Popular Culture

Jan Jipson and Ursi Reynolds

JAN

Flying down the 401 in Ontario at eighty miles per hour—trying to convert "km" to "mph" so I will know if I'm speeding in Canada. I imagine myself to be Thelma or Louise before the Grand Canyon became the inevitable climax to their lives, stretching the boundaries of the possible, traveling free, no hesitation. As I drive I listen to a Bob Dylan tape, one of my favorites—"Just Like A Woman." I hear the line, "And she breaks just like a little girl" and I shudder. Did I ever really notice what he was singing? I fast-forward to "Like a Rolling Stone," but the feeling of power and energy leaves me.

I thought back to a xerox from a 1960s *Seventeen* magazine that a colleague had shared with me . . . something about being "blessed" to be a woman. I probably first read it as a teenager. I wonder how articles like that had affected my friends and I in the 1960s and had influenced our collective socialization as women. I considered how insidious those magazines were, how subtly the song lyrics shaped our expectations of life.

I pull into Burger King, my young son clamoring for a cold drink. The Kid's Meal special is Pocahontas; we draw a blonde, blue-eyed, plastic John Smith. Erik is disdainful, comments in his own imperious way on colonial multiculturalism and decides the doll will fit in his Jurassic Park collection. I start a different road tape, "Boys on the Side," and catch Bonnie Raitt and later Whoopi Goldberg singing versions of "You Got It."

Multiple perspectives, now, in 1995: "Everything about you tells me you're my man/best friend . . ."—take your pick. But has anything really changed, I wonder? The buoyancy of my cross-country drive turns to distress as I once again acknowledge that the often distorted representations of women and children are still disrupting the possibilities I imagine for myself and my kids.

Two summers ago, Ursi and I had the opportunity to discuss similar issues of representation with the participants in a graduate seminar in teacher education. I recall clearly what they said about their early socialization and the effects of popular culture on them and on the students they teach.

It was supposed to be the best course I had ever taught. I wanted to stretch my perceived limits of what I could do. It was an opportunity to put together pieces of my work for the past four years, my personal wanderings, struggles with imposing my ideas and beliefs on my students, further experiments into the implementation of feminist pedagogy—a perhaps final revisiting of the fiction-as-curricular-text issues that Nick Paley and I had been examining for five years, a still tentative excursion into being a constructivist teacher, into an emergent curriculum extending from the shared life experiences of all of us in the class. It was going to be an extension of my ongoing exploration of Rob Proudfoot's (1986) Relational Education model, facilitating student construction of personal meaning within the context of an examination of issues related to contemporary society and with respect for the multiple contributions of women and people of color. Ursi shared my interests in examining issues related to women and children in the popular culture. She agreed to join me in coteaching the course.

URSI

The course was a graduate seminar, "Issues in Education: Women and Children in Popular Culture," designed to explore contemporary social issues surrounding women and children as they are represented in the various media of the popular culture—in news media, television, film, toys, music, art, and literature. We planned to rely on media as curricular text—there would be no traditional academic material in print form. Our agenda was to explore the possibilities of using media and technologies to foster critical analysis, and we mapped the contours of the course with several guiding questions. Is popular media a useful curricular text for teacher education? If so, what practices foster its success? If not, what are the constraints?

In immersing participants in the seminar in popular media rather than in customarily preferred print text, we extended an invitation to participants to consider the place of media in not only their own lives but in the lives of children and families. Although the course was not dedicated to media theory or critical analysis or feminist theory, these were all elements of it. Concerned with prevailing cautionary views of the effects of popular media on children and youth, we proposed that participants scrutinize the traditionally low status knowledge forms of popular culture for presented realities of women and children.

We delighted in the fact that the group was diverse in gender, age, nationality, status, race, sexual orientation, social experience, and political awareness. Even though they were all university students their routes into the university experience varied dramatically. Because the seminar was small we could provide a variety of means of discovery and we could provide support.

There were, however, questions of possible ambiguity enmeshed in the concept. Would the participants understand our media choices? Would they connect their personal judgments to media imagery? Would they investigate why the top shapes more easily than the bottom and would they connect themselves as persons and teachers? Could our reliance on media-as-text promote a level of analysis to inspire and even motivate social action? To focus our concerns we decided to observe dual aspects of student experience. We articulated several questions: How did situating issues of women and children in popular media influence the growth of our students as educators? We decided to collect several tangible expressions of student knowledge, attitudes, beliefs, and values. One was observational and recorded data from seminar sessions, and the other was reflective journals and written assignments. Although both were rich informational sources, we were ever mindful of the inherent difficulties in making inferences about experiential process.

JAN

Anticipating interactions in the seminar, we also had other concerns. What range of perspectives would our participants bring to the experience? Would they find our media selections engaging? Would our process facilitate analysis? What levels of participant resistance might be stirred by documenting our process?

*   *   *

In this chapter we share our reflections and experiences as coteachers and those of the seminar participants as we collectively responded to the multiple media presentations. Underlying the actual engagements of the seminar was a shared commitment on the part of the instructors to feminist pedagogy and an overt dedication to applying a model of nonsynchronous parallelism as a theoretical frame of analysis. We hoped to juxtapose a theoretical analysis of the materials with the daily experiences of the participants within the cultural context in which they lived.

As we shared our ideas and struggled to meld them into some sort of mutually acceptable plan, we identified three places of intersection that were to form focal points for the seminar—landmarks to guide our progress through the unmapped terrain of a new course.

1. In comparing our various histories as educators, mothers, and single parents, we repeatedly returned to issues related to the oppression we had experienced because of and through our gender, social-class backgrounds, and racial, ethnic, and religious identification, particularly as they were repeatedly activated by the media and within the popular culture.

2. Having identified these issues as core to our personal understanding of women and children in popular culture, we agreed on the construct of nonsynchronous parallelism as a starting point for the exploration of specific representations of the experiences of women and children in the popular culture.

3. And finally, we identified our desire for a comprehensive examination of multiple forms of media and for diversity through the inclusion of textual events representative of multiple gendered, cultural, class, and ideological perspectives.

Our goal and destination? To facilitate a critical exploration of how media constructs particular representations of women and children through its objectified images of victimization, powerlessness, beautification, and consumerism. The vehicle? A detailed examination of representations of women and children in print media (newspapers and magazines), film, television, toys, children's institutions (museums, parks, and amusement parks), and more traditional artifacts such as music, dance, drama, fiction, art, and poetry.

Theory on the Side

We were working with the layered notion of nonsynchronous parallelism (McCarthy, 1988) to analyze the perceptions of culture-sensitive teachers to issues of power and inclusion. We felt it could be useful as a point of view from which participants might interpret media messages and apply them to women's and children's issues.

It was a conceptual and teaching challenge to introduce the parallelist position in one evening's activities and discussion. As the discussion unfolded participants warmed to the elements of subjectivity, particularity, and variability that make up the nonsynchronous aspect of the parallelist position. We were again mindful that self as the center of knowing is as crucial to adults as it is to the children with whom we are concerned.

The discussion began with the clarification of the meanings of single-cause theory, parallelism, nonsynchrony, and the production of difference. Seminar participants offered personal experiences to illustrate that categories are often mutually exclusive since one cannot, for example, alter one's gender by achieving monetary wealth. They cited examples of personal life decisions marked by particular and situational needs and informally expanded the original categories to include age, ability, and sexual preference. Together, we generated several themes that became central to our analysis: (1) our private and public lives are inextricably interwoven with economic, cultural, political, and social spheres of society; (2) our individual needs and social events are historically and situationally variable; and (3) popular media does not reflect the multilayered realities of authentic people and groups.

We ended the first session by soliciting written responses to the question: What is popular culture? One participant wrote:

> Everything that impacts me? Stuff that controls me? Keeps me from self-actualizing? Opinions of people I respect? Where I am from (personal history, ancestry, culture)? What I'm afraid to be—What I think I am? Fads? Artificial constructs?—Maybe there's a whole subset of popular culture out there that doesn't affect me because either I know nothing of it or am nonplused by it.
>
> How do I feel about it? I feel angry about the "things" in it. I still fall under the power of . . . and at the same time I realize if a person doesn't make some peace around that, it's too much bad news. Sometimes I see it in terms of a deficit—like the things that get their hooks in you that you can't shake—the big mothers like love/romance—and then there are the lesser hooks—popularity, beauty, success, etc. I think it creates isolation, depression, self-doubt, that one has to struggle against—proportionately to whatever else one has either balanced it against or managed to stuff off. It becomes convoluted at some point. Like do I shave my pits because it's what I've chosen to do or because I'm not comfortable with the other side of it? It's confusing when you think of actually living out the results of dictates of popular culture. . . . I think it comes in part from all the stuff you "picked up" when you were little, carried forward, made sense of and will pass down.

Subsequent sessions focused on selected aspects of the popular culture as represented in various contemporary media. Dialogue journal writing was included as a regular seminar assignment to encourage personal responses to the interwoven content and experience of the seminar. Themes of oppression, identity, power, and relationships pervaded the participants' writings. Excerpts from their journals and papers revealed the meaning of these themes in the lives of the participants. By reflecting on their own experiences with the popular culture, participants began to relook at the experiences of the children with whom they were currently working.

Free to Be You and Me and Other Mythologies

To begin the second session, we showed "Still Killing Us Softly," a documentary about gendered advertising to illustrate connections between popular images and political, cultural, and economic issues. In the debriefing discussion the participants explored wide-ranging themes from the film, including: objectification, imposed standards of beauty, physical perfection as ideal, sexualization of childhood, an emphasis on heterosexuality, the linking of sex and violence, separation of love and sex, devaluation and contempt of women, devaluation as normal, contempt of women's bodily processes, promotion of artificiality, consumerism and conspicuous consumption, issues of health, racism, and ageism, trivialization of rape, trivialization of social movements, denial of gentleness, and validation through sexually pleasing men.

In discussion, often contextualized within stories of their own life experiences, participants peeled away the layered messages of the film. They described how women are cued by the media to strive for power through physical appearance and observed that advertising promotes women against one another by imposing beauty norms representing class superiority. They discussed elective plastic surgery as an issue of social class, children's toys with sexual characteristics as exploitive economics, and *Vogue* as soft porn. They asked, "Are there parallels between the third-wave women's movement and the ever growing popularity of Victoria's Secret?"

Kathy, in a journal stuffed with cartoons, ads, poems, photographs, and dried flowers, began by reflecting on the concept of nonsynchronous parallelism:

Dear Diary: Will I go to hell if I look at this model instead of the relational model? [Robert Proudfoot's (1988) Relational Model of Education had provided a core theoretical frame for her teacher preparation program.] This model reminds me how effectively "they've" confused values, class and economics. I don't even see class anymore as more than artificial. It seems like focusing on the wrong stuff. Is class ever an issue if you're middle-class? When I worked in an office where people weren't really required to be whole people at all—or use their minds much—the trade-off was clothes— how you looked—that's where $$ was spent—It was a trade-off of clothes for minds—there was a sort of happiness in looking good. . . . When I was a kid, one woman who I thought was the most powerful in the world [would] sit at a piano and play hymns and silly songs like the "possum song"—and I never wanted to be anywhere else. And I think her arms sagged underneath.

To further analysis of implicit messages and explicit advertising, we showed segments from a popular children's video from the 1970s, "Free to Be You and Me." Participants characterized Marlo Thomas, Rita Coolidge, and Kris Kristopherson as fashionable and smiling shades-of-white at the hearth of an idyllic farmhouse fireplace. In the animated story sequence, they felt that even though at first glance the characters were appealing the film was laden with racial, ethnic, gender, age, and parenting stereotypes. Reflecting on contemporary television, they concluded that, sadly, the messages in kid's videos haven't changed much in twenty years.

Kathy also had a strong reaction to "Free to Be You and Me": "I've never seen it before. It has that sort of we're all alike feel to it. There's something in it that made me think of the fear of change. If we can make it the 'same' will we be OK? If you buy your son a baseball mitt, marbles, basketball, it helps keep you safe in your memory of 'sameness,' a built-in historical, cultural connection to all that perpetuates what you value, feel sure in and are—but WE ALL DO THAT—it's the struggle of culture emerging."

Making the News

We began exploring the news through print and identified values underlying the portrayal of women and children in a current selection of newspapers and magazines. Our focus question was, What is the message about women and children that popular print media would convey to a person unfamiliar with our culture?

An informal tally of newspaper articles revealed that among the many stories in the press the most frequent themes were women's bodies, women and their relationships with social institutions, women's jobs and professions, reproduction issues, hurt children, poverty, and homelessness. Many of the magazines were directed at the women's market and emphasized themes such as reproductive rights, entertainment figures, high culture and fashion, sexuality, super moms, child care, beauty tips, home management, and jobs.

In looking at print advertising, we asked several questions: To whom are these ads directed? How does advertising fragment consumers into groups and why is this done? How and why do people perceive advertising images differently? These questions generated lively cutting and pasting as the ads were assembled and summarized into categories including selling products with body parts and phallic imagery, creation of product image through women's ethnicity, and women as consumers of expensive products and adornment.

On the Front Line

We continued with a series of TV clips from local stations, brainstorming questions such as: Is today's TV news the same as in the past? What alternatives are there and how do we find them? How are editing decisions made? Whose voices are missing? How does TV news affect democracy?

Carol commented on the selective tradition in television editing:

> Issues that affect poor families, for example, were presented not by poor families but by other people who also made the decisions about what to say and how to present it. I realize that news people do get comments from the people involved, but then they select the voices they want heard, so they might as will skip the work of finding ordinary folk to interview and say whatever they want the audience to believe. It's more insidious to include real voices, though, because it lends a greater aura of truth and reality.

In contrast with mainstream television news, we viewed a PBS program about television news called *The '90s*. At a demonstration directed at network coverage of the Gulf War, the roving cameraperson interviewed Lady Atterly of *Mr. Rogers' Neighborhood* fame. She offered a concise and scathing critique of TV war coverage and its implications for children. The participants were inspired by the heroine of children's TV in her role as eloquent media activist.

We posed several summarizing questions: Are the stories on TV news symptoms of larger stories that are not made explicit? What are the motives and rewards for the news decisions made behind the camera? If we could learn more about this story, what would we like to know and how am I affected as an individual and an educator?

Cruising Through the Days of Our Lives

On the fourth evening we turned our attention to television entertainment. Participants had been asked, as a homework assignment, to watch a variety of programs including advertisements, situation comedies, soap operas, and Saturday-morning cartoons. Journal reactions to their viewing experiences were emphatic.

Allie, in comparing print advertising with print news media, commented:

Images of sex and violence are common to both, but they are presented so differently that it's difficult to relate them. In the news, women and children are victims of violence, including sexual and economic violence. In advertising, women invite sexual violence.

The ads, of course, are more and more alarming; even those aimed at very young children use sex and music to sell. Commercials for candy, juice, gum, and the like imitate adult images in a really disturbing way. There's also the element of which toys are advertised to boys and which to girls, and how they're presented. That's just as bad, with the loud, harsh music, fast voices and action for boys and their hideously deformed, water-filled baby dolls.

During the soap operas, especially, the ads were geared toward women viewers, and it was obvious who was in charge. Several ads depicted women with physical ailments (PMS, constipation, and a C-section); they couldn't deal with it and took drugs. Another woman, with heartburn, received an antacid with calcium in it ("Besides, it's got something my body needs!") from a man with heartburn.

The most incredible were commercials during sports events, which were on early in the evening and which Alex [her son] watched with his dad. It's not the decency factor in the half-naked women parading around. I appreciate and admire all kinds of human figures and think more, not less, should probably be exposed. It's the fact that all of the women are, of course, young, thin, tall, white (but suntanned), and not always blonde but never too dark. Dark-haired women are used to indicate a real mysterious and sexy type, probably a little bad. Dark-skinned women are virtually nonexistent unless an element of real exotica is desired. In addition to the extremely limited version of what it means to be attractive, the actions are distressing, too. Do I want my child to believe that women spend most of their time walking around in bikinis or tight, short skirts, looking hungrily at men drinking beer? . . . Especially as the kids grow older, they will begin to see more and more such images of beauty, desirability and passivity. When I wonder about how my sons will construct their versions of reality, I think about my own conflict between personal experience and the "reality" represented in the media. Although I was told I could do anything, I was smart, I was pretty (but it's better to be smart than pretty, and soon, I KNEW that I would never be pretty enough, good enough, sexy enough, never anything enough, except maybe smart), but who cared? Smart doesn't show up in photo shoots. . . . It makes me angry that I spent so much time disliking myself, because it isn't just the physical appearance and the knowledge that you'll never achieve the ideal. It's completely tied in to who you are as a human being. My sons will never experience that same distress, although they'll have their own problems, some of which the media will undoubtedly contribute to. But the messages of who women are, what they should look like, what they should do, will affect them nonetheless as they deal with women and girls in relationships in their lives and work. Will they really know that girls and women are people?

Allie also wrote about network television programs:

I watched *Designing Women*, the same episode we saw clips from in class. Issues brought up by this one episode included working women (do they ever actually do any work?), reproductive technology (the man won't have his sperm frozen; "I guess I'm just an old-fashioned guy"). Weight loss (it's worth risking lung cancer to fit into that size 10), and race, gender and power relations (both between the women and their foil, their black male employee, and between the woman wanting another baby and her old beau who won't make a baby with her).

Sex, Power, and Videotapes

Films and videos were the focus of the next class. *Santa Sangre*, a film that looks at the violence of colonialist oppression through the experiences of a circus troupe, was juxtaposed with *Men Don't Leave*, where the sex, religion, and pain were veiled under the cover of blankets, smiles, and humor and with a home video of children's circus pretend-play.

Carol reflected in her journal:

Santa Sangre hits me as the most powerful piece of media we have viewed in this class, especially in line with the subject of divorce as what follows for women and children. Basically the breakdown of the family structure, caused mainly by divorce, leaves us in a place of no role models, no givens, and, in a sense, chaos. Women and children are left searching for answers that have not yet been answered. Women have the strain of two roles; that of mother and breadwinner, and the children have to endure the fear, stress, and exhaustion their mothers are going through. The main woman in *Santa Sangre* displayed this type of role search. She is first seen as a priestess defending her temple, a woman defending her home, which is going to be destroyed. In the next scene her son runs to her and begs her to come down from her perch; now seen as mother with a child begging for her life. As the film progresses she is also seen performing in the circus (the working role) and as a lover, wife, and jealous woman. No one role seemed to be predominant; she had no roots but lived out the chaotic circus of womanhood. . . . I certainly feel the class that pervades our society because of the loss of structure. As a single mother of a toddler I continually try to evaluate my roles as both breadwinner and mother. . . . I strongly identify with the frustration and depression felt by the main character in *Men Don't*

Leave. The financial pressure of being solely responsible for children in overwhelming and very isolating. How strong can women actually be? How much can we give? . . . Breaking down to the point of not functioning at all is the scariest of all.

As we considered her words, we asked ourselves again: Who is creating this image of stress, of undefinable chaos and helplessness? Does it portray the real experiences of women who are workers and mothers? In contrast to Carol, Allie wrote:

I am finding it difficult to discuss the impressions for this class session. Watching the children's circus video, I was immediately struck by all kinds of messages that I consider to be a problem. For example, the lion tamer and ringmaster are always in control, with their whips and loud voices; the dark-skinned faces were covered with white makeup; the children of all colors were made to look identical, needing no individual character; the women are on display, helping make things look good. There are a lot of things in the real world that I believe children shouldn't be exposed to; just because it's reality doesn't mean that children had better wake up and smell the coffee. I also wouldn't go to this other extreme of deliberately promoting a version of reality that is so sanitized and artificial as this video of the circus. I tend to look at visual images as they're presented, without being able to analyze them very well, such as examining my responses to the images as manipulated or provoked by certain elements of the presentation. Sometimes it's really obvious, such as sobbing violins or a very fast pace. Usually, though, I don't think about what it is that brought out my responses, and I'm having a hard time doing it. With the circus video, it's pretty easy, because it is so obvious and nonsubtle.

The film *Santa Sangre*, however, is still very difficult for me to think about, even a couple days later. I don't really want to look closely at it, because the bottom line is that I don't see a reason for making this film. But it's hard for me to think about the music or camera angles, for example, in terms of how they affected my perception, or to look at how women and children are represented. If this were something I read instead of watched, I might be able to consider the messages the writer intended. Visual images, however, are too direct and powerful. I can see how the juxtaposition of the bizarre and the familiar takes me to the point of rejecting the images I see, but then forces me to look again. I wondered why the teen slasher/horror movies I used to watch didn't disturb me, even though they were gory and graphic. I think it's because a film like *Santa Sangre* is much more real, with real people in the context of their lives. Both the characters and the plots of most horror movies are so stupid and far removed from reality, viewers don't need to care about them; you just go for a scare. Those movies are just to make money: I can understand that. But the message of Santa Sangre is that violence and affection are both random, and there is no evil and no good.

The Archaeology of Toys

For this session, participants were asked to visit Toys 'R' Us as an assignment prior to class. When they arrived for the evening class, they were
informed that they would be participating in a structured dramatic play
experience. They were to pretend that they were archaeologists from the
twenty-first century who had just discovered an important dig from the
twentieth century. Their visit to Toys 'R' Us had, in fact, been an excursion to a preserved museum of 1990s toys. A variety of toys and other
cultural artifacts were scattered about the room, and it was suggested
that they examine the materials and try to determine what the values of
the material culture of that "ancient" society might have been like.

Finally, they were told, a guest expert from the twentieth century had
been located, someone who had miraculously escaped the nuclear
holocaust. This individual would be arriving soon to share with them his
recollections about the significance of the found objects in their own
historical time. When five-year-old Erik arrived and proceeded to lecture
them on the use of transformer toys, the participants were taken aback.
They had obviously expected an adult authority.

Allie commented:

> Playing the archeologist was a fun experience, but I would have been too
> self-conscious to role play on my own. What if I looked stupid, or didn't do
> it right? It was fun to look at different objects and try to imagine what they
> might be, if we didn't know they were toys. Religious icons? Ceremonial
> props? Work tools? It was hard to pretend that we wouldn't know anything,
> though, about this society only a few hundred years in the future. It oc-
> curred to me that details like that never bother kids when they pretend;
> they just incorporate or ignore major conflicts in their script.
>
> One of the most important characteristics of toys is their gender-typing.
> In my archaeologist role, I wouldn't necessarily know whether male or fe-
> male was preferred. Although it seems obvious that boys are preferred, with
> the more promoted and exciting toys geared toward them, in the future or
> in another society, what's quieter, less promoted, less available, could indi-
> cate greater value. In my real-life roles, however, I am indeed concerned
> about the obvious promotion and preference of toys for boys. In my opin-
> ion they are not more interesting or exciting, but they are certainly pre-
> sented as such to children who haven't had opportunities to form their own
> ideas. One of the most striking differences is in bicycle names: at Toys 'R'
> Us, boys can buy *Outrageous, Hands Off, Cobra, Challenger, Untamed, Black
> Hawk.* Girls can choose from *Miss Rocker, Frills, LA Lady, Sprinkles, Sweet
> Dreams.* . . . Bicycling has always seemed to me like a pretty unisex activity,
> and I think it still is. But "what's in a name" can be pretty powerful. It seri-
> ously concerns me that commercial culture promotes very narrow and
> rigid gender roles while children are working on establishing their own gen-
> der identity and appropriate roles and behaviors. Kids are usually afraid to

do anything that might look different or weird to their peers, so girls stick to an exaggerated girliness and boys stick to violence, noise, and action. Our expert guest, Erik, already knows this. Like my own son, he hasn't experienced a gender-stereotyped childhood, yet he does understand and apply those rules.

I had an interesting conversation with Karen, who I work for, about Ninja Turtles and other such toys. A boy gave Karen's daughter a Ninja Turtle figure for her fifth birthday, and she plays with it in ways not depicted by the manufacturers. She makes little beds and houses for it and had adventures. She also has *My Little Ponies* and all the other faddish toys that look so appealing and attractive on TV and in their packages, including Barbie.

Allie went on to write:

Of greater concern to me are the images of the relationships between men and women, appreciate roles and behaviors of girls and women and children as sexually desirable objects. What my sons see at home has virtually no relationship to what they would see in magazines or on TV. I wonder how they will make sense of what they see represented in popular culture in comparison to their experiences at home. I can't try to actively teach them anything about it: I can respond to what they see, ask questions that create "oppositional meanings," but I don't always know what kinds of connections they're making or will make.

The Institutionalization of Childhood

We examined video examples of children's institutions—schools, day care centers, and play groups—to examine the informal portrayals of children. The participants noted the characteristics of each institution by listing the rules for participation that they could discern. They were disturbed to see children used as props in some of the home and classroom videos and to also see their classroom projects used for political purposes. They discussed the effects of forced compliance and physical restriction. They observed that when children are wild in outdoor play they are rejecting the inhibition and self-control they must practice in classrooms. They concluded that since dominant groups maintain their power through imposition of control, adults who are controlling in institutional settings are protecting the values of their dominant group, in this case, adult teachers.

Yet they realized that maintaining the control required by institutional systems produces stressed teachers who feel they must rehearse children for parental approval. They recognized that teachers who appear constantly energetic and overdirecting with demands for compliance are also constrained by the boundaries of the institutions within which they teach.

The seminar group was particularly captivated by an exposé of bad day care that ran on *Prime Time Live*. In the video, children appeared to be exploited to generate money for the day care proprietors. The program seemed to suggest that mothers should not work outside the home because so-called affordable day care is bad day care.

We wondered at the possible purposes of this program. Even though at face value it appeared to provide important information, and thus to promote social action and the improvement of child care services, we felt that the underlying message was contradictory. The message to parents was that they should feel guilty about their child-care arrangements because there are no constructive solutions to the need for child care. The example of "good" day care on the program was a highly adult-controlled setting where children recited their ABC's for the camera. The seminar participants, many of whom were early childhood educators, moaned at the choice of curriculum and talked about the current public confusion about what really was "developmentally appropriate."

The Universal Experience:
It's a Small World After All

Other institutions of childhood—children's museums, zoos, neighborhood playgrounds, and theme parks—were discussed as preservers of particular perspectives on the lives of children in our culture. Contrasts were made between the videos of children performing in a play circus, a children's video about circuses, and *Santa Sangre*. The cuteness and choreography of made-for-kids videos starkly contrasted with the pain and danger portrayed below and between the "circus acts."

The participants observed that toys and institutions of childhood support and reflect one another. One participant mentioned the example of a dollhouse-like miniature day care center, using teeny versions of the manufacturer's own commercial play equipment as props. Jean mentioned day care and school play sets with unvarying female teacher dolls and traditional settings with ABCs and 123s on the walls: "An important element of institutions is that they define normalcy for their participants. There is definitely one predominant version of schools, the most important institution for most children."

Another participant commented:

> The kindergarten class performing their circus was just as irritating as the video, *Day at the Circus,* and more depressing because it was real. The adults in that setting had no respect for children's interests or abilities; child-created activities and costumes would have looked sloppier but a lot more charming. As my child approaches kindergarten, I am becoming

more and more disturbed about the messages he might soon receive. Although his first experience will, allegedly, be developmentally appropriate, it won't take long for him to realize that there are right and wrong ways of doing most everything (including thinking), and however kids do them is likely to be the wrong way. Adults don't always know what kids want or need.

Day care isn't institutionalized like schools are, but the cultural values surrounding day care are as defined as if there were one national bureaucracy running everything and publishing guidelines. Day care provides perhaps the most obvious demonstration of this society's lack of value placed on children.

Everyone knows the facts, though, that very few families have a stay-at-home parent (mother, almost always—even fathers at home usually have "something" on the side). Even when the family has two parents. Single parents obviously can't even consider the option of having one parent stay home. So who will take care of the children? Whose responsibility is it? Who pays for it? The news special we watched made it clear that it is the parents' responsibility to find day care, and that they'd better watch out! I meant it when I said that the message to viewers is, "Mothers, stay home with your children!" Of course I know that isn't an option for most parents, and even when it is, it shouldn't be taken just because of fear. The first message I got from this report was that the team was proud of its investigative work. While they may have uncovered important information that the public really needs to be aware of, I wonder whether they cared about this in terms of the children involved or were just pleased that they got their hidden cameras in there. This also brought up the ethical question of how they could observe a child being hit, or sitting in his own vomit, and not intervene. I realize that good journalists are not involved or biased, but maybe we need to rethink good journalism. It's a hopeless feeling sometimes: Are children *ever* going to be a priority?

High Culture: Still Talking About My Girl

Finally, we looked at more traditional, venerated cultural representations of women and children—Sendak's opera *Where the Wild Things Are*, selections of poetry, fiction, art, and dance.

Mary wrote:

One day last summer my husband Todd and I heard a group of South African musicians performing on television. When Todd made an admiring comment about the beauty and power of their music, another person present scornfully said something to the effect of, "Let me know when they've produced a Beethoven." It's clear that some types of culture are considered higher than others. The hierarchy includes the least accessible representations of culture at the top and the most accessible, maybe television sitcoms, at the bottom. Some people believe this is a universal hierarchy, with African nations as a whole, for example, below Western cultural achievements. Identifying the highest forms of culture is related to the producers of that culture; white males in this society will define their productions as higher than productions of women or people of color. This is one problem: This division allows the experts to acknowledge fine black literature, black art, women's literature, etc. But these are in their own, separate categories, not accepted as "high culture" within the mainstream. Another problem is that unless all forms of high culture are considered equal, then someone has to determine criteria for evaluating it. This isn't to say that all forms of culture are not equally *valid* for their creators and their audiences. But what about aesthetic standards? Can there be any that reflect more than one (dominant) perspective regarding what that means?

Specialized knowledge, or some kind of "in," is necessary to understand all kinds of things. I realize that only some of them are considered by the "experts" to be the best and worthy of the gold seal or whatever, but that's yet another different problem. Do I set my own standards, or do I accept what experts tell me is best? Classical music is, by definition, classical. It's what you listen to if you've got class.

Finally, we asked, whose experiences, production, and artifacts were represented as part of the high cultural literacy for children? To whom does high culture belong?

I Take You with Me:
Popular Culture/Women and Children

And so, what did we learn? What *is* the place of popular culture and its critique in the lives of teachers? Does it represent a tightrope to be transited between social/political expression and our daily, lived experiences as educators? Does it provide a rationale, an incentive, a support for engaging in social change? Does it even really exist at all in our lives? Do we deny its power? Or are teachers able, as Madeleine Grumet seems to suggest, to commute comfortably "back and forth between the actual and the possible"?

The narratives of the teachers included in this essay point to the importance of examining the popular culture as an arena of representation where race, class, gender, ethnicity, and sexuality and economics, history, culture, politics, and the like collide and intersect. The media and textual choices for the seminar generated a broad array of perspectives on curricular, social, and pedagogical issues related to the representation of women and children in the popular culture. In assembling this collection, we attempted to provide a diverse and sometimes conflicting bricolage, layering different positions and images across each other and extending our understanding of the impact of these images in the common spaces, familiar feelings, and seemingly universal experiences of teachers.

Many of the participants in the seminar, from their very earliest memories of *Romper Room* and *Howdy Doody*, reported an intuitive awareness of the distortions imposed by the culture around them, an awareness, however, unvalidated in their daily lives. Many felt they had actively resisted the imposition of cultural stereotypes and, with their lives, tried to create alternative possibilities for themselves and their children. The text of the seminar, therefore, was not new for them but rather a formalization of the intuitions, memories, and suspicions of their past experiences.

As we encountered the multiple images of women and children in the popular culture and deconstructed their varied meanings, participants reflected back, reminiscing about past images and previous understandings of what it meant to be female—a woman—in the twentieth-century United States. Rereading the journals months after their writing, savoring the reactions, stories, and language expressing resistance to gendered, classed, and racially stereotyped media messages, and holding in mind the model of parallelism with the evocative concept of nonsynchrony that foregrounded the multiple voices, we were moved by the boldness with which the participants confronted personal experience in their own cultural, political, and economic spheres. Their words speak to us in direct and understandable voices, and their images, as Jo Anne Pagano (1990) says, "recreate realities consistent with themselves." Their explorations of media-constructed notions of womanhood and childhood reflect a movement toward the explicit naming of oppression as it is reflected through the popular culture.

Most of the participants' written narratives engaged the media in a personal rather than a professional way, but several also described teacher expectations. For example, a public school teacher planned to adapt the course itself for secondary home economics students. She felt that certain of our media choices would be useful in her work with teen parents and that she could develop others more appropriate for adolescents. Several other participants expressed desires to teach their own students to critically analyze media and its role in shaping society. Early education teachers expressed desires to work with families to help them understand the role of media in the lives of young children. Several also described a need for media literacy in public schools.

There were numerous examples in the personal journals of the participants of the internalization of the assumptions that private and public realities are composed of economic, cultural, and political spheres; that individual needs and social events are historically and situationally variable; and that media does not reflect the multilayered realities of authentic people and groups. As the course progressed we saw the discussion shift from a focus on the effects of media on women and children somewhere out there to the effects of media on me as an individual and through me upon my own children, my students, and their families.

Two conclusions emerged around the educative process. Some participants perceived difficulty in extracting the invisible from the visible in media messages, and most participants expressed evolving awareness of the value of personal and particular interpretations of media messages. Participants frequently wrote of the conceptual challenge of no longer "looking at" media but beginning to discern underlying messages. This engaged their imaginations, and the class discussion was animated.

Another result of the excitement of discerning media messages was the increased sensitivity to particularity. A natural consequence of the diversity of the group was differences in perception of the effects of media on individuals within society. The concept of nonsynchrony was helpful here, and personal stories were exchanged about responses to media that differ from one time and situation to another. Numerous connections were made between personal responses to media and larger social and cultural influences. Much of this discussion focused on gender and economics.

Intertwined with the perceptual and interpretive differences was a group process that invited a merger of experiences and perspectives. This process resulted not only from sharing a theoretical framework for analysis but also from sharing stories back and forth in an interactive rehearsal of personal histories. As participants discussed the dreams promoted by the media and as their memories were activated through the images, class discussion, and writing, connections were made around the relatedness of people to one another and to social systems.

Participants expressed universal apprehension at the enormity of addressing the inequities promulgated by the popular media. In spite of their willingness to participate in the assignments, the participants often expressed overwhelmed feelings when confronting the magnitude of the perceived negative influences of media on and about women and children. As facilitators of the seminar, we became concerned that raising awareness would contribute to a sense of weakness rather than a sense of strength. Yet even as participants expressed apprehension they sometimes made statements and gestures of commitment for change. Several of them investigated and discussed alternatives to the status quo. Their narratives indicate that for the most part the participants increased their ability to perceive their own evolving perspectives as related to their work with children and families. Because we hoped a positive sense of political efficacy would be supported, we were pleased with the many examples our participants provided of engagement of the delicate relationship between individuals and the social fabric.

A consequence of group process was the generation of examples of connections between media stereotypes and schooling. In their writings, several participants focused on expanding awareness of women, children, schools, and culture. For example, in a summary paper on children's play and women in the workplace, Allie described the implicit messages in some action figures she saw in a toy store.

> The fact that toy manufacturers represent women in the workplace does not mean that they are depicted as competent professionals in their field. Combined with the additional information children acquire about what women should be doing and where they should be working, teacher "action figures" merely reinforce the cultural belief that women's role is taking care of and educating children. Messages for adults are made more explicit. As the news special on the horrors of day care showed, women are doing a very poor job of caring for our children. In addition, the condemnations of the U.S. educational system that frequently appear in newspapers and books imply and sometimes state that teachers are not doing their jobs. The message appears to be that the institutions of childhood are the appropriate place for women to be but they aren't doing it well.

Neither of us, as facilitators of the seminar, could determine whether the expectations of individual participants toward their own students were changed as a result of the seminar, since we cannot fully know their prior perspectives. As with any innovative curricula there are inherent unknown results. We know, because participants told us in many ways, that there were dynamic personal results. Seminar discussion was illuminated by the individuality with which participants engaged the course content.

Our original teaching agenda included the identification of corporate and institutional power, recognition of self-censorship, and awakening to conditioning. We set out to introduce concepts and methods of analysis that represented our own ideologies, and, as we anticipated, the participants made of the course what they would. In retrospect, we believe that as a result of the seminar participants mediated their own historical and cultural experiences in ways that will be constructively reflected in their practice.

Fay Crosby (1982) writes about the media controversy over the conflicts women experience in their multiple roles of mother, wife, and worker. She describes the fixation on the conflict between roles as a diversionary tactic deflecting attention from the real conflicts within roles: sex discrimination at work, gender expectations at home, and the tradition of rugged individualism in which each nuclear family is supposed to be a self-sufficient entity. Our experience with this seminar confirms her suggestions. Participants were able to see through the transparent images promoted by the popular culture to construct particular perspectives about women and children. In their identification of these images, participants acknowledged their own socialization as well as their continued resistance to the limits implied. In the creation of their oppositional meanings, they defused, partially and for a brief time, the power of the popular culture.

In this chapter we have explored the impact of the popular culture on children and teachers through a selected representation of contemporary media and artifacts. In our collaboration with our participants we hoped to initiate a multilayered dialogue between our experiences as educators and our understandings of how the popular culture has impacted our thinking. As the collectors of these works we resonate with the centrality of the issues to our participants' lives. Memories and narrative connections to family members, friends, and participants form the frame through which they, like us, have woven their beliefs and their theories into their lives. As coauthors, in reflecting on their work, we share the sense of wonder and play, the angst and hesitation that envelops their work as teachers. Finally, we recognize, as feminist educators, that we also position our beliefs centrally in our teaching as both artifact of analysis and as a pedagogic strategy for understanding.

References

Carr, W., and Kemmis, S. (1986). *Becoming critical: Education, knowledge, and action research.* London: Falmer Press.

Connelly, E. M., and Clandinen, D. J. (1988). *Teachers as curriculum planners: Narratives of experience.* New York: Teachers College Press.

Crompton R., and Mann, M. (1986). *Gender and stratification.* Cambridge, England: Polity Press.

Crosby, F. (1982). *Relative deprivation and working women.* New York: Oxford University Press.

Duelli Klein, R. (1983). How to do what we want to do: Thoughts about feminist methodology. In G. Bowles and R. Duelli Klein, eds. *Theories of Women's Studies.* London: Routledge and Kegan Paul.

Giroux, H. A. (1983). *Theory and resistance in education: A pedagogy for the opposition.* South Hadley, MA: Bergin and Garvey.

_____. (1986). Curriculum, teaching, and the resisting intellectual. *Curriculum and Teaching* 1(1–2): 33–42.

_____. (1988). *Teachers as intellectuals: Toward a critical pedagogy of learning.* South Hadley, MA: Bergin and Garvey.

Giroux, H. A., Penna, A. N., and Pinar, W. F., eds. (1981). *Curriculum and instruction: Alternatives in instruction.* Berkeley, CA: McCutchan.

Grumet, M. (1988). Body reading. In W. F. Pinar (ed.). *Contemporary curriculum discourses.*

Grundy, S. (1987). *Curriculum: Product or praxis?* London: Falmer Press.

McCarthy, C. (1988). Rethinking liberal and radical perspectives on racial inequality in schooling: Making the case for nonsynchrony. *Harvard Educational Review* 58(3): 265–279.

Pagano, J. (1990). *Exiles and communities: Teaching in the patriarchal wilderness.* Albany, NY: SUNY Press.

Proudfoot, R. (1986). *Model for the synergy of relational education: The dynamics of cultural interaction and connection.* Unpublished manuscript.

14 McDonald's, Power, and Children: Ronald McDonald (aka Ray Kroc) Does It All for You

Joe L. Kincheloe

IN HIS BOOK *The Hawkline Monster: A Gothic Western* (1974, 11), the late Richard Brautigan develops the character, Cameron, who is a counter:

> Cameron was a counter. He vomited nineteen times to San Francisco. He liked to count everything that he did. This had made Greer a little nervous when he first met up with Cameron years ago, but he'd gotten used to it by now.
>
> People would sometimes wonder what Cameron was doing and Greer would say, "He's counting something," and people would ask, "What's he counting?" and Greer would say, "What difference does it make?" and the people would say, "Oh."
>
> People usually wouldn't go into it any further because Greer and Cameron were very self-assured in that big relaxed casual kind of way that makes people nervous.

I can relate to Cameron, for I, too, am a counter. McDonald's also is a counter—and like the people who noticed Cameron's peculiar proclivity, most Americans don't go very far in analyzing the company's propensity for counting or, for that matter, anything else about the fast-food behemoth. Like Greer and Cameron, the company's self-assurance (that is, its power) must make people a little nervous.

I was destined to write about McDonald's, for my life has always intersected with the Golden Arches. As part of my undergraduate comedy shtick I told my listeners (truthfully) that I had consumed 6,000 McDonald's hamburgers before graduating from high school. In junior high and high school we were allowed to go off campus to eat. My friends and I (before we had our driver's licenses) would tromp through the Tennessee woods rain or shine to McDonaldland—by high school we drove. After six years of three-hamburger lunches, not to mention the Wednesday-night burgers with my parents and several more on weekend nights after cruising with friends, the count began to mount. A secondary bonus for my fifteen-cent burgermania involved the opportunity to count my cholesterol numbers as they crept higher and higher. Ray Kroc, the man who made McDonald's a household name, would have been proud.

Somewhere in my small-town Tennessee adolescent consciousness, I understood that McDonald's was the future. I couldn't name it, but the standardized hamburger was a symbol of some vague social phenomenon. Like Italian or Polish immigrants of another place and time, I was ethnic (hillbilly). And like all children of traditional ethnic parents I struggled for an American identity free from the taint of ethnicity. Though it hadn't yet assumed the mantle of all-American symbol around the world, I knew that the McDonald's of the early 1960s was mainstream America through and through. As such, my participation in the burger ritual was an act of shedding my ethnic identity. Understanding the company's regulation of customer behavior, I complied readily, knowing the menu in advance and placing my order quickly and accurately. My parents, in contrast, raised in the rural South during the early twentieth century, were lost at the ordering counter—never understanding the menu, always unsure of the expected behavior; the effort to shape their customer conduct was a bust.

On a very different level, however, my parents were seduced by McDonald's. Students of media have come to understand that readings of film, TV, and TV commercials are idiosyncratic, differing significantly from individual to individual. So it was in my home. As victims of the Great Depression in southern Appalachia (a double economic whammy), my mother and father came to see excessive spending as a moral weakness. Eating out, when it was possible to prepare food at home, was especially depraved. My father would darken the door of McDonald's only if he was convinced of its economic "good sense." Indeed, advertisers struck an emotional chord when they pitted fifteen-cent McDonald's hamburgers and twelve-cent french fries as an alternative to the extravagant cost of eating out. To my self-identified working-class father, eating McDonald's was an act of class resistance. He never really cared much for the food—he would have rather eaten my mother's country ham and cornbread. But as we McDined, he spoke with great enthusiasm about how McDonald's beat the price of other burgers around town by fifty or sixty cents. Such statistics made him very happy.

Like others in peculiar social spaces around the world, my father consumed a democratic, egalitarian ethos. French teenagers accustomed to the bourgeois stuffiness of French restaurants could have identified with my father's class-resistant consumption, as they are known to revel in the informality and freedom of the restaurants' "American atmosphere." The inexpensive fare, the informal dress, and the loud talk are class signifiers (Leidner, 1993). Such coding is quite ironic in light of the company's right-wing political history, its manipulations of labor, and its cutthroat competition with other fast-food enterprises. That McDonald's continues to maintain an egalitarian image is testimony to the power/expertise of its public-relations strategists. And here rest the major questions raised by this essay: What is the nature of these public-relations strategies? What do they tell us about McDonald's? And how do they affect American culture—its kinderculture in particular?

Shaping Culture, Shaping Consciousness

Few Americans think in terms of how power interests in the larger society regulate populations to bring about desired behaviors. In America and other Western societies political domination shifted decades ago from police or military forces to the use of cultural messages. Such communications are designed to win the approval or consent of citizens for the actions taken by power elites (Giroux, 1988). The contributors to this book in their own particular ways are involved in efforts to expose the specifics of this process of cultural domination (it is often labeled hegemony). The process takes place in the everyday experience of our lives. The messages are not sent by a clandestine group of conspirators or devised by some secret ministry of propaganda; neither are they read by everyone in the same way—some people understand the manipulative intent and rebel against their authority (Goldman, 1992). The company's role in these power dynamics illustrates the larger process. If any organization has the power to shape the lives of children from Peoria to Moscow, it is McDonald's.

The construction of who we are and what we believe cannot be separated from the workings of power. Americans don't talk much about power; American politicians don't even talk about power. When the subject of power is broached in mainstream sociology, the conversation revolves around either the macro level—the political relations of governments—or the micro level—the personal relations between two people (Abercrombie, 1994). Power, as the term is used in this essay, is neither macro nor micro—nor does it rely on either legality or coercion. Power, as it has evolved at the end of the twentieth century, maintains its legitimacy in much more subtle and effective ways.

Consider the power generated by the company's use of the media to define itself not simply as an American institution but as America itself. As the "land we love" writ small, McDonald's attaches itself to American patriotism and the cultural dynamics it involves. Ray Kroc understood from the beginning that he was not simply selling hamburgers—he was selling America a vision of itself (Luxenberg, 1985). From the all-American marching band to the all-American basketball and football teams to the all-American meal served by all-American boys and girls, the all-American of the Year—Ray Kroc—labored to connect the American signifier to McDonald's. The American flag will fly twenty-four hours a day at McDonald's, he demanded. Using the flag as a backdrop for the hamburger count, Kroc watched the burger numbers supplant the Dow Jones closing average as the symbolic statistical index for America's economic health. In the late 1960s and early 1970s, Kroc saw the perpetually flying flag as a statement to the war protesters and civil rights "kooks" that McDonald's (America) would not stand for anyone criticizing or attempting to undermine "our" country (Kroc, 1977).

One of the reasons Americans don't talk much about power is that it works in such a subtle and hard-to-define manner. Ask Americans how McDonald's has shaped them or constructed their consciousness, and you'll draw blank stares. What does it mean to argue that power involves the ability to ascribe meanings to various features of our lives? Return to the McDonald's all-American ad campaign. Kroc and McDonald's management sanctioned the costliest and most ambitious ad campaign in American corporate history (Boas and Chain, 1976). All this money and effort were expended to imbue the hamburger—the McDonald's variety in particular—with a star-spangled signification. And it worked in the sense that Americans and individuals around the world began to make the desired connection. Described as the "ultimate icon of Americana," a "cathedral of consumption" where Americans practice their "consumer religion," McDonald's, like Disneyland, transcends status as mere business establishment (Ritzer, 1993). When McDonald's or Disney speak, they speak for all of us. How could the Big Mac or Pirates of the Caribbean mislead us? They are us.

Just as Americans saw mystical implications in the deaths of Thomas Jefferson and John Adams on July 4, 1826, the fiftieth anniversary of the Declaration of Independence, contemporary Americans may see mystical ramifications in the fact that Ray Kroc and Walt Disney were in the same company in the U.S. army. Both having lied about their age, the two prophets of free enterprise–grounded utopian Americana fought the good fight for the American way. It takes nothing away from the mystery to know that Kroc described Disney as a "strange duck" (Donald? Uncle Scrooge? Daisy?) because he wouldn't chase girls (Kroc, 1977).

No expenses were spared, no signifiers were left free-floating in the grand effort to transfer reverence for America to McDonald's. The middle-class cathedral was decorated as a shrine with the obligatory plastic eagle replete with powerful wings and glazed, piercing eyes. A banner held in the bald eagle's beak read "McDonald's: The American Way" (Boas and Chain, 1976). These legitimation signifiers work best when they go unnoticed, as they effectively connect an organization's economic power to acquire property, lobby Congress, hire lawyers, and so on to its power to ascribe meaning and persuade. In the process the legitimated organization gains the power to create and transmit a view of reality that is consonant with its larger interests—American economic superiority as the direct result of an unbridled free-enterprise system.

A recent ad campaign paints a nostalgic, sentimentalized, conflict-free American family pictorial history. The purpose of the ad is to forge an even deeper connection between McDonald's and America by creating an American historical role for McDonald's where there was none before. You can almost hear the male voiceover: "Though we didn't yet exist, we were there to do it all for you—McDonald's then, McDonald's now." We're all one big, happy family with the same (European?) roots. "We" becomes McDonald's and America—"our" family (Goldman, 1992). The only thing left to buttress the all-American image would be some type of Santa Claus connection. Kroc's public-relations men quickly made their move, inducing Kroc himself to distribute hamburgers to Chicago's street-corner Santas and Salvation Army workers. Newspapers noticed the event and, to Kroc's delight, linked Santa Claus to a chauffeur named McDonald's. The legend grew when the public-relations men circulated a story about a child who was asked where Santa had met Mrs. Santa. "At McDonald's," the child was reported to have said. Wire services picked up the anecdote, sending it to every town in the country (Boas and Chain, 1976). Whether with big ad campaigns or bogus anecdotes, McDonald's has used the media to create an American mythology.

Like other giant international corporations of the late twentieth century, McDonald's has used the media to invade the most private spheres of our everyday lives. Our national identifications, desires, and human needs have been commodified (that is, appropriated) for the purposes of commerce (Giroux, 1994; Kellner, 1992). Such media usage grants producers a level of access to human consciousness never before imagined by the most powerful dictator. One way such power is illustrated is in the resistance McDonald's elicits as signifier for America. Time and time again in the company's brief history neighborhood organizers have reacted to its efforts to enter their communities. Seeing McDonald's as a form of cultural colonization that overwhelms locally owned businesses and devours local culture, individuals have fought to keep McDonald's out. In the 1970s opposition became so intense in New York City that Kroc ordered high walls built around construction sites to keep them hidden from local residents. At the same time in Sweden, radicals bombed two restaurants in hopes of thwarting "creeping American cultural imperialism" (Boas and Chain, 1976). For better and for worse, McDonald's had succeeded in positioning itself as America.

McDonald's Is a Kids' Kind of Place: E-I-E-I-O

Contrary to the prevailing middle-class wisdom, childhood is not and never has been an unchanging developmental stage of humanness. Rather, it is a social and economic construction tied to prevailing perceptions of what constitutes the "natural order" (Polakow, 1992). Forces such as urbanization and industrialization have exerted significant influences on the nature of childhood—as have the development of media and the techno-power it produces for those financially able to afford it. By the term *techno-power* I am attempting to illustrate the expansion of corporate influence via the use of recent technological innovation (Kellner, 1989; Harvey, 1989). Using techno-power, corporations like McDonald's have increased their ability to maximize capital accumulation, influence social and cultural life, and even help mold children's consciousnesses. Since childhood is a cultural construction shaped in the contemporary era by the forces of this media-catalyzed techno-power, the need for parents, teachers, and community members to study it is dramatic. Let us turn now to McDonald's and the late-twentieth-century construction of childhood.

Even the name—"McDonald's"—is kid-friendly, with its evocation of Old McDonald and his farm—E-I-E-I-O. The safety of McDonald's provides asylum, if not utopian refuge, from the kid-*unfriendly* contemporary world of child abuse, broken homes, and childnapping. Offering something better to escape into, the company's TV depiction of itself to children as a happy place where "what you want is what you get" is very appealing (Garfield, 1992). Thus, by the time children reach elementary school they are often zealous devotees of McDonald's who insist on McDonaldland birthday celebrations and surprise dinners. Obviously, McDonald's advertisers are doing something right, as they induce phenomenal numbers of kids to pester their parents for Big Macs and fries.

McDonald's and other fast-food advertisers have discovered an enormous and previously overlooked children's market. Children aged five to twelve annually spend $4.2 billion of their own money. They influence household spending of an additional $131 billion each year. Of this $131 billion, $82 billion goes to food and drinks (Fischer et al., 1991). Every month nineteen out of every twenty kids aged six to eleven visit a fast-food restaurant. In a typical McDonald's promotion where toys like Hot Wheels or Barbies accompany kids' meals, company officials can expect to sell 30 million to child customers. By the time a child reaches the age of three, more than four out of five know that McDonald's sells hamburgers. As if this level of child-consciousness colonization were not enough, McDonald's, along with scores of other companies, has targeted the public schools as a new venue for child marketing and consumption. In addition to hamburgers for A's programs and advertising-based learning packets for science, foreign language, and other subjects, McDonald's and other fast-food firms have attempted to operate school cafeterias (Hume, 1993; Ritzer, 1993; Giroux, 1994).

Make no mistake about it: McDonald's and its advertisers want to transform children into consumers—indeed, they see children as consumers in training (Fischer et al., 1991). Ellen Seiter (1993), however, warns against drawing simplistic conclusions about the relationship between advertisers and children, as have, she says, many well-intentioned liberal children's advocacy groups. ACT (Action for Children's Television), the leading voice against corporate advertising for children, fails to capture the subtle aspects of techno-power and its colonization of childhood. Seeing children as naïve innocents who should watch only "good" TV, meaning educational programs that portray middle-class values, ACT has little appreciation of the complexity of children's TV watching. Children at the end of the twentieth century are not passive and naïve TV viewers. As advertising professionals have learned, children are active, analytical viewers who often make their own meanings of both commercials and the products they sell. These social and psychological dynamics between advertiser and child deserve further analysis.

One of the most important of these dynamics involves the recognition by advertisers that children themselves feel oppressed by this middle-class view of children as naïve entities in need of constant protection. By drawing upon the child's discomfort with middle-class protectionism and the accompanying attempt to "adjust" children to a "developmentally appropriate" norm, advertisers hit upon a marketing bonanza. If we address kids as kids—a dash of anarchism and a pinch of hyperactivity—they will love our commercials even though parents (especially middle-class parents) will hate them. By the end of the 1960s, commercial children's TV and advertising were grounded on this premise. Such video throws off restraint, discipline, and old views that children should be seen but not heard. Everything, for example, that educational TV embraces—earnestness, child as an incomplete adult, child in need of correction—commercial TV rejects. In effect, commercial TV sets up an op-positional culture for kids.

One doesn't have to look far (try any middle-class home) to find that children's enthusiasm for certain TV shows, toys, and foods isolates them from their parents. Drawing on this isolation, children turn it into a form of power—they finally know something that dad doesn't. How many dads or moms understand the relationship between Mayor Mc-Cheese and the French Fry Guys? Battle lines begin to be drawn between children and parents, as kids want to purchase McDonald's hamburgers or action toys. Conflicts in lower-middle-class homes may revolve around family finances; strife in upper-middle-class homes may concern aesthetic or ideological concerns. Questions of taste, cultural capital, and self-improvement permeate child-adult interactions in such families. The child's ability to negotiate the restrictions of adult values is central to the development of an independent self. A very common aspect of this development of independence involves the experience of contradiction with the adult world. Children of upwardly mobile, ambitious parents may find it more difficult to negotiate this experience of contradiction because of the parents' strict views of the inappropriateness of TV-based children's culture. Thus, the potential for parent-child conflict and alienation may be greater in this familial context.

A covert children's culture has always existed on playgrounds and in schools. The children's culture of the past, however, was produced by children and propagated through child-to-child contact. Today's post-modern children's culture is created by adults and dispersed via television for the purpose of inducing children to consume. As they carefully subvert middle-class parenting's obsession with achievement, play as a serious enterprise, and self-improvement–oriented "quality time" (a subversion that in my opinion probably contributes to the public good), advertisers connect children's culture to their products. McDonald's commercials reflect these themes, although less blatantly than many advertisers.

Attempting to walk a tightrope between tapping the power of children's subversive culture and the possibility of offending the middle-class guardians of propriety, McDonald's has developed a core of so-called "slice-of-life" children's ads. Casting no adults in the commercials, advertisers depict a group of preteens engaged in "authentic" conversations around a McDonald's table covered with burgers, fries, and shakes. Using children's slang ("radical," "dude," "we're into Barbie") to describe toys in various McDonald's promotions, children discuss the travails of child-hood with one another. In many commercials children make adults the butt of their jokes or share jokes that adults don't get (Seiter, 1993; Gold-man, 1992). Subtle though it may be, McDonald's attempts to draw some of the power of children's subversive culture to their products without anyone but the kids knowing. Such slice-of-life ads are opaque to the degree that adults watching them don't get it—they don't see the advertiser's effort to connect McDonald's with the subversive kinderculture.

The Bloody Fight for Conformity, Courtesy, and Established Virtue: McDonaldland, Ronald, and Ray

TV ads often serve as postmodern myths, as they resolve cultural contradictions, portray models of identity, and glorify the status quo. Although all McDonald's ads accomplish these mythic functions to some degree, none do it better than ads and promotions involving McDonaldland. To understand the mythic dynamics of McDonaldland, one must appreciate the psychological complexity of Ray Kroc. Born in 1902 in a working-class neighborhood on Chicago's West Side into what he called a "Bohunk" (Bohemian) family, Kroc was obsessed throughout his life with proving his worth as both a human being and a businessman. Having failed in several business ventures while in his twenties and thirties, Kroc had much to prove by the time the McDonald's opportunity confronted him at the age of 52 (Boas and Chain, 1976). Kroc defined McDonaldland the same way he defined himself—through consumption. Driven by an ambition to own nice things, Kroc's autobiography is peppered with references to consumption: "I used to comb through the advertisements in the local newspaper for notices of house sales in the wealthier suburbs. . . . I haunted these sales and picked up pieces of elegant furniture" (Kroc, 1977, 27). Watched over by the messianic Ronald McDonald, McDonaldland is a place (your kind of place) where consumption was not only the sole occupation but the means through which its inhabitants gained their identities.

McDonaldland is a kid's text fused with Kroc's psyche that emerges as an effort to sell the system, to justify consumption as a way of life. As central figure in McDonaldland, Ronald McDonald emerges as a multidimensional clown deity, virgin-born son of Adam Smith, press secretary for free-enterprise capitalism. He is also Ray Kroc's projection of himself, his ego creation of the most loved prophet of utopian consumption in the McWorld. Ronald's life history begins in Washington, D.C., with Willard Scott, currently the *Today* weatherman. Struggling to make it as a junior announcer at WRC-TV during the early 1960s, Scott agreed to play Bozo the Clown on the station's show. When Scott donned the clown suit, he was transformed from Clark Kent to Superman, bumbling Willard to Superclown. The local McDonald's franchisees recognized

Scott's talent and employed Bozo as a spokesperson for McDonald's. When the show was canceled by WRC, McDonald's lost a very effective advertiser. The local McDonald's owners worked with Scott to create Ronald McDonald (Scott's idea), debuting him in October 1963. Ronald was so successful, creating traffic jams every time he appeared in public, that the local operators suggested to the Chicago headquarters that Ronald go national (Love, 1986).

After a lengthy debate over whether they should employ Ronald McDonald as a clown, a cowboy, or a spaceman, corporate leaders and advertisers settled on the clown. Dumping Scott because he was deemed too fat for the image they wanted to promote, the company in 1965 hired Coco, an internationally known clown with the Ringling Brothers and Barnum & Bailey Circus. Beginning with his first national appearance in Macy's Thanksgiving Day Parade on November 25, 1966, the deification of Ronald began. The press releases on Ronald issued by the McDonald's Customers Relations Center are sanctification documents cross-pollinated with frontier tall-tale boasting. "Since 1963, Ronald McDonald has become a household name, more famous than Lassie or the Easter Bunny, and second only to Santa Claus" (McDonald's Customer Relations Center, 1994).

All of the other characters in McDonaldland, the company's promotional literature reports, revere Ronald—aka Ray Kroc. He is "intelligent and sensitive . . . he can do nearly anything. . . . Ronald McDonald is the *star.*" If children are sick, the promos contend, Ronald is there. Even though he has become "an international hero and celebrity," Ronald is still the same friend of children he was in 1963. Ninety-six percent of all children, claimed a bogus "Ronald McDonald Awareness Study" fed to the press, can identify this *heroic* figure (Boas and Chain, 1976). Ronald was everything Kroc wanted to be: a beloved humanitarian, an international celebrity, a philanthropist, a musician (Kroc made his living for awhile as a piano player; Ronald has cut children's records). Even the sophisticates—a group whose affection Kroc sought throughout his life—loved Ronald, Kroc wrote in his autobiography. Unfortunately, he would have to settle for it vicariously through Ronald. Abe Lincoln, too, had been rejected by the sophisticates of his day; as twentieth-century Lincoln, Kroc prominently displayed the bust of Ronald adjacent to the bust of Lincoln on a table behind his desk at the Chicago headquarters (McCormick, 1993; Kroc, 1977).

According to the promotional literature designed for elementary schools, Ronald "became a citizen of [the McDonald's] International Division" in 1969 and soon began to appear on TV around the world. Kroc was propelled to a new level of celebrity as the corporation "penetrated" the global market. Now known everywhere on earth, Kroc/Ronald be-

came the Grand Salesman, the successful postindustrial Willy Loman—
they love me in Moscow, Belgrade, and New York. Stung by a plethora of
critics, Kroc was obsessed with being perceived as a moral man with a
moral company that exerted a wholesome influence on children around
the world. Kroc wrote and spoke of his noble calling, establishing his
"missions" with the Golden Arches as part of his neo–white man's burden. "I provide an humanitarian service," Kroc proclaimed: "I go out and
check out a piece of property [that's] not producing a damned thing for
anybody," he wrote in his epistles from California. The new franchise
provides a better life for scores of people—"out of that bare ground
comes a store that does, say, a million dollars a year in business. Let me
tell you, it's great satisfaction to see that happen." Kroc/Ronald personi-
fied the great success story of twentieth-century capitalism. Kroc's and
his franchisees' fortunes came to represent what happens when one
works hard in the free-enterprise system. McDonaldland and the Mc-
World—signifiers for the McDonaldization of the planet.

The convergence of the growth of international megacorporations
and the expanding technological sophistication of the media have
prompted a new era of consumption. Some analysts argue that the central feature of the postmodern lifestyle revolves around the act of consuming. In McDonaldland Ronald McDonald serves as CEO/archduke
over his fiefdom of consumer junkies. The Hamburglar is "cute" in his
addiction to hamburgers. According to the literature provided to schools
about McDonaldland, the Hamburglar's "main purpose in life is the acquisition of McDonald's hamburgers." Grimace is described as "gener-
ous and affectionate . . . [his] primary personality attribute is his love for
McDonald's shakes." The most important passion of Captain Crook is
his love of McDonald's Filet o' Fish sandwiches.

As free-enterprise utopia, McDonaldland erases all differences, all
conflicts; social inequities are overcome through acts of consumption.
As such messages justify the existence of extant power relations, conformity emerges as the logical path to self-production. The only hint of difference in McDonaldland involves Uncle O'Grimacey, the annual Irish
visitor who speaks in brogue and is defined by his obsession with Sham-
rock shakes. The emphasis on standardization and "sameness" is so intense that all Ronald McDonald actors go to school to make sure they
conform to a uniform image. The training system is so rationalized that
students are tracked into one of two groups; throughout preservice and
in-service experiences the clowns are either "greeting Ronalds" or "performing Ronalds." The most compelling manifestation of conformity in
McDonaldland involves the portrayal of the French Fry Guys. As the only
group of citizens depicted in the Hamburger Patch, these faceless com-
moners are numerous but seldom seen:

They tend to look, act, and think pretty much alike. Parent French Fry Guys are indistinguishable from children, and vice versa. They are so much alike that, so far, no individual French Fry Guy has emerged as a personality identifiable from the others. They resemble little mops with legs and eyes and speak in squeaky, high-pitched voices, usually in unison. They always move quickly, scurrying around in fits and starts, much like the birds one sees on sandy beaches (McDonald's Customer Relations Center, 1994).

As inhabitants of a McDonaldized McWorld, the French Fry Guys are content to remove themselves from the public space, emerging only for brief and frenetic acts of standardized consumption—their only act of personal assertion.

Life in McDonaldland is conflict-free—the Hamburger Patch is a privatized utopia. It is late-twentieth-century America writ small, corporate-directed and consumer-oriented. Questions such as distribution of income among classes, regulation of corporate interests, free trade, minimum wage, and collective bargaining traditionally elicited passion and commitment—now they hardly raise an eyebrow. The political sphere where decisions are made concerning who gets what and who voted for what is managed by a small group. Their work and the issues they confront are followed by an ever-decreasing audience of news watchers tuned to CNN and C-SPAN. Politics, Americans have concluded, is not only useless but far worse in the mediascape—it is boring. It can't be too important; it gets such low Neilsens. The political structure of McDonaldland reflects this larger depoliticization with its depiction of the inept and superfluous Mayor McCheese. The school promotional literature describes him as a "silly" character not "to be taken seriously." As a "confused and bumbling" politician, Mayor McCheese would rather spend his time in the privatized space of McDonald's, eating cheeseburgers. The lesson is clear to children—politics doesn't matter, leave McDonald's alone, let these business*men* run their business the way they see fit.

The benign nature of capitalist production, with its freedom from serious conflict of any type, portrayed by McDonaldland and Kroc/Ronald is a cover for a far more savage reality. Business analysts, for example, liken McDonald's operations to the U.S. Marine Corps. When a recruit graduates from basic training (Hamburger University), he believes that he can *conquer* anybody (Love, 1986). Motivated by an econotribal allegiance to the McFamily, store operators speak of faith in McDonald's as if it were a religion. Kroc openly spoke of the Holy Trinity—McDonald's, family, and God in that order (Kroc, 1977). Released from boot camp on a jihad for a success theology, these faceless French Fry Guys have forced thousands of independent restaurant owners out of business (Luxenberg, 1985). Competing fast-food franchisees tell of their introductions to recent Hamburger University graduates and other McDonald's managers with amazement: "We will run you out of business and bury you," these Khrushchevs of fast food proclaim.

No matter how ruthless business might become, there is no room for criticism or dissent in McDonaldland. "I feel sorry for people who have such a small and wretched view of the system that made this country great," Kroc (1977) wrote in his autobiography. The "academic snobs" who had criticized McDonald's tapped a sensitivity in Kroc's psyche that motivated counterattacks until the day he died. This love-it-or-leave-it anti-intellectualism finds its McDonaldland expression in the Professor. Described as the proud possessor of various degrees, the Professor is a bumbling fool with a high-pitched, effeminate voice. As none of his theories or inventions ever work, he meets Kroc's definition of an overeducated man: someone who worries about inconsequential affairs to the degree that he is distracted from the normal problems of business. Kroc never liked books or school and saw little use for advanced degrees: "One thing I flatly refuse to give money to is the support of any college" (Kroc, 1977, 199). Intellectuals don't fit into the culture of the Hamburger Patch.

As much as the Professor is effeminate, Big Mac, McDonaldland's policeman, is manly. The promotional literature describes him as "the strong, silent type. His voice is deep and super-masculine; his manner is gruff but affectionate . . . his walk is a strut. His stance is chest out, stomach in." The gender curriculum of McDonaldland is quite explicit: Big Mac as the manly man; Birdie, the Early Bird, as the pert, nurturing female. As the only female in McDonaldland, Birdie is faced with a significant task. She is the cheerleader who encourages the male residents to jump into the activities of the new day. "Her enthusiasm and energy are infectious . . . her positive attitude is emphasized by her bright, perky, cheerful voice" (McDonald's Customer Relations Center, 1994). Once the McDonaldlanders have gobbled down their Egg McMuffins and are off to their respective occupations, Birdie retires to the sidelines as a passive observer.

The Kroc influence is alive and well in the gender dynamics of the corporation. Referring to himself in the third person as "Big Daddy," Kroc expressed a sometimes disturbing misogyny in his handling of company affairs. Ray's personality, one colleague observed, would never allow a woman to gain power (Love, 1986). To Kroc, women were to take care of frills, leaving the important work to men:

> Clark told me I should hire a secretary.
> "I suppose you're right," I [Kroc] said. "But I want a male secretary . . . I want a man. He might cost a little more at first, but if he's any good at all, I'll have him doing sales work in addition to administrative things. I have nothing against having a pretty girl around, but the job I have in mind would be

much better handled by a man. . . ." My decision to hire a male secretary paid off when I was hospitalized for a gall bladder operation and later for a goiter operation. [The male secretary] worked between our office and my hospital room, and we kept things humming as briskly as when I was in the office every morning (Kroc, 1977, 48–49).

June Martino was a very talented woman who had been with Kroc from the earliest days of his involvement with McDonald's. Corporate insiders described her as a gifted businesswoman whose expertise often kept the company going during difficult times. Kroc's view of her reflected his view of women in general: "I thought it was good to have a lucky person around, maybe some of it would rub off on me. Maybe it did. After we got McDonald's going and built a larger staff, they called her 'Mother Martino.' She kept track of everyone's family fortunes, whose wife was having a baby, who was having marital difficulties, or whose birthday it was. She helped make the office a happy place" (Kroc, 1977, 84).

Such attitudes at the top permeated all levels of the organization and were expressed in a variety of pathological ways. Management's sensitivity to sexual harassment was virtually nonexistent well into the 1980s. Interviews with women managers reveal patterns of sexual misconduct involving eighteen- and nineteen-year-old women employees being pressured to date older male managers. Reports of sexual harassment were suppressed by the company bureaucracy; women who complained were sometimes punished or forced to resign. One successful manager confided that after she reported harassment, company higher-ups stalked her both on and off the job. She was eventually forced to leave the company. Not surprisingly, such an organization was not overly concerned with women's complaints about the exaggerated gender roles depicted in McDonald's commercials and promotions. From Birdie as cheerleader to Happy Meals with Barbies for girls and Hot Wheels for boys, McDonald's has never escaped Kroc's gender assumptions (Hume, 1993).

McDonald's perpetuates what Allen Shelton (1993) refers to as a hegemonic logic—a way of doing business that privileges conformity, zealously defends the middle-class norm, fights to the death for established virtue, and at all costs resists social change. As a passionate force for a Warren G. Harding "normalcy," McDonald's is the corporation that invites the children of prominent civic, military, and business leaders to the opening of its first McDonaldland Park—but leaves the daughters and sons of the not-so-rich and -famous off the invitation list. This hegemonic logic holds little regard for concepts such as justice or morality—McDonald's morality is contingent on what sells. This concept is well illustrated in the company's emphasis on the primacy of home and family values in its advertising.

We've Got Ourselves a Family Unit:
Home Is Wherever Ronald McDonald Goes

Kroc and his corporate leaders unequivocally understood their most important marketing priority—to portray McDonald's as a "family kind of place." As they focused on connecting McDonald's to America and the family, they modified the red-and-white ceramic takeout restaurants to look more like the suburban homes that had sprung up throughout America in the late 1950s and 1960s. Ad campaigns proclaimed that McDonald's was home and that anywhere Ronald goes "he is at home." Like many other ads of the late twentieth century, these home and family ads privilege the private sphere, not the public sphere, as the important space where life is lived. As an intrinsically self-contained unit, the family is removed from the public realm of society; such a depiction, however, conceals the ways that politics and economics shape everyday family life. The greatest irony of these ads is that even as they isolate the family from any economic connections they promote the commodification of family life. A form of doublespeak is discernible in this situation: The family is an end in itself; the family is an instrumental consumption unit whose ultimate purpose is to benefit corporate profits and growth.

McDonald's ads deploy home and family as paleosymbols that position McDonald's as the defender of "the American way of life." Kroc (1977) never knew what paleosymbols were but he understood that McDonald's public image should be, in his words, a "combination YMCA, Girl Scouts, and Sunday School." Devised to tap into the right-wing depiction of the traditional family under attack from feminists, homosexuals, and other "screwballs," these so-called "legitimation ads" don't sell hamburgers—they sell social relations. In the midst of social upheaval and instability, McDonald's endures as a rock of ages, a refuge in a world gone mad. McDonald's bring us together, provides a safe haven for our children. The needs the legitimation ads tap are real; the consumption panacea they provide is false (Goldman, 1992). After its phenomenal growth in the 1960s, McDonald's realized that it was no longer the "cute little company" of the 1950s (Love, 1986). From Kroc's right-wing perspective, he saw the antiwar, civil rights, and other social movements of the late 1960s as repugnant to all of his American values. Such views, when combined with the marketing need for McDonald's to legitimate itself now that it was an American "big business," made home and family the obvious battlefield in the legitimation campaign. As the public faith in corporations declined, McDonald's used the paleosymbols to create an environment of confidence. Going against the grain of a social context, perceived to be hostile to big business, the ads worked. The lyrics of accompanying music read:

> You, you're the one.
> So loving, strong, and patient.
> Families like yours
> made all the states a nation.
> Our families are our past,
> our future and our pride.
> Whatever roots we come from,
> we're growing side by side (quoted in Goldman, 1992, 95).

The world of home and family portrayed by the McDonald's legitimation ads is a terrain without conflict or tension. In an ad produced during the early 1980s, as Reagan's family-values agenda was being established, a typical white middle-class family is returning to the small town of Dad's childhood. Excited to show his preteen son and daughter his childhood world, Dad tells the family that his old house is just up the street. As the "Greek chorus" sings "things have changed a bit since you've been around" as background music, Dad is shocked to discover new condominiums have replaced the old house. Dismayed but undaunted, Dad tells the family that his old friend Shorty's house is just around the corner. Shorty's house is also gone, replaced by a car wash. From the backseat the daughter tells her disappointed father that she hopes the place he used to eat at is still standing because she's hungry. Dad immediately begins to look for the unnamed eating place; the background chorus sings: "In the night, the welcome sight of an old friend." The camera focuses on Dad as his eyes brighten and a smile explodes across his face. The camera cuts to a car pulling into McDonald's, and the chorus sings: "Feels so right here tonight at McDonald's again."

Once again consumption at McDonald's serves to solve the problem of change. The consumptive act in this case serves to affirm family values in a world where the larger society threatens them. Nothing has changed at McDonald's, as Dad tells the perky, young counter girl that he had his first Big Mac at this McDonald's. The camera focuses across the dining room to a short man expressing surprise and disbelief. Of course, it is Shorty. As Shorty embraces Dad we find out that Dad's childhood name was Curly—ironic in the fact that he is now bald. The camera retreats to frame the old friends embracing in the light cast by the Golden Arches. Dad is at McDonald's, he is *home* with old friends and family. McDonald's made it all possible (Goldman, 1992). The turbulent 1960s are finally over. We (America) have "come home" to the traditional family values that made us great. The chorus has already reminded us that it "feels so right . . . at McDonald's *again*." The key word here being "again." Reagan, whose candidacy Kroc and the McDonald's management fervently supported, has brought back traditional values—McDonald's wants viewers to know that McDonald's is an important aspect of the traditional family-values package.

In the final scene of this "Home Again" commercial, the camera shoots a close-up of the son and daughter. Having just watched the embrace between Dad and Shorty, the daughter turns to her brother and says with ironic inflection, "Curly?" Her brother shrugs and rolls his eyes in recognition of the generational rift between Dad's understanding of the scene as compared to their own. The camera tells us the reunion is irrelevant to the son and daughter as it focuses on the attention they pay to the hamburgers sitting in front of them—the only time, by the way, McDonald's food is displayed in the ad. McDonald's wants it both ways: the adult identification with Reagan, America, and the return to traditional family values; and child identification with the subversive kinderculture described previously. The subversive kinderculture subtext of this ad involves the children's shared recognition of the father's fatuous pursuit of a long-dead past and his embarrassing public display of emotion. Dad blows his "cool pose." The "Curly irony" is the overt signifier for these deeper generational divisions—differentiations described by advertisers as market segments.

The grand irony of this and many other ads is that under the flag of traditional family values McDonald's actually undermines the very qualities it claims to promote. The McDonald's experience depicted does not involve a family sharing a common experience—each market segment experiences it in a different and even potentially conflicting way. The family depicted here, like so many American middle-class families, is an isolated unit divided against itself. In terms of everyday life McDonald's does not encourage long, leisurely, interactive family meals. The seats and tables are designed to be uncomfortable to the point that customers will eat quickly and leave. In the larger scheme of things, family values, America, and home are nothing more than cynical marketing tools designed to legitimate McDonald's to different market segments. Kroc himself made his feeling about family very clear—work comes first, he told his managers. "My total commitment to business had long since been established in my home" (Kroc, 1977, 89). The cynicism embedded in McDonald's ads and scores of other ads undermines the social fabric, making the culture our children inhabit a colder and more malicious place. Such cynicism leads corporations to develop new forms of techno-power that can be used to subvert democracy and justice in the quest for new markets. Such cynicism holds up Kroc/Ronald as heroes while ignoring authentic heroes—men and women who struggle daily to lead good lives, be good parents, and extend social justice.

References

Abercrombie, N. (1994). Authority and consumer society. In R. Keat, N. Whiteley, and N. Abercrombie, *The authority of the consumer.* New York: Routledge.

Boas, M., and Chain, S. (1976). *Big Mac: The unauthorized story of McDonald's.* New York: E. P. Dutton.

Brautigan, R. (1974). *The Hawkline monster: A gothic western.* New York: Pocket Books.

Fischer, P., et al. (1991). Brand logo recognition by children aged 3 to 6 years. *Journal of the American Medical Association* 266(22): 3145–3148.

Garfield, B. (1992). Nice ads, but that theme is not what you want. *Advertising Age* 63(8): 53.

Giroux, H. (1988). *Teachers as intellectuals: Toward a critical pedagogy of learning.* Granby, Massachusetts: Bergin and Garvey.

_____. (1994). *Disturbing pleasures: Learning popular culture.* New York: Routledge.

Goldman, R. (1992). *Reading ads socially.* New York: Routledge.

Harvey, D. (1989). *The condition of postmodernity.* Cambridge, Massachusetts: Basil Blackwell.

Hume, S. (1993). Fast-food caught in the middle. *Advertising Age* 64(6): 12–15.

Keat, R., Whiteley, N., and Abercrombie, N. (1994). Introduction. In R. Keat, N. Whiteley, and N. Abercrombie, *The Authority of the Consumer.* New York: Routledge.

Kellner, D. (1989). *Critical theory, Marxism, and modernity.* Baltimore: Johns Hopkins University Press.

_____. (1992). Popular culture and the construction of postmodern identities. In S. Lash and J. Friedman, *Modernity and identity.* Cambridge, Massachusetts: Basil Blackwell.

Kroc, R. (1977). *Grinding it out: The making of McDonald's.* New York: St. Martin's.

Leidner, R. (1993). *Fast food, fast talk: Service work and the routinization of everyday life.* Berkeley: University of California Press.

Love, J. (1986). *McDonald's: Behind the arches.* New York: Bantam.

Luxenberg, S. (1985). *Roadside empires: How the chains franchised.* New York: Viking Penguin.

McCormick, M. (1993). Kid Rhino and McDonald's enter licensing agreement. *Billboard* 105(8): 10–11.

McDonald's Customer Relations Center (1994). Handout to schools.

Ritzer, G. (1993). *The McDonaldization of society.* Thousand Oaks, California: Pine Forge Press.

Seiter, E. (1993). *Sold separately: Parents and children in consumer culture.* New Brunswick, New Jersey: Rutgers University Press.

Shelton, A. (1993). Writing McDonald's, eating the past: McDonald's as a postmodern space. *Studies in Symbolic Interaction* 15: 103–118.

About the Book and Editors

For corporate America, children—and their parents' money—are one of the most targeted groups in our consumer society. There are TV shows, movies, video games, toys, books, and restaurants that are specifically directed at children—all of which has produced a "kinderculture" run by marketing and advertising executives. Through a series of entertaining and insightful essays, Kinderculture: The Corporate Construction of Childhood explores some of the icons that shape the values and consciousness of children, from Beavis and Butt-Head to Barney, from Disney movies to Nintendo.

Contributors drawn from the fields of education, sociology, and popular culture analyze the profound effects and the pervasive influence of these corporate productions in a style parents, educators, and general readers will welcome. Arguing that the experience of childhood has been, with or without our consent, reshaped into something that is prefabricated, Shirley Steinberg and Joe Kincheloe bring home to readers the impact our "marketing blitz" culture has on our children—and on our beliefs about childhood.

Shirley R. Steinberg teaches part-time at Adelphi University. She is an educational consultant and drama director. Her latest book is *Ain't We Misbehavin'? A Pedagogy of Misbehavior* (in press), and she is the coauthor with Joe L. Kincheloe of *The Stigma of Genius: Einstein and Beyond Modern Education* and *Changing Multiculturalism: New Times, New Curriculum*. She is also coeditor (along with Kincheloe and Aaron Gresson) of *Measured Lies: The Bell Curve Examined*. Steinberg and Kincheloe coedit the journal *Taboo: The Journal of Culture and Education* and several book series. Her current research involves issues of diversity, popular culture, and curriculum.

Joe L. Kincheloe teaches cultural studies and pedagogy at Penn State University. He is the author of numerous books, including *Teachers as Researchers: Qualitative Paths to Empowerment; Toil and Trouble: Good Work, Smart Workers, and the Integration of Academic and Vocational Education*; and (with Shirley Steinberg) *Thirteen Questions: Reframing Education's Conversation*. Kincheloe and Steinberg travel frequently presenting workshops and keynote addresses on popular culture, critical pedagogy, and issues of race, class, and gender. Kincheloe and Steinberg are the parents of Ian and Christine, Meghann, Chaim, and Bronwyn; they love '57 Chevys, screamin' guitars, and the Atlanta Braves.

About the Contributors

Eleanor Blair Hilty teaches at Western Carolina University. The author of many articles and chapters on teacher education and children, her next book is *Political Dimensions of Educational Psychology: Learning in Critical Perspective.*

Alan A. Block teaches at the University of Wisconsin–Stout in Menomonie. His recent books include *Occupied Reading: Critical Foundations for an Ecological Theory* and *I'm Only Bleeding: Education as Violence Against Children.*

Jeanne Brady is an assistant professor at Penn State University. She is the author of *Schooling Young Children: A Feminist Pedagogy for Liberatory Learning.*

Linda K. Christian-Smith is a professor in the Department of Curriculum and Instruction and Human Services, University of Wisconsin, Oshkosh. She is the author of *Becoming a Woman Through Romance* and *Texts of Desire: Essays on Fiction, Femininity, and Schooling.*

Jean I. Erdman is the chair of the Department of Curriculum and Instruction and Human Services, University of Wisconsin, Oshkosh. Her work has been published in many journals and books; she is currently the poet laureate for the *Wisconsin State Reading Association Journal.*

Henry A. Giroux is the Waterbury Chair Professor at Penn State University. His latest books include *Fugitive Cultures: Race, Violence, Youth, Pedagogy* and *The Politics of Hope: Culture and Schooling.* He is internationally known in the areas of critical pedagogy and cultural studies.

Aaron David Gresson III teaches at Penn State University. A well-known writer, he is the recent author of *The Recovery of Race in America* and *America's Atonement: Recovery Pedagogy and Media Culture in Transitional Society* (in press).

Jan Jipson is an associate professor of education at Carroll College. Her recent books include *Repositioning Feminism and Education: Perspectives on Education for Social Change* (coauthor) and *Daredevil Research: Re-creating Analytic Practice* (with Nicholas Paley).

Douglas Kellner is a professor in philosophy at the University of Texas at Austin. He is the author of *Media Culture* and *The Postmodern Adventure* (forthcoming).

Peter McLaren is a professor in the Graduate School of Education at UCLA. He is the author of numerous books on popular culture, critical pedagogy, and politics. His most recent books are *Counternarratives* (with Giroux, Lankshear, and Peters) and *Critical Pedagogy and Predatory Culture.*

Janet Morris teaches communication studies at the University of Windsor, Ontario. Her research interest includes evaluation of media literacy programs and related education policy.

Murry R. Nelson is a professor in curriculum and instruction at Penn State University. A fervent collector of baseball cards and an expert on the history of sports, he is the author of *The Future of Social Studies* and *Children and Social Studies*.

Eugene F. Provenzo Jr. is a professor in education at the University of Miami. His recent books include *School Teachers and Schooling: Ethoses in Conflict* and *The Educator's Brief Guide to Computers in the Schools*.

Ursi Reynolds teaches early childhood at The College of the Redwoods in Northern California; her work is in media and technology and multicultural education.